TOTAL
RESPECT

'MY LIFE ON THE DOORS'

ANTHONY
THOMAS

WITH

(Best-Selling Non-Fiction Crime Writer)

LEE WORTLEY

Dedication

Dedicated to family and friends who have passed, on my journey through life.

And my fellow comrades in battle

Nigel Cleaver

Paul Curtis

Paul Elliot

Darryl Worrel

Bernard 'The Boss' Driscoll

Gone, but never forgotten.

We would also like to shout a big thank you out to our friend, Michael Nesbitt (author of the hugely popular Britain's Gangland Magazine) for his incredible work creating and designing the books cover.

CONTENTS:

FOREWORD

Julian Davies

(Author of Three best-selling books: Street Fighters, Bouncers and Hookers)

Back in 1996, I was asked to pop into a local gym and help a young boxer along with some sparring now and again. I was told the lad was my height and a little lighter than me. When I met him the first thing, I noticed was that he was 3 inches taller and about 2 stone heavier. We sparred a few rounds and became good friends ever since. That was the start of our friendship, we had the same interests and living close to each other we became training partners. He was always in the local paper for boxing, and people started to be aware that he was becoming a good fighter, inside and outside the ring.

I decided to write a book called 'Street-fighters' and travelled the country interviewing men who fought on the streets. Big Shirl came everywhere with me with these interviews, and we had a great time.

Most Sunday's Shirl would pop down my house for a cup of tea, and he would tell me stories about bouncing the night before. He said that I should write a book on door work and if I did, he would tell me loads of stories to put in it, which he did. When I finally released a book called Bouncers, the book done well, and I have him to thank for the idea and interviews. I wrote another book about hookers (not the rugby type), but he didn't have any stories for that one.

I have seen him at his highest, like when he sat in my garden laughing his head off because the night before he had fought a whole rugby team. The lowest being when he got knocked out in a gang fight, someone put a solid glass gin bottle over his head, and another man had stabbed him. I went to the hospital to see him, and he said to me that he will catch up with them, and he did.

A few years ago, I developed an inoperable brain tumour, and they have only given me a few years. I'm not allowed to drive, and Big Shirl has driven me to every doctor's appointment, every scan, and all I have to do is buy him dinner at a local café. However, every time I get in that car, it's like Death Wish 6 with the big fella.

Shirl had me some extra work on a new film about the fighter Lenny McLean in London. I tell him I'll do it, but I'm not having my beard cut off. "Don't worry, they can use you like that because they want you to be a pikey" he assures me. After getting lost another 3 or 4 times on the way there, we turn up at the venue to mix in with other extras waiting for makeup. It's my turn, and I sit down while one of the makeup artists gels my hair and gives me a side parting. I'm just about to get up when she tells me she must cut off my beard. I said it was ok because my mate said we were playing gypsies and we wouldn't need to shave. The lady then tells me that my friend has lied to me. She then cuts off my beard and leaves me with a moustache, which she then dyes darker to make it stand out more. After she puts eye shadow and blusher on me, I look to my right Big Shirl is screaming laughing at me shouting out, "I knew they were going to do that to you."

We have been filming all day and are shattered. We get to our hotel room where he has booked a double room. The hotel manager takes a look at us with big gay moustaches and make up and says wouldn't you rather a double bed than two singles. I tell him that we are extras in a film, I'm not gay, and if I was, I could do a lot better than Shirl. Then Shirl tells the manager, "No, he couldn't mate" and the manager just looks at us with a shocked face.

We filmed the next day and start driving home, 5 minutes from the venue he goes through a red light and nearly killed some Chinese kid on a motorbike. Then shortly after he crosses lanes, a lorry driver swerves and starts beeping his horn and swearing at us. I reclined my seat right down and pulled my hat over my eyes. The idea that I was about to die in the car, I'd rather go in my sleep, not knowing that I'm going out through the windscreen at 90 miles an hour. I start to fall asleep, but shortly after I'm woken by Shirl shouting out his window, "I didn't know it was a fucking bike lane, you cockney prick, with that I drifted off to blissful sleep.

We came up with the idea for our own internet comedy show, and now we have loads of followers. In the Juggy and Shirl show, he plays someone a little thick and bit of a baby with things. It is so much fun when some druggie scum watches the videos and think Shirl is like that in real life, they always come unstuck.

I have lost count of how many people he has knocked out or been in a ruck with, in the past. This book is not only violent, emotional, but funny as hell too. I trust Shirl with my life, and he is the greatest friend ever, I'm lucky to have him in my corner.

Good luck with the book big man,

Julian

INTRODUCTION

Adrenaline pumping, fist-clenching, brow scowling, that's how you see me, isn't it? Well, it isn't true! Ok, so I am all those things, but only at times when you rile me. Indoors, I'm as soft as a pussycat, the big bear with a face full of glitter and lip-gloss, applied by my three sweet girls. You see to them, I'm simply Dad, the big daft nutter that brings home the Maccy D's. I've played Santa by day and a raving lunatic at night; so, in some ways I'm the real-life Jekyll and Hyde. However, to those closest, I'm just me, the boy my Mother bounced upon her knee. Big Shirl or Shirley, that's how the majority refer to me, so read on and you'll soon find out, what this boy from the valleys is all about.

Trouble was stirring. I was surrounded and terrified. I was a young boy, ya 'see, and at this stage of my life, I was ill-equipped to deal with bullies. It was do or die, you could almost taste the violence, overbearingly palpable, and as real as the fear running through my quivering bones. A beating was imminent, and I had nowhere to hide. I could run, but these boys' would soon catch up with me; I mean, I wasn't the sveltest or agile of children, to say the very least - I was a "fat boy," or that is at least what the bullyboys kept telling me. Their taunts were getting heavier, accompanied by hand gestures, a warning of what was to come, I legged it (ran off) as fast as my 10-year-old out of shape frame could carry me. I could hear their footsteps getting louder and louder, an indication of how close they were getting. My breathing was heavy and laboured, like a gazelle hunted by a murderous feline pack. This must be

9

similar to hyperventilation, the air was there, but I had no way of taking it in, every gasp I took seemed to make me weaker and more fragile, and the only alternative I had, was to stop and accept my fate, and I couldn't be more frightened than I was in that moment. I came to a halt and was immediately kicked to the floor, everything went foggy, and the last image I could see through my blurry eyes was my front door, the entrance to my house; the bolt-hole that up until this day I had used as a comfort blanket, when, SMACK! I took another boot to the head and everything from that moment on went hazy, I was done, battered, bruised up and whimpering, and this was the turning point for me; a life-changing, seeing-of-the-light epiphany, and the very last day, I ever got bullied.

Shoot to the year of our third millennium, the year 2000. A local bully is making himself known, and everyone in this roughhouse pub known as The Vulcan are intimidated by his provoking insults. Every individual he eyeballs for a fight turns their head the other away - even the other doormen were weary, and unsure – simply because this six-foot four-inch club-bouncing lunatic was just waiting for the wrong word from someone's lips, a word that would be taken as an invitation for him to make his move. Our unmerciful eyes met, as the gorilla meandered his way over, entitled, and confident, stepping into my space. The whole of the pub slowly lift their heads, and BANG, with one clean power shot I 've almost taken his head off, (Warrens words not mine,) a right hook so alarming, it's sent him to sleep where he stood. At that moment, his enormous back hit the concrete pillow that was holding him up, and he then slips in "staccato motion," down, landing in a heap on the floor. This boy might think twice about his role as a bully the next time he visits one of my doors.

So, there you have it, two extremely similar encounters, with incomparable conclusions.

A first-hand, panoramic view into the world of,

Big Shirley.

Most of the people who know me, or at least know of me, will tell you that, I am, and have always been a lifelong researching lunatic into the life and legacy of London's most respected Gangland enforcer - Lenny 'The Guv'nor' McLean. Now, my fascination with Lenny was never just about his power as a fighter; no, it was more to do with the respect he earned on his way up the proverbial tough-guy ladder. In London town and beyond, Lenny was regarded as the ultimate bouncer, a man among men with the muscle to back it – and in my world; the valleys of Merthyr Tydfil, I was, and remain, one of the same. My role as a fist-fighter was never a chosen career path for me; it was quite simply thrust in my face as tiptoed into my youth, and from that day forward, I have known no other world. Since the very first day, I stood in that lonely pub doorway; my life has been one hellish battle after another.

Now, as many fighting men would tell you, the life of a doorman can be devastatingly taxing. The difficult task I undertook, as I worked my way up, from a reasonably quiet little pub, quickly accelerating to the top of the "bouncers' league table" to become head doorman of our town's largest and liveliest of clubs, duly noted by the Merthyr club-land hierarchy. Now, as gratifying, as this may seem, in the wildest of times, this promotion almost took its toll on me, not to mention the strain it put on those people I hold dearest behind my castle walls - my family. To say it has been disturbing, relentless, and unforgiving at times, would be a herculean understatement. From fighting for my life against an unholy amount of ale fueled and raging rugby players. To separating scantily clad women, in jealous bouts of extreme cat-clawing violence, while young Boy's without goal or ambition hit the town, on the promise or the merest glimmer of a bunk up., an encounter that was never to come to fruition. And after drinking their body weight in their chosen "tipple," they feel the need to take out their anger on some innocent bystander; to fight - a misplaced reward for some sexual relief they missed out on that night!

The battles, the brawls, the head butting of walls, mark my words people; "through my eyes," I have seen it all. I've had threats at my door, by one. Two. Three, and more, armed to the teeth with chains, bats, and bars galore. Now, as a rule, I've never used a tool, for my fists have always got me out of the scariest of brawls. I've had hits on my life, but I've seen them off with ease; for the most part, a word in the right direction would efficiently appease.

Nevertheless, I've never been one to 'piss-n-moan,' because as a result of this, I've managed to afford myself a reasonably comfortable existence - as I plied my trade in the only way, I knew how. Now, at 49, and with battle scars as trophies for trying to govern this unruly little town, I think it's about time I settled down. It's been one hell of a journey, with an enormous amount of strife, so the time is upon me to hang up the gloves in favour of a more tranquil and healthy life.

Therefore, as we stride toward the year 2020, and I tread ever closer to my 25th year on the door. It is at this point in my life I feel that, through blood, sweat, and anguish, I have earned in ample amount, the stripes, and honours to bring you an image inducing account. A thought-provoking glimpse into my world as pub and club bouncer, minder, and bodyguard. A thankless job, with very few personal rewards, and an ever more woeful pay packet. An underrated position of protection that has, on occasion, seen my mortality flash before my very own eyes. My death! A hard pill to swallow for my wife who waved me off as I stepped out into the night to protect your children from the dangers that lurked outside. From the lunatics that brought trouble to our club doors, the dealers, the pill-poppers, and more, that preyed on the partygoers, to line their filth-laden pockets with your honest to God, hard-earned gravy. Well, listen, someone had to do it; somebody had to be the one to go into battle, and unfortunately, destiny chose me as its first line of defense.

Now, as you peer through the letterbox of my mind, and read about the stabbings, the knife attacks, and the shootings, you'll be at peace knowing that you're reading this, safe and unscathed from the comfort of your dwelling. These tales that I have collected over the years will evoke every one of your emotions. The words written for your inspection will shock you, stun you, and at certain points maybe even educate you as you dip your toe tentatively into the murky world of a doorman from the valley. However, first, I need to tell you how it all began.

CHAPTER ONE

(Growing up in the Valleys)

I was born in the famous fighting town of Merthyr Tydfil in South Wales on July 11th, 1970. Merthyr had been famous for its champion boxer's, the likes of Howard Winstone, Johnny Owen; Eddie Thomas, and of course, the legendary "Tylorstown Terror" Jimmy Wilde. In the peak of the 19th centuries Industrial Revolution, the districts of Merthyr housed four of the greatest Ironworks in the world, and this, with its promise of a better life, brought my great grandfather's over from Ireland, and also Carmarthen, to make a living working and settling here.

I was the first born of three brothers, and for the first three months of my life, we lived in a rat-infested flat in Dowlais, until my parents had had enough, so for a couple of months they moved us in with my Nan on the famous old "Gurnos Estate." The Gurnos, was a housing estate that housed a handful of notable names, like fellow author Des Barry and screen actor, Richard Harrington (of whom I body guarded a few years ago), to name just two. 'See, I was in good company, right from the start.' It's strange because I always felt that I would be drawn back to the area where I grew up, and only last year, I moved back to where it all began. Mind you, I hope it isn't an omen, because apparently a report was done in 2011, and it was suggested that the life expectancy of a man living on "The Gurnos" was a non-too-healthy fifty fucking eight. Fuck me, we had better get a move on with this book. Anyway, I've got nine years to go yet, so let's get back to the story.

Back to the 70s, and new houses were being put up on the estate, one came up on the opposite side to my Nans, and my parents made this our family home for the next thirty years or so. My mother had worked in various pubs, and her family had run the Old Angel public house in the town for quite a while. A few years later, when she was about twenty-one, she met my dad, who had spent two years as a radioman in the Malaya war and had recently returned home. My dad did not go into much detail regarding what had gone on there; however, he did mention one story about him, and his mates being stuck in some trench up against about twelve of the opposition. Unfortunately, for my Dad and his chosen career path as a radioman, he was seen as the ultimate threat, and for that reason, these men were trying their best to take him out first. I don't know why, but that story always stuck in my mind, I guess it's because my Dad always seemed reluctant to tell me the end. Because when I asked him, 'what happened next Dad?' all he would say was, 'Well look, Son, it was either them or us, and we were the ones that came home.'

As I got a little older and wiser, I realised that in those few words from my Dad, what with me being so young, he did not want to go into too much detail about it. Dad also tried his hand at boxing and had a couple of bouts in the Army; he must have been quite decent because he won the first couple; nevertheless, he suffered his first defeat and decided that boxing wasn't for him.

As a boy, along with my younger Brothers Barry and Steven, respectively, I have no recollection of any sort of fighting thrust upon us. The earliest thing I can remember was being taught how to play darts since my father was a champion of Merthyr three years in a row and would come

15

home with massive trophy's all of the time. We had a dartboard in our passageway, and there would play for hours and hours on end. Being kids, we would even pretend that we had won our Dad's trophies and present them to one another. All of which couldn't be further away from fist fighting.

Growing up seeing my dad-winning trophy after trophy, made my thirst to win something one day paramount. I entered a football competition when I was young as a goalie (goalkeeper) because someone had pulled out, anyway, we lost 10-0, on the upside to this, I was awarded a little trophy, and I was proud of it. When I was about 18, my two mates were entering into running competitions. Now, like I said I wasn't a small boy, and I wasn't stupid, I knew I wasn't going to win any competition's; however, I finished a few races and was awarded a medal, and this I was wholeheartedly happy with.

It was different with us and fighting. You see, most people have fighters in their families, and it filters through the family DNA and becomes part of a man's make-up. People like this are born to fight, but in my case, in my adolescents, I shied away from it - I hated fighting! Maybe it was there in the genes somewhere but had to be found as I found out recently that maybe one of my great, great, grandfathers Cornelius Holland was an Irish bare-knuckle fighter who used to travel and fight on the boxing booths. Therefore, as the saying goes, 'it's either in you or it's not,' and for years and years, I had nothing in me, but it would eventually turn up.

Throughout junior school, I was picked on quite a lot; I could never understand why, and like many kids back in the 70s, I just bottled it up. Perhaps the bullying was due to

16

the weight I was carrying; in addition to that, I had this big mop of Shirly Temple style curly hair, hence the nickname Shirly. Imagine growing up on a rough estate as a young lad, with a girly nickname like Shirley. Well, as you can imagine, it set me off on a bit of a bumpy road.

I can remember being with my brother Barry a few times who was two years younger than me and he was getting picked on, and some of the lads would say to me, 'aren't you going to stick up for your brother?' and at that time I didn't want to know. One day at school, a boy who was a year younger than me hit him, and again, I did fuck all about it; I just went home like a big baby. When I think back, I remember how it hurt me so much, knowing that I didn't do a thing; even at such a young age, and not known as a fighter, it was still killing me inside.

The earliest memory I have of being involved in what I would deem as a fight was when I was a 10-year-old boy at junior school; I remember it like it was yesterday. It was a boy that lived close to me; his name was Derek, and he was a right bully, would make people kiss his shoes, why I don't fucking know, but he did, and I was next, he had pulled me down to the floor and he's screaming at me to kiss them, a big crowd has gathered and I'm just about to pucker up when I thought it can't get any lower than this so he's just standing there looking all cocky so Iv wrapped my arms around his legs and rugby tackled him down, we ended up wrestling on the floor and I managed to get on top of him and in those days at that age was counted as a win, it then got broke up, but he never picked on me again.

I went home that night with my head held high; I felt on top of the world. Not long after, on my way home from school, a boy called Jason picked a fight with me, I hit him as hard as I could in the face, and he just laughed and immediately beat the shit out of me. At that moment, I remember thinking that I wasn't a fighter; it just wasn't my thing. I was still getting bullied for no reason whatsoever, and as a result, I had a few more scraps (fights) but always came second. I honestly thought at that time that I'd get bullied for the rest of my life. I was too scared to tell my parents and to get out of going to school; I would lie and say, I was ill. However, my Mam and Dad were having none of it, and I was promptly sent off to school - the bullying continued.

I was down by the river with my mates one day, when a rival gang ran at us, a few of our mates ran away, but Steve who was half my size stuck with me, and even though we got smashed to pieces we just laughed it off on our way home. As I said, Steve wasn't the biggest of boys, but he was like a little terrier. He saw these bullies picking on me and would go off his head, screaming at me because I wouldn't fight back. He would try and unearth my temper by punching me full force in the arm, but I'd laugh at him, and he'd say, 'c'mon Shirl, the size of you, you could kill them!' I would say nothing and smile. Funny really, because recently, after a great many years, he and I have reconnected and spoken about it in length. We still laugh like lunatics about those crazy days growing up.

I was playing at my mate house, David, one day, when out of the blue, and for no reason at all this boy who was at least a couple of years older than me started to beat me to a pulp; to be honest, he battered me that much that I was struggling to breath. Unbeknown to me, someone had run over to my house to tell my parents, next thing my mother Lynda is steaming up the street with my Dad Terry closely

18

following behind. My Mum was screaming at the top of her voice, 'where does he live?' Anyway, one of my mates pointed her to the opposite corner house, and as I'm still having trouble breathing, she dragged me over to the house. With that, my Mum knocks heavily at the door, and immediately his father answers, 'where's your boy?' My Mum demands, as the boy comes flying out and my mother swings for him. At this point, the father got in the way, and Mum smashes him too. By this time, my father is in the garden, and he drags Mum away. I glance over at the bullyboy, whose face is a picture, and with that, his dad grabs him and hurries him back into their house.

By the time I got to Pen-Y-Dre secondary School, I was becoming more streetwise. Oh, I was still having the beatings, but I was getting a bit bigger and stronger by the day, perhaps this could work in my favour - as a deterrent. It wasn't until secondary school having been bullied once again, that I finally began to believe in myself. The culprit on this occasion was a big stocky boy who was ranked in the top five toughest lads in our form. Now, every school has their top ten hardest boys; it's a ridiculous list made up by someone who has probably never even fought before, someone who stands egging the bully on from the safety of an urging crowd. Anyway, it just so happens that this particular boy was his chosen number-five – and he's looking for me, and me being me, I bottled it and went home early.

I woke the next day with the "fear" staring down on me; I was petrified and tried my best to convince my Mother to let me have the day off school; she was having none of it, so reluctantly off I went. I was with my mate Kevin later that day, and he was winding me right up trying to get me to fight this boy, but I was shitting myself. Then as we are walking down a corridor the boy's waiting for me with about four of his mates, and he shouted over to me, 'Oi, I've been looking for you,' and I thought to myself, 'Right, I've got nothing to lose' and walked straight up to him and smashed him clean in the mouth. He didn't go down, but he didn't laugh at me like the other bullyboy I mentioned earlier. You see, like most young boys, I had no idea how to punch properly, but eh, it was a start, at least I'd showed him that I wasn't a pushover, and we ended up wrestling with each other on the ground. As luck would have it, I began to get the better of him, and I ended up on top of him, punching him in the face. However, seconds later, a teacher came running and pulled us apart, the bully is bust up good and bleeding, and I haven't a mark on me. The teacher sends the two of us off to see the headmaster, and at this point, I didn't give a fuck and says to him, 'right, we'll finish this off later,' to which he pleads, 'I'm sorry! I've had enough! It's over!

Therefore, after a relatively easy fight, I was placed straight in at the number five spot on the 'toughest-boy-list.' I was happy with my newfound fighting credentials, and for some reason found the list worthy, as opposed to what I thought when I wasn't on it. Later that day, I met up with my mate Kevin again, and he said, 'see Shirl, I don't know what you were worried about. I knew you could do him.' I let the bullyboys mates off, and to be honest, I ended up being really good friends with them all in the end.

One time, I was collecting for a bommy (bonfire) with a local gang; I must have been about 12 at the time. What we used to do was raid other local gangs' bonfires for their wood and tyres etc. However, on this particular day, it all went seriously wrong and backfired on us. We had gone down to a place called Lakeside, and as we were down there, one-half of this other gang was lying in wait to ambush us. There we were grabbing all of this gangs' tyres and other bommy bits, and as we were running up this hill, we've run smack-bang into them; there was about ten of us in total, but we'd split up, and a few of us are hiding in a bunch of fern bushes nearby. All of a sudden, everything's gone quiet, so my mate Colin and I make a move onto the streets, and immediately, five of the other gang pops out from nowhere. Colin and I are now fucked, with nowhere left for us to run. Being a lot older and bigger than us, they hold us up against a brick wall, and one of them pulls out a big fucking knife, and I've almost pissed my pants as he's holding this knife up, threatening to slit our throats and kill us.

I start to cry as I'm begging for my life, he then puts the knife against my throat as the other boys are holding my arms, and I daren't move a muscle; too scared to move in case he cut's me. The gang leader then says, 'it's your lucky day,' as he puts the knife back in his pocket. It was obvious to them that they had scared the living daylights out of us, and they then start punching and kicking us, they gave us a right good hiding before eventually letting us go. Immediately Col and I sprinted off as fast as we could, and after a while, the two of us still in disbelief as to what had just happened. The pair of us had been battered senseless, and there we were still laughing. To be honest, I think it was a mixture of nerves and shock more than anything; that, or just the fact that he and I were happy to be alive.

A few weeks after this, we sadly lost another member of our gang called Stuart in a swimming accident in a local river. It was terrible because I'd only been with him a few days earlier, collecting wood and that for our bonfire, in addition to that, Stuart, and I used to swim in that river together all the time. It was a horrible time in my young life, and the first funeral I had ever been to, which affected me for many years after – to be honest, it still does. Stuart was a great lad and a right character, just like the other boys we knocked around with.

Our gang was made up of some right nutters, and because of this, I remember not wanting to go out with them very often because some of the stuff they were getting up to just wasn't for me, and even then, it was clear to see that some of them were on a one-way path to prison – or worse. On one occasion, they decided to do over the local sweet shop, and when they went into detail about the amount of chocolate and sweets they had seen in this lock-up, I just had to be in. I guess it was on that day that I acquired my love for many cocoa bean delights. Anyway, about four of us done the 'chocolate heist,' and was carrying as much as we could from this lock-up down the Gurnos; we ended up stashing the whole lot in my front of house shed, you wouldn't believe your eyes; a whole fucking sweet shop right there in my shed. Mind you, I was scared shitless with the thought of it all stashed in there, especially knowing what a hiding I'd get if my Mum happened to come across it, but when you're kids, you just don't weigh all the odds up properly. Anyway, I was right about some of the boys' and the destiny that was waiting around the corner, because a few years later, a few of them ended up in jail.

I remember someone telling me that one of them had pinched a tractor and tried knocking down some prison walls to help his brother escape - right crazy fuckers they were. I did come unstuck this one night with them and ended up getting arrested by the police. I got caught pinching on a building site by a security guard, the boys got away, but they kept me until the police arrived, who then took me to my house where I was giving a verbal warning, if not for my age I think I would have got worse. If I'm honest, I was more scared of what my mother was going to do more than the police.

I had a few pets when I was a kid, earliest I remember was this dog named Spot. He was full of energy and kept escaping out of the house until he came unstuck and one day was hit, and killed by a car, it broke my little heart. Then one day my dad's brother Freddy turn's up with this little black Labby pub, which we named (as you would expect) Blackie. This dog was adorable but just would not stop barking at people as they passed the garden. We also kept a pet rabbit at the bottom of the garden; I arrived home one day to find that the nutty dog had somehow managed to open the cage, well, I won't go into detail, 'cos it was so upsetting at the time and still is.
About a year later, some prick threw some meat over the fence and Blackie the Labby died - turns out he'd been poisoned. These were such sad events, and for that reason we never had pets again.

I'm now about 13 years of age, and I was good mates with this boy called Ian. I'd be over his house most night's watching all the new videos that were out. Now, Ian's sister's boyfriend's name was Paul Coffey, who was a big lump of a man and a rugby player for Merthyr at the time. Paul started taking Ian and me down to the local rugby club with him every Saturday, and we'd have free food, play pool, and then watch him smashing player's up. Most weeks, he'd be involved in fights, and the crowd loved him; I was in awe of him and thought, 'I'm going to be like him one day.' Moreover, who would believe that the little boy of theirs called, Ryan would follow in his father's footsteps and even play on the same team as me later on in life.

I'm now in my first year as a fully-fledged teen; 13, and I'm getting bigger and bigger by the day; 'well I guess that's the free school meals for you' I was a bit of a glutton too, because if someone didn't want their meal ticket, I'd have it off them and be straight back up to the food hatch for seconds, not to mention the hamburgers that I'd sneak into my trousers pockets when the dinner lady had her back turned.

I had heard there was a boxing class in another school at night, and it was only a few miles from where I lived, so over a few days, I built up enough courage to go with my mate, Paul Miles. I must have been about 13 at the time and did not have a clue. The trainers at the time turned out to be my future cornermen, Howard Williams and Gareth Donovan. I remember Gareth giving us ropes and telling us to skip for 30 minutes in this corridor, and that was just for starters. Anyway, after a few sessions, I could not get my head around it and called it a day. Nevertheless, I did tell all my mates in school that I was now a boxer.

I'd always loved boxing, as did my dad, and he would show me how to throw a punch properly, I used to love it but had no idea that I'd ever be good enough to get a proper fight, in a real boxing ring.

Growing up, I did all the usual stuff, from joining the Scout's, and a few years later, I even joined the RAF cadets. I started playing rugby for the school team, too, and that was where the fights started to happen. Game after game all it would be was fighting with the rival teams; due to the fights and how capable I was, I very quickly started picking up a bit of a reputation, and for this reason by the time, I left school, the bullying had almost completely stopped. I was almost fifteen stone by the time I left school, and I was still growing, and training, and had also started weight training as well with a mate of mine, Flynny.

I left school with no qualifications whatsoever; school just wasn't for me, and from me saying that you would imagine that I never went to school, but I did; not once did I ever go bunking off, or skipping lessons, but for some reason, none of it ever sunk in. Therefore, in my mind, I just felt that the last five years of my life had been a complete waste of time, apart from the fact that I had met some fantastic people along the way.

CHAPTER TWO

(Madder by the Day)

The crazy days of adolescents were just a shadow in my wake. I was turning into an adult, bigger in size, and more prominent in nature; out of control - and not a thing in this town-filled-dole-drum could stop me. It was a phase, or at least I hoped that's what it was. A period of mania that I simply had to go through. However, would the next few years flag up a brainwave of realisation; realisation that I was for all intents and purposes a lost fucking cause. Only time would tell - or would it?

After leaving school we held a party in a local nightclub, now this was the very first time I'd stepped foot in the place, and already we were having a bit of a run-in with a gang of boys who were bullying everyone. These boys were a lot older than us, and one of them is picking a fight with one of my mates Martin, so I jump in and tell him to fuck off. Immediately the boy turns his attention to me and starts forcing his head into mine at the bar. However, unfortunately for him, the more he sticks his head into mine, the more I just laughed at him, laughing right up in his face; I'm goading him, and his ego is under attack. With that, one of the club's bouncers escorts me out along with my mate, and he demands that I "run along." I couldn't believe it, why they hadn't thrown the other boy out as well, seemingly, even the door staff were wary of him at the time. The following day I was informed that these boys wanted a fight with me, and I was bricking it. There was I sat in my mums, eagle-eyed, staring intently through her window, wondering what the fuck had I started. Thankfully, nothing came of it.

With my schooldays behind me, it was time to step out into the big bad world and choose a career path, so off to Merthyr College, I went to study computers and electronics. I was sixteen at the time, and every Friday was drink night, the boys and I would get ourselves in some right states, we would start drinking homebrew at my mate Paul's house, and then we'd move on into town, and as a rule we always ending up in the Kirkhouse or 'Kooler's,' as it is now known.

I met Paul or 'Milesy' as we called him at school and spent the majority of my spare time at his house, drinking his homemade beer. To be honest, this alcoholic pond-water tasted like piss, but it did the job. However, it was due to its potency that we ended up scrapping with various gangs and other people most Fridays. We got banned from our first pub 'The Eagle, at sixteen for being underage, oh, and we also called the landlord some very unpleasant names as well. Fortunately, a couple of months later, the landlord allowed us back in, but it wasn't too long after that we got barred for fighting again.

One night, Milesy and I had gone into the local curry house called Hing Hong's because we were starving-hungry, we were in a right fucking state – pissed out of our brains. Up until then, we had had a quiet night, and then a couple of drunk boys came in, and for no apparent reason, started a fight with us. Anyway, these fellas were ever so much older than us, so we left. Now one of these fellas lived near Milesy, and we knew that he had his own business, which was a pop round (he delivered fizzy drinks locally in his van.) Pissed off and gutted that we had had to leave our

27

food, we shot off up this back alley out of the way, and Milesy said to me, 'I've got an idea, Shirl. Let's go and smash his van up?' I smiled in agreement, and the next thing you know, we're stood three feet away from his precious fucking pop van. Anyway, we've found ourselves a couple of big house bricks and smashed his van right up and immediately legged it into Miles's house laughing our heads off like a couple of crazed hyenas'. Eventually, we met up with the boys a couple of years later, and unfortunately for them, we got our own back.

A couple of weeks later and a few of us were out again, it's the end of the night, and we were outside this club where some food vans were parked. It had been another crazy night, but we hadn't had any trouble at all, which was surprising because there were about seven of us. There we were, quietly sat eating our food and minding our own business, when out of nowhere these three boys decide to start on my mate Stephen. Stephen was a year older than us and was in the RAF, but he was out on leave and didn't need any shit. Now, these boys can see that all of us are staying quiet, and there's police passing by every couple of minutes, but their taunts and threats are getting heavier. So, I said to my mate, 'what the fucks all that about,' and trying to keep the peace, he said, 'oh, fuck 'em, Shirl, just leave it.'

However, I am thinking to myself, I've gone all the way through school being bullied, and it was still fucking happening. This was the first time I had stayed quiet, and they probably thought we had all bottled it.

A couple of minutes later, and while still eating their food, they decide to walk past us, they were still making stupid threats; goading, and then one of them walked up to

28

Stephen and went to push him. Now, it takes a lot to get me going, but this fucker was asking for it, so I've stepped in front of Stephen, and without saying a word, I've smashed him clean in the face. I'd had loads of fights in the past, and in my mind, I had done an excellent job. However, up until today, I had never actually knocked anybody out, but that was about to change. For the simple reason that for the past few months, I had been training on the weights with another mate of mine called Flynny, and as a result, I'd become one hell of a lot stronger. Anyway, as I've hit him, his eyes have gone into his head, and he's spark-out-cold where he stood. This boy has hit the floor hard. I couldn't believe it; it seemed so easy. Then within a split second, his mate has come at me to have a go too, so I've smashed him as well, and his eyes have also gone back into his head like the other one, only this one had lost all control of his body and fell smack-bang onto his face. I was shaken for a second because he looked like he was dead, and having seen this, the third of the bullies fucked off. By this point, people had come running from everywhere, either to have a bit of nose at what's happened or maybe even to join in. I started to scream at whoever was there, but the boys then pull me away before the police turn up. The boys were still unconscious on the floor as we left. On the way home the boys treat me like a hero, I don't think they had ever seen anybody get knocked out before, let alone two of them in the same number of seconds. After that night, they looked at me in a different light. I found out a week later, one of the boys from that fight had suffered a broken jaw, but fuck 'em, they deserved it for all their bullying, and anyway, how many others had they started on in the club in the past.

A couple of weeks later and I was over my mate's house having a cup of tea on a Saturday afternoon like usual, making plans to go out later that night. We were discussing what had happened the night before has I had not gone out, and they had been jumped by another gang, anyway, a little more on that story later.

There was this local boy who had recently been released from Borstal, now this boy was a nutter, and was known for his fighting. I'm sitting on this wall drinking tea, and he's walking towards us with his girlfriend. With that, I heard him holler across, 'what did you just say?' Now I haven't even looked at him, so I replied abruptly, 'what the fuck are you on about?' to which he says in a threating tone, 'did you just call me a cunt?' So, we've established at this point in my book that I'm no mug and that I can throw my fists around a bit, but that's the last thing I'd call this fucking lunatic; I thought he was well out of my league. At this stage in my life, I thought he would easily flatten me, especially if you believe all the hype surrounding his reputation. Now I'll be honest with you and tell you straight; I was shitting myself - big time. I was sat there thinking, oh no, it's happening again, I'm being picked on simply because I'm the biggest – or the fattest if we're brutal.

Anyway, he's still hurling abuse at me to fight him, and a crowd has started to gather around us, even my mother and father were there; someone must have run; knocked at my house and told them. The boy is still stood there, taunting, so my mother went off and phoned the police. Nevertheless, my mam's actions have made me look like a right wanker, and I thought I've got to do something - and soon. Then he made the biggest mistake, stepping right over the mark; it was like a red-rag-to-a-bull, as he started abusing my mother and father, that's done it, now it's time

30

to go to work. I immediately steamed in and smashed him into a nearby wall. I managed to overpower him, getting him in a headlock and fucking pummeled him with punches until my father stepped in and stopped me.

Nevertheless, this lowlife is still making threats, so I gave it to him again. Yet again, I was stopped, only this time he's had enough and decides to walk off, and this time it's me hurling the threats, and I'm laughing at him. My mates looked at me and said, 'Shirl, why the fuck didn't you do that earlier?' They were, of course, correct. I'd beaten this so-called nutter to a pulp, and it was easy. There is a funny side to the story, and that is that my mother had phoned the police saying that her little "innocent," 17-year-old boy was getting picked on. Therefore, the police expected to turn up and witness me battered and bruised, but the reality was that I had to try to explain that I'd actually beaten him up - talk about dropping yourself in it. The police were ok about it though and said that there was a warrant out for his arrest anyway, due to him robbing a shop an hour earlier. I bumped into him about two weeks later in town, he glanced at me for a second, but immediately put his head down, and that was another bully that had bitten the dust. Right, back to my mate's story the night before.

They had been in a bit of a row in a pub called the Great Escape, which was run by an ex-pro boxer and trainer named Eddie Thomas. They were outnumbered by about twenty of these "rockers" and had cuts and bruises as a result, and they weren't at all happy. Therefore, we stepped in and planned to take a couple of cars with five boys in each and pay them a visit that evening.

We arrive; it went off, and although we did a better job than the boys did the night before, we just had no chance, there were just too many of them. However, we managed to get out of there in one piece, and I remember Eddie hitting me over the head with a sweeping brush outside to alert me because I had this boy on the floor. Anyway, we got ourselves away from the place but planned to let it simmer for a few weeks in the hope that they would forget, and then we would go in heavy and finish the job.

About a month later, on a Saturday night, we had been out all day in our local pub and decided to go to town. We stopped off at a pub called the Vulcan, a rough old pub and well known for its fighting and violence; even the owner kept two Dobermans out the back in case of emergencies. Now at the back of the pub, there were two pool tables, and guess who's playing pool; you got it, about six of these rockers from the Great Escape, nice and relaxed and without a care-in-the-world. A few minutes later, all hell has let loose; its mayhem and the place has erupted. Me and one of my pal's nicknamed Curly, who's only about 5 foot 4 inches tall, but built like a bull go at this big fucker. Now, this lump must have been about six-foot-five and towered above the pair of us. Not to mention the fact that he had a pool cue as well, so it looked like the odds are stacked.

Nonetheless, we weren't going to let that stop us as we knocked him onto the pool table and battered him senseless. I managed to get the cue out of his hand and hit him over the head with it, by which point he's cowering and covering his head, pleading for us to stop. Our gang battered the lot of them that night, and to be honest, I don't think they got a single punch in. The downside was that we got chucked out of the pub by the owner, who was threatening to let the dogs out. Don't ask me how, but through all the fighting, I'd only gone and lost one of my trainers; the boys took the piss out of me for the rest of the night for that one. I went back to the pub a few hours later, and the owner gave it back to me, not before informing me that we were all barred, so that was that. Everything calmed down with those boys after that fight, although we did cross paths with the rest of them one day, and they didn't want to know – especially in light of the Vulcan incident. Years later, I became friends with some of them, and we buried-the-hatchet, putting it down to us being kid's growing up.

A mate of mine was going to pay some man a visit who had been chatting his girlfriend up, and he asked me if I would go down to watch his back; I agreed to it and took another pal of ours called Flynny with us in case it came-on-top. Anyway, it's the day of reckoning, and we wait until it's after hours so that there will be no witnesses about, and then jump in his car, and make our way down to the pub that he worked at; the pub was cited on the bank of some canal (the relevance of this will become apparent very shortly.) Now instead of turning the car round so that we could make a quick exit if it gets too heavy, my mate wasted no time, slammed the brakes on, and jumped out of the car in a mad temper storming his way over to the doors of the said pub. At that point, I'm shaking my head, thinking, 'what the fuck is he doing,' as he's banging his fist on the heavy doors. The supposed offender answer's, and my mate immediately goes at him; fist flying like a lunatic, so Flynny and I start to get out of his car when all of a sudden five drunk men come running out through the doors, and a couple of them go straight for me. One of them smashes me in the mouth, which busts my lip, I go flying back, and they are on me again. Now, these are men,

33

not boys, but they're as drunk as fuck, so I manage to hold on to them, and the three of us go flying into the canal, we're in three feet of water, and I'm throwing punches around everywhere. (I can laugh about it now, but at the time, I was scared shitless, and I think they knew it.) Anyway, they let go of me, allowing me to get out of the water and order us to fuck off out of there. We're going, but as I glance across, I can see my mate getting back into the car while shouting abuse at them; he's calling them all the bastards under the sun. I said to him, 'for fuck's sake, let's get the fuck out of here,' the three of us were bust up bad, and all our clothes had been ripped off us. Mind you, I was the only fucker who looked like he'd been swimming with the pike and rusty bike chains, but we still laughed about it as we drove home. My mate's father found out and went back down that night, but this time they wouldn't open the door - probably because they knew him and were aware of his reputation, turns out, they called the police in fear.

A little while later, we caught up with the boy and his mates in a place called Strikers, and they all ended up with their comeuppances. I'd started playing for a local youth rugby team round this time known as, Dowlais, and every week for about a year would we be fighting non-stop. It got so bad that the local W.R.U threatened to chuck our first team out of the league if we didn't stop fighting; our club even got one of their players a well-known hard man, Ken Morgan, to have a talk with some of us. The talk calmed us all down for a bit - but unfortunately, not for too long. Nevertheless, I managed to stay on with the youth side for three years, and I even picked a trophy up for the most promising player of the year, which saw me promoted to the senior team. Dowlais was well known for attracting some of the hardest men in the town, formidable names that up until this point I'd heard only stories about while growing up, and here I am at the same club, and eventually even training and playing with them.

When I wasn't at rugby training in the week, the lad's and I would be down the local shop buying all kinds of potent booze, and as usual, we would get in a right state. One night we got into an argument with this local gang known as, "the Gurnos shop boys," there was only five of us; outnumbered by their hefty fifteen, so as you can imagine, we got ourselves out of there sharpish; cos' let's face it us boys were crazy, but we weren't fucking stupid.

Word soon got around that these boys were looking for us. So, the boys and I went back over there one night, and as luck would have it, there were only about five of them this time too. They began pleading with us a bit, saying that it wasn't them that want trouble, but one of the leaders.

Anyway, we arranged to meet him for the following night at seven o clock, but we needed a plan. Therefore, I said to the boys: 'if we all go over there, we will all end up getting battered,' I said, 'if just two of us go, the rest of the boys won't start jumping in.' The boys were happy enough for me to go, but said that they would be close by, in waiting, in case it went tit's up, so that was that - the plan was formed.

A few days later, my mate, Kevin, picked me up with twenty minutes to spare, and I'm there nonchalantly tucking into pie and chips at my mam's house. Anyway,

Kev says to me, 'eh Shirl, what's happening, we've got to be there by seven, haven't we?' He must have thought I had bottled it, and carries on with, 'how come you're so relaxed?' to which I replied, 'I'll beat the boy easy,' and if there was any chance that I was going to lose, then I was going to spew my pie n chips up all over him. 'You're fucking mad, you are Shirl.' Kev said. We made our way to the shops, and as we got closer, I spotted about twenty of them gathered there waiting, and I did start to get a bit nervous.

Putting my nerves aside, I walked straight over to them and said. 'Right, where is he then?' Immediately one of them piped up with, 'he hasn't turned up yet!' Then suddenly, out walks one of them like Clint Eastwood; drops his jacket to the floor and says: 'I'll fight you?' Now I knew this boy was probably the hardest one out of the lot of them, which was obvious; otherwise, he wouldn't have stepped up in the first place. Therefore, without giving him a second's notice, I grabbed him and threw him smack bang into these shop shutters, and he hit them so hard that he immediately collapsed to the floor, and I jumped on top of him and pummeled him with a flurry of punches. Next thing you know, his gang is pulling me off him, telling me to calm down, but my heads gone and I'm offering each and every one of them to fight me - only to no avail. Steadily I calmed myself down a bit and says, 'tell your leader he's having it when I get hold of him,' while the other boys are still spread-eagle on the floor as my mate and I walk off with me the victor; cool as a cucumber as Lenny Mclean would say. I couldn't believe that not one of them had the balls to fight me.

A week later, I was out with two of my mates, and we'd been clubbing, and as we were sat outside the club, who do we bump into, only the leader and his mates. Now, the boy I'd battered up at the shops was in the middle of being arrested for fighting again, so this other so-called leader starts shouting, 'c'mon, round the back of the club?' Now things are quite even because there are three of them and three of us, well two of us really, cos our third boy just held our coats. I went at the fucking leader, and I'm pummeling him with rights and lefts, he was fucked and, on the floor, then, all of a sudden I felt someone else hit me from behind, and as I turned around there was this boy stood there going, 'c'mon then, I've got a black belt in Karate.' I looked at him for a second and then smashed him up too. We jumped straight into a taxi and got the fuck out of there before the police turned up, rumours were going around a couple of days later that the leader's jaw was broken, and that the police were looking for me. Things settled down, and I never heard any more about it; I'm guessing that the 'Wanted-Shirley' rumours were simply bullshit.

It's now 1988 and I'm coming up to my 18th birthday and it was about this time that I going to make my police cell, debut. I was out for my mate's birthday and we were up the Gurnos estate club drinking. Being young and foolish we decided to have a competition who could drink the most of this new German lager called D pills; this stuff was like fucking rocket fuel – anyway, I won albeit with a certain amount of cheating, but hey, who was to know. Now due to the amount of lager I had drank in such a short space of time meant that by the time we got into town - I was absolutely fucked! I hadn't a clue what I was doing; anyway, at the time we ended up in a pub called 'The

Court of Requests.' Now this place was a right shithole at the time and downstairs was a proper drug den, I hated drugs, so we stayed out in the beer garden. Everyone's fucking about having a good time when all of a sudden, and for reasons I cannot explain, I picked up a breezeblock and launched it through a plate-glass window. You see, like I said I was fucked. Everyone is looking at me in complete shock. I mean it wasn't even funny – it was futile and pointless. Next thing I know I'm being rugby tackled to the ground by three men, and they're holding me down. However, I'm off my head; laughing like a fucking psychopath, and still making jokes and acting up when the police arrived. The boys that were with me were still in shock, they knew I'd gone too far this time. Anyway, I was very quickly handcuffed, and carted off to the local police station.

Having been in the cell for a couple of hours, I was starting to sober up, when I heard this voice outside, shouting, 'when you get out of here, I'm going to bastard kill you!' Oh, crap, I thought, it wasn't funny anymore because this was my mother, and I'm telling you now, she doesn't sound ready for a whimsical story - this was all I needed.

Apparently, there had been a big fight with the skinhead's in the town that night, so the cells were full of these nutters, too, and on hearing my mother, they were laughing their heads off at me. I remember one of them shouting: 'fuck me, son, you're safer in here than outside!' My father was there too but must have had enough of the waiting and left at about 3.30 in the morning. As for me, I had to stay there a bit longer for mugshot and autograph signings, and then they let me go about two hours later. To be honest, being released into the arms of my raging Mother was probably the scariest time in the whole sorry situation and arriving home that morning; stepping through my front door was terrifying. I'll leave the rest to your imagination.

The very next day (on the proviso that I pay for the window) the police made a phone call to my house to inform us that the pub was willing to drop all of the charges. I guess my Mother must have stated her case quite well, and it must have hit home with the police, and for that reason, I was lucky and was let off without being charged. Mind you, it did end up being a costly night out, but not quite as expensive as the night my mate was about to encounter a few weeks later.

This time we're on it again, four of us this time, and as usual we're all pissed up. I had calmed down a little after the performance with the window. However, one of my mates, Flynny had been arguing with someone, and he was in a bit of a temper. Walking across the college bridge on our way back into town, Flynny, still raging, started hitting some panels of a window with the heel of his hand; he's only tapping them though, I think he was just trying to impress us. Anyway, the other boys' and I decided to give him a helping hand and we're kicking the windows with him; we must have smashed about four of them when I said to him,

'Look, if you're going to hit them, hit them properly like we just have. Don't fucking tickle 'em Flynn!'

Next thing you know, he's punching 'em full force with his fists, which is something I had learnt not to do many years ago when I put my fist straight through a telephone box and split my knuckle open, leaving my hand in a bad way for a long time. As we were approaching the end of the bridge we noticed that there were police at either end – we were definitely fucked, I thought. Moreover, I certainly didn't fancy doing a Butch and Sundance style jump into the river below to getaway. So, considering what I'd been pinched for just a few weeks earlier, I was sure I was going to get sent to prison.

The police tackled us! Insisting that we had put the windows in and that they had been watching us as we were walking across the bridge, we contested this saying that we hadn't smashed anything. Now, there weren't any cameras around there so they couldn't totally prove it. Nonetheless, one of the cocky fuckers said, 'can you all remove your shoes, as we are using them for evidence?' By this point, we were all laughing, that was until we realised that he was being serious. 'I'm fucked again,' I thought to myself, and next thing you know, one of the coppers notices that Flynn's hand was pissing blood all over the place. With that, Flynny was arrested; he took it on the chin though, taking all of the blame himself. I'd never been so relieved in all my life. They took Flynn away, got a result with him, and let the rest of us off. Happy with the result, we made our way up to the local curry house, laughing our heads off on the way. Flynny ended up with a considerable fine and paid it all himself.

After leaving school with no qualifications at all, I went to various job interviews, but unfortunately, I was always turned down; work was tough to find. I ended up working for a building firm, labouring for my father, for a poxy seven quid a day. The money was shit, but after five days, I had 35 quid in my pocket, that was well enough money for a whole weekend of drinking back in the 80s. I also picked up a bit of labouring work with my uncle Jeff as well at the time.

As the title suggests, we were getting madder by the week, and it always seemed to be me that was the front man, with mad Miles in the wings, winding me up. Whenever we met up on a Sunday, after a night out, all you would hear was, *did you hear what Shirly did last night?* - I was relentless. We had been on a good little run, and the police could never pin anything on us.

I was in my second year of college but dropped out in the end because I felt that I was getting nowhere fast. There I was, with no qualifications from school, and now I'd fucked up college too – people were trying to help me, but it just wasn't sinking in - I had no interest whatsoever. Over time, I applied for a bunch of jobs and had plenty of interviews, but unfortunately, I failed them all.

Eventually, I was given the option to go on what was called a Nacro course, with the slogan: 'BE WHO YOU WANT TO BE!' And all that crap. It was a Plastering course, and as luck would have it, my dad was a plasterer; so, I thought it might be a handy trade to have under my belt, and it could also be invaluable to me in the future. However, after just a month into the course, I lost interest, and after hooking up with some new mates, I started missing lessons. I was knocking around with a boy called Jason, and another boy who had recently passed his driving test, anyway, this other boy said, 'I've got my dad's car boys, do you fancy going for a spin?' Well, I must admit, this sounded far better than being stuck in plastering all day long, so we agreed to go with him for a ride. Within minutes of getting in his car, he's speeding, and he's gone around this bend and totally lost control - flipping the car over three times. There was I, wedged behind the seat screaming for my life when finally, the car came to a stop - upside down. I'm frightened and a little dazed, but thankfully I was still alive.

A few minutes later, Jason and the driver have disappeared, while I was stuck screaming my head off in his Dad's fucking car. Turns out the boy had done a runner because he had taken the car while his dad was on holiday without him knowing. A group of men from a garage opposite dragged me out, and another was seeing to Jason, whose arm was fucked. The police turned up, and Jason and I were sent to the hospital for a check-up. After an extended stay in A&E, Jason and I took the long walk home to break the news to our parent's, we were scared shitless for the outcome, but happy to be alive, and then what did we do? *You got it: straight out on the piss.*

It was around this time when I started having some sort of OCD episode, it was tiring, not to mention soul-destroying. I would have to count to certain numbers in my head, touch things so many times, and I even developed a minor bout of Tourette's. In addition to this, I also adopted a strange little twitch where I'd chuck my head back now and again and lick my lips a hundred times until they were red-raw and scabby. I had this for years, and even to this day, I still have my moments, *mind you I try my best to hide it.* I never went to see my doctor about any of it. I simply put it down to some kind of cross-wiring in my head.

This one night, I'd been out drinking with Jason and another mate I'd met on the plastering course named John, who we nicknamed, 'Ganga' down to his love of cannabis. I never had done a drug in my life, but it was the thing to do back then, so a few of the other boys and I started smoking. A little later on, as we were going through town,

42

we noticed some roadworks outside this shop; all of a sudden, Ganga pushed me down this hole, which was about 5feet deep. If I'm honest, I don't think he realised just how deep it was because he had a right game trying to pull me back out. I was as black as fucking coal, covered head to foot in mud, mind you, I was way too drunk to give a fuck, and just carried on drinking in the next pub, with all eyes on me. Sometime after, I managed to get my own back on Ganga, you see, a mate of mine Kevin was in the police force, so I got him to make out he was on duty and arrest Ganga, it was hilarious, my copper mate even had him up against a wall and everything; searching him, until we all broke out laughing.

We had a bit of trouble with skinhead gangs at the time. This one night, they'd smashed my mate in the face on our way home but left the rest of us alone 'cos they could see we were a lot younger. A year later, we visited a club called the Scala; unaware that it was a skinhead club we just went in. Now, there were about eight boys with me. I was quite drunk and had just bought myself another pint and put it on the pool table, which apparently, was a bit of a "faux pas" in this club. Anyway, the next thing you know, these skinheads start ripping into me, so I've chucked the pool cue at them, called them all a bunch of wankers and left. As I left the pub, about four of them followed me outside, so I've hit the one closest to me full in the face, and he's gone down. Immediately the rest jump on me, I was outnumbered and swinging like a mad man. Next thing you know I'm on the floor holding my nuts. Now, I don't know if you've ever been kicked in the bollocks by someone wearing a pair of calf-length doccies (Doctor Martin boots) but it hurts like fuck! I was debilitated to say the least. Fortunately, two of my mates ran in to help me.

The rest of my lot were inside the pub, still shitting themselves, but by this point, I was back up on my feet, and we were up against seven of them. I manage to knock another one of the fuckers down; this gave us a bit of breathing space and a little time to get ourselves away! We had given theses skinheads a good go, and all we had ended up with were a few bruises. I thanked my two mates but immediately realised that I'd left my jacket in the fucking pub, so went back in to get it – alone.

As I approached the club, the rest of my mates who had bottled it came walking past me with their heads down. I called them a bunch of wankers and carried on over to the doors. As I walked in, I noticed a couple of skins on the door so I said to them, 'Oi, I want my fucking jacket!' My mouth was bleeding like fuck, and I think that this gave them the impression that I didn't give a fuck, and they were right, 'cos I didn't! I mean, let's be honest, if they had wanted to, this lot could have done me again right there and then, but they didn't, and one of them just went and got my jacket. Apparently, I earned a lot of respect from the 'skinheads' that night, and years later ended up good mates with some of them.

A couple of weeks later, two of my mates had a bit of a tear up in a club and had taken a bit of a beating from this bloke who was a so-called tasty fucker and a bunch of his mates. As luck would have it, the very next night while out with a few of my mates, we bumped into him in a pub called 'The Castle Hotel.' Anyway, he start's threatening the boys' again, and thinking that we were bottling it because we left the place, he followed us outside, however, as soon as he got within arms-reach of me; I've belted him straight in the face: dropping him on his arse, my mates joined in, and we beat the living crap out of him. Mind you, we had it away

44

on our toes in case the police turned up, and never had any trouble off that bully, ever again.

Talking about tasty fuckers, I'll tell you about another well-known hard man who started trouble with me one night. It was New Year's Eve, and it had been a good night until this point when right in front of us this nutter was having a row with his girlfriend, he then proceeded to get up and kicked a pint glass straight at us.

Being leary, we all laughed and cheered, but he took umbrage to this and immediately ran at me (the biggest of our bunch), again! We went hurtling straight onto a table; it collapsed, and we were rolling around in a shitload of glass. I managed to get off him, and then all my mates started to kick the shit out of him. With that, his misses jumped in, she was going off her head and then she bottled one of my mates. The hard man got himself up and went next door to get his cousin - who was fucking enormous, so we got the fuck out of there and ended up in the road laughing our crazy heads off. We later found out that night that his cousin had run in the club and knocked three other boys spark out, thinking that it was us. We gave the town a wide berth for a while, just in case they were still looking for us.

I did see the boy a couple of years later when I was bouncing; he came up to me and said, 'you don't remember me do you?' However, I was straight back at him and replied, 'of course I can remember you! I was fighting you in a pub a few years back!' A look of shock came across his face as he put his hand out and said, 'no hard feelings mate, eh?' He and I became good friends a few years later when I joined a gym that he was running.

Another night we had gone to the local Indian curry house, now, I was utterly fucked again, and trying to think of things to do for a laugh. Now, my mate's neighbour's Son was home on leave from the army, and they were in the curry house too, and they're sat right behind us. Anyway, I've finished my food double-quick, and decided to lift my table up in the air for a laugh, now, I know you're all thinking 'what on earth's funny about doing that?', and to be honest I ain't got a fucking clue. All I can say is that when I was young, I was clearly a bit dumb; so, I just found it funny. Noticing that I'd done this, one of my mates decided to do exactly the same thing with his table - obviously, he was as dumb as I was. With that, we ran for the door! Now, some of the boys that hadn't been observing my, 'table up in the air' trick, stood stunned and bewildered, and unbeknown to us as we got to the front doors, we realised that they were in fact locked – SHIT! The owner of the restaurant must have realised that we were about to play the fools' and locked them just in case.

There we were, ten of us crammed in this little hallway, with my mates' trying everything possible to open the front door. I'm on the other side of the entrance holding another door shut, trying my best to stop the bunch of "machete-wielding-Indians" from killing us. I was laughing at them through the glass, calling them all the fuckers under the sun, while some of the boys are screaming, 'we are going to die!' By this time, I'm in full- on-psycho-mode, screaming at them and laughing. It occurred to me that the more terrified I got, the more raging I became. Nonetheless, I'm stood there thinking, 'if they open this fucking door, we're all going to get chopped up into little pieces – it was less than funny now.

Thankfully, and not before time, one of the boys happened to notice a window open above the door, and within a split second, the old nutcase from the army was up and out of it like John Rambo up a mountain and opens the door from the outside. The boys' scattered out onto the street like rats scuttling up an alleyway. While I'm standing holding onto the door for dear life, well, not for much longer, 'cos with that legged it, getting myself out of there. With the amount of mayhem, you'd swear there was a bomb going off in that place, and we must have missed the police by seconds has I watched them arrive from an alleyway. Another lucky escape and something to laugh about for years to come.

Another night I was in a Chinese curry house called Hing Hongs. I'd been playing up in that place for years, and how I had never been banned is anyone's guess; I imagine it was like the rest of my antics - just a part of growing up. Obviously, looking back at it now, it was stupid and childish; nevertheless, I made it up to the owner ten years later when I worked next door to the place and sorted a whole load of trouble out for her.

We arrived at Hing Hong's and took over two tables: four of us on each. Halfway through eating, I borrowed one of the boy's lighters, turned around and pretended to be talking to one of my mates as I was setting fire to their tablecloth from underneath. I then turned back to my table and continued to eat my food as if nothing was wrong, while all the time smirking. A couple of seconds later, there was a load of screaming, and the boys from the other table are running around like headless chickens, as the waiters were running around throwing buckets of water over the burning table, and then the owner threw the lot of them out.

Realising what I had done, the boys on my table started laughing like fuck as the tablecloth was in flames. I've got my back to them, pretending that I knew nothing about it and carried on eating my food as if nothing was wrong. When we left, the woman said that the other lot were banned for life, but we were ok. I caught up with the boys' outside and told them, of course, they weren't very happy, but found the funny side of it and couldn't help but laugh.

Another local pub of mine was the Gurnos Tavern; it was a well-known rough pub, where you'd always end up fighting. One night I was outside, and two of my mates were fighting each other over a stupid argument. Anyway, I went to break them up when two boys said to me, 'oi, fucking leave them to fight!' I thought you cheeky fuckers, so you want to see a fight do you, as I steamed into them and smashed them up instead. Next thing you know, I'm getting hit over the back with a sweeping brush by the landlady - I thought to myself, what's the fucking score with these people and their brushes, and again, we all ended up getting banned. I did go back to the tavern a few years later; however, the first night back in, I got banned again; this time though, it was for life. The pub was demolished a few years later.

CHAPTER THREE

(Going off the Rails)

It had reached the stage where every weekend had to have a story to tell; what with Milesy, winding me up, the fact of the aforementioned was in part already written. It's difficult to believe that this wind-up-merchant is now a respected schoolteacher, but in those days, he was as mad as a hatter, whatever that fucking means, reference Merriam: (a person who makes, and sells hats,) well anyway, he was fucking crackers. I was also getting madder by the hour, much to the point that if I didn't do something off the wall, or risky, it would be deemed in my lunatic head as a boring night. We would do anything, from smashing windows in garages to half-inching clothes off of washing lines; we'd pinch potted plants and set fires to skips, and fight with gangs for a hit, – an idiotic young boys fix.

For a laugh, someone dared me to go up on the roof of a nightclub called, The Zone, and move the hands of the local clock. Therefore, pretending to use the club's toilet, I snuck up the scaffolding that was erected for repairs on the outside of the building and climbed through the window. I was about 100 feet up in the air, drunk as a skunk, balancing across this roof when the bouncers began yelling at me to come down. They couldn't actually see me, so I hid out of eyeshot for at least an hour; there was no way they were going to risk their lives coming out to check. I then knocked on the toilet window and snuck back in as if nothing had happened.

Boxing Day the following week and there were loads of us boys out, we were in a place called the labour club, playing up merry hell as per usual. Most of the boys were jumping up and down on cars, and in the meantime one of our mate's knocked some boy off his motorbike in the middle of the road, and they immediately started fighting; it was mayhem, everyone trying to outdo one another, nevertheless, with our boys, there's only ever one winner, me!

As we were on our way to the local nightclub, my mate spotted a dead pigeon on the floor. Its guts are hanging out, and a couple of the boys were spewing. I asked the boys if they minded it tagging along with us, as I concealed it inside my jacket and snuck into a nightclub. No sooner had we got inside, I started to throw it across the room, and watched on while every fucker in the room was looking up in the air in shock thinking there a live pigeon in the club. All the girls were screaming, as it landed on them… how I never got caught with that one, I don't know. I was a bouncer's nightmare, a complete prick.

Another night Milesy had wound me up all night, he had bet me that I couldn't pinch a JCB, and drive it home, I couldn't even drive a car let alone one of these fucking things. Nevertheless, dumb fuck that I was just had to give it a try. The police nearly had us again as they chased the boy's away from there while I was still sitting in it, hiding out of the way.

Half an hour later, I caught up with the boy's, and they bet me a pound, yeah, I know, a fucking pound note, that I couldn't jump across some car bonnets. There was about five in a row, and I managed to do two of them when all of a sudden, I slipped and landed flat on my back, I thought I was fucked, the rest of the boys ran off laughing, to the

50

calamitous noise of me running across the car roofs' and bonnets to getaway. Noticing the flashing lights from the nearing police sirens, I got up and ran like a fucking banshee. Nothing was safe when I was on top form, I would pinch anything that wasn't locked down, I would even nick bags of coal and Christmas trees from the local garage, and when I arrived home I'd be stinking; hiding my clothes in-case my Mam found them and twigged.

I had another run-in with the police; I didn't get caught or anything but, I heard they were looking for me, so I went and gave myself up. I had been in a fight a month or so earlier with these boys. What had happened was my mate's sister was getting hassle in work off this boy, and one-night, he caught up with him and a fight a broke out. I'd had a good few beers at this point, and the next thing this boy was trying to head-butt my mate through a local Kebab shop window. After a few more minutes, I had had enough of what I was seeing and went over and punched the boy straight in the head dropping him to the floor. Immediately, a few other boys joined in, and all hell let loose. A few of us managed to drag my mate away before the police got there, at which point the boy and his mates were fighting with another bunch of boys while luckily, we had made our way up the street. However, a month or so later my mate and I were up at court on a charge of GBH,

I had to laugh at one part in the boy's statement, because he said that as he was fighting my mate, got hit on the back of the head, with what he believed to be a hammer; I was dying to tell the copper that was interviewing me that it was actually my right hand that he'd felt. The only bit that really pissed us off was that they were trying to say that we pinched all of their jewellery. Now, we didn't mind a fight, but we weren't no pincher's, anyway we were due to appear in court when we get a phone call the day before saying that it had all been thrown out. Not long after this my mate started to calm down, which was good because he was due to go off to college, which was the best move he ever made.

I've never had much luck with work; when I was young while I was labouring for my dad, I got electrocuted on a wall, that'll teach me for touching bare wires. I also crashed a milk float into a garden and lost my gaffa hundreds of pints of milk, not to mention the woman's fence that I had knocked down. As I'm sure, you can imagine I didn't keep that job for long. Another time I was working upstairs at this house above a local convenience shop, the builder who I was working for popped out for an hour, and as I've walked past a water tap, I've knocked it and the water's gushing out all over the fucking room. Besides, these were the days before phones. Anyway, I've panicked and run down the stairs, by which point there was that much water spraying out that the whole shop was flooded but fortunately this boy with a bit of savvy ran outside and turned the water off. To be honest, I could have cried, and again, it wasn't long before I lost that job as well.

Sometime after, my dad and I started working for this builder, we had a good run with him until he tucked the whole firm up. We tried for months to get back the money he owed us: all to no avail. If it happened today with my reputation, it would be a different story, but at the time, I didn't have one, so we just left it.

A few people tried tucking me up when I did a bit of plastering on my own too. I was on the job working in this

big building that sold settees and carpet's etc. Anyway, I'd
given this big Indian man a price for 5 days work; I think it
was about £300 at the time. Now, to get the job done a bit
faster, I did a few extra hours at night and completed the
work in just four days,' and when I went to get paid, he
tried to

palm-me-off with less, saying that it was fair because it had
taken me less time. I explained that I'd worked on through
the evenings, accenting that in fact, I had done more hours
over fewer days, but he said quite adamantly, 'No! No! No!
I'll pay you £50 less!' I could feel the colour drain from
my face as I started yelling at him, and he got in my space,
so I just lost it and smashed a table, which flew up in the
air. I also threw my plastering hawk at him and waved my
sharp trowel about threatening to cut him. To be honest, I'd
never seen a man back down so quickly, he was pleading
that he was sorry, and ran off to get the rest of the money. I
had my brother Steven working with me as a labourer, so I
asked him to grab all the tools, and that we were leaving –
we didn't even finish the job.

I was now in my twenties and still playing rugby, only
now, I was in the senior team, inevitably fighting most
games. I don't know what it was, but every time I put on
those fucking rugby boots, I turned into an animal. I
couldn't even begin to imagine the number of fights I've
had on a rugby field, but it must be a lot because I was
even up against the W.R.U for my violent misbehaving.
During one game, we had five people sent off and had to
appeal against it in front of the committee in Cardiff Arm's
Park; it was either that or be chucked out of the league.
Mind you, I still got a guilty at the hearing, but fortunately,
two of the other boys got off with it, which meant we could
stay in the league – thankfully.

I remember fighting this well-known hard man from the valley one Saturday afternoon; most of my team were scared shitless of him, and he was throwing his weight around on the field. I was only about twenty-three at the time, but I didn't give a fuck who he thought he was. He'd gone into one ruck and stamped on one of our boys' heads, so I've gone straight at him, landing on top of him with a flurry of punches. With that, he managed to roll on top of me and then someone broke us up. Everyone there thought he was going to try and do me after the game, but he didn't, he just came over and shook my hand. I went back to his club a little later - he didn't say a word, and the respect I had from my team on the bus on our drive home was unbelievable.

This one night I was walking home drunk with my mates Flynny and Mark, we'd been up the local garage to get some food when I bump into a boy who I'd known while growing up. He asks us if he could walk home with us for a bit of company and went on to say that he had robbed the garage of porn mags and chocolates ten minutes before. He had been inside for the last couple of years when all of a sudden started giving the big hard man story, showing us his scar where he'd been slit with a machete right across his stomach, over some drug deal in prison – I'm sure he thought he was John Mcvicar.

After about five minutes of non-stop bragging, he began to do our heads in but insisted on telling us that he had changed and was no longer like he was years ago and that he was as hard as nails, and a force to be reckoned with. At this point, my mates were walking in front of us chatting away, when 'Mcvicar' starts telling me about this other boy who was in prison with him. Supposedly, the boy was in jail for burglary, but also apparently, for sexually abusing some old woman. Anyway, 'Mcvicar' reckoned they were best mates and that the boy had taken the wrap for him, so I said to him, 'what the fuck are you on about?' To which he replied, 'well, you know the old grannie who he supposed to have raped?' I nodded in acknowledgment, and he went on, 'yeah, well the other boy inside didn't do it; it was me!'

Now I thought to myself, what the fucks is he telling me this for the dirty bastard, and I've smashed him straight in the face and dropped him to the floor. I was just about to stamp on his head when my two mates pulled me away and asked me what the fuck was going on. I called the lowlife all the dirty cunts going, he as he's shouting to me, 'you're fucking mad, you are. I was only winding you up!' Well, that's it, my heads gone, and I've smashed him in the face knocking him down again. My mates were screaming at me to leave him alone, so I then explained to them what the boy had said, and my mate changed his tune, saying, 'go on Shirl knock the dirty fucker out.' However, my mate banged him instead, knocking him spark out. While he was on the floor, I opened up his jacket, and pinch the mags and chocolates from him, and we walked off laughing. I don't know if there was any truth in what he'd told me, but I didn't give a fuck – he was a prick. To be honest, I have not a clue if what he was saying was right, because the clown was always a bit of a 'Walter Mitty' fantasist! I almost bumped into him a couple of years later when I walk into a shop in town, and he was in there abusing the staff, his arse went when he spotted me and quickly left the shop.

Talking about garages, one particular night me and some of the boys were walking home drunk "again," and went into a local garage. Now, the doors were usually closed, but a taxi driver had left them open, so about four of us went in. Immediately after stepping foot over the threshold, I pulled a porno mag (Adult Magazine) down from the top shelf and opened it up. Then suddenly, this boy came from behind the counter and snatched it right out of my hands, while 'effing-n-blinding (swearing) at me. This boy obviously didn't know who I was, and with that, I flipped my lid. I picked up a box of Terry's chocolate orange and launched it straight at him; hitting him in the face, he looked at me in all shocked but proceeded to chuck a bag of sweets back at me; it looked like a fucking "Bugsy Malone" fight scene. Oh, it's all happening now, I thought, as I launched a couple of mars bars at him, and by now, my mates were laughing their heads off while loading up their pockets with sweets and chocolates. I was thinking to myself, shit, we better get the fuck out of here before the police turn up. At that moment, the boys' and I got out of the shop and ran, in speedy fashion up the street and hid behind an embankment – the Police turned up minutes later, so we all split up, making our way to a mate's house for a late drink. One of the boys Phillip said he'd never seen anything like it before, as he pulled a magnum bar from out of his trousers laughing. Once again, it was a lucky escape; mainly because the shop had CCTV, but thankfully, nothing came of that little incident either; which was fantastic, imagine reading the headline on that little story in our local paper.

One of the maddest things is I ever did for a laugh was to eat a toilet cube; you know little blue cake that sanitizes men's urinals. Well, I have put one in my mouth and start chewing it like a sweet - the boys were wrenching but laughing at the same time. Mind you, it was not so funny an hour or so later when I was walking home, feeling faint as I was hallucinating and talking shit. My mates' Mark and Jeho, ended up carrying me home. The effects of that little juvenile trick had me spewing all night. My parents thought I was drunk, and I was in a bad way for a good couple of days after, with the taste of that detergent-drenched-lozenge, persistent. Not to mention the boys', as they gesticulated pissing up against me for the forceable.

I was still fighting week in week out on the rugby field. One week this boy came into a ruck late and stuck his head into one of our players, I immediately spotted him, and smashed him straight in the mouth, knocking a bunch of his teeth out, he was flat out on the floor, and nobody had seen it. The funny thing was he ended up playing for us the following year and would pull his false teeth out after games and say to everyone while laughing, 'see these gnashers (teeth) look, Shirly did this to me!' To be honest, I felt a bit of a twat, even though he'd deserved it at the time.

One Saturday, we were playing this team up in the mountains, I was a sub at the time because of an injury, and, watching this big number 8 throwing his weight about; he was punching and stamping on most of our team. With about 20 minutes left to go the coach said to me, 'warm-up Shirl, you're going on Son - and that big fucker in the number 8 shirt is all yours!' Well, I was only on the field for about 5 minutes, and we had one knocked out number 8 grazing on the grass. I remember watching them carrying him off, while my captain Bluffis caught my eye winking at me. We still lost the game though, I mean, I can do a lot of things, but I can't perform fucking miracles – but anyway, my job was done.

Another time I'd drank two pints of "ultimate orange" (banned to consumers) before a game of rugby and was running around like a fucking lunatic for an hour and a half, most of the other boys on our team could only take half a pint.

Anyway, 3 o clock the next morning I was still buzzing and still drinking like a lunatic in my mate Gary's pub before getting myself out of the place at about 6 o clock in the morning. Now there's a shortcut to my house across this football field, but the only thing is there were a couple of horses in it, now I'm not a fan of horses, but I'll do anything for a bet.

Anyway, I thought I'd save myself half an hour and take a risk. However, halfway across the field, one of these things comes towards me; I'm still pissed up and panicking, so I gave the horse a right hook belt right on its chin. Well, his whole head moved, and he made a terrible noise, so, there I was doing a Linford Christie style hundred-meter sprint without the suggestion of a glance behind me, right across the field. When I finally got to the end of the field, I start spewing up everywhere, I turned around, and the horse hadn't so much as budged from its spot. To this day, I still have no time for Shergar and his pals, and from that day forward, I made sure I took the long road.

One summer, we went on holiday and rented a house for a week in Newquay, Cornwall with my mate Lyn and his misses. It was at the time that my mates and I had taken up smoking a bit of weed, oh, and sniffing vodka up our noses- for some silly reason. Now, that's an experience I certainly wouldn't recommend to anyone, although it sort of started a trend off, and the locals couldn't get over it. One night a couple of us ended up in the sea, fucked out of our heads amongst the fish and the seaweed. Later, we had a competition in a pub who could pinch the maddest object, which was no easy task because to get to our house, you had to go past the local police station. Shortly after, there was I with a 3-foot tall garden gnome tucked under my arm, how I didn't get caught and locked up for that little jaunt, I'll never know. Mind you, I still lost; my mate beat me by sneaking into a bed and breakfast lounge and pinching an even bigger fucking ornament. *'Better luck next time Shirl.'*

I also had a thing about water (I was terrified of it) and I'd had a few escapes in my time with it as well. The thing is, I can only swim about a length, but I just love jumping in from great heights (I'm a lunatic). I once jumped off the Newport Bridge, drunk, and why, I hear you ask? I couldn't tell you, and I later found out that it was a local suicide spot because of the mud underneath. Another mad night I went down the local weir in our town drunk, the police turned up, and one of my mates told them that we were just tickling fish, and thankfully, they let us off with a warning. I went down there 'drunk' again a few years later, only this time I almost lost my life – let me explain…

Right, the drop on the weir was about 10 feet high, but because of the water, it was like one massive big slide. Anyway, my mate Davies and I slid down it together, the boys are crying laughing at us and usually when you stop at the bottom it's about 3ft deep, and you could walk to the side, but it had been raining all week, and the current was too strong, instead of stopping, we end up getting chucked about downstream, I tried my best to get to the bank but just couldn't make it, I was now panicking and getting really tired, I started to swallow water has I was going under and the water was freezing has it was winter, I ended up about 30 yards downstream clinging to this branch for my life, Davies had got to the bank a little bit further on downstream, I eventually made it to the bank and just lied there exhausted, but happy I was still alive, we walked all the way back round talking about how lucky we were, the other boys thought we were dead by the way the current had taken us downstream, I learned my lesson that night, and I wouldn't go down there again.

My luck finally came to an end in the Zone Night club, I'd been drinking cider and whiskey chasers and was dancing like a lunatic, I got asked by a bouncer to calm down but silly fucker me carried on, he came at me again and said 'fucking calm down, you prick', so I've pushed him flying and the next thing I know I've got five bouncers on me, they then carry me out of the club, now I'm struggling like fuck when all of a sudden they drop me to the floor in this corridor, then they all decide to punch and kick fuck into me, but one of them is right going for it, but the harder they kick me, the more I'm laughing at them, they must have thought I couldn't have been right as I was taking a right hiding and just laughing at them. They then pick me back up and chuck me out of this side entrance, I'm lying on the floor looking up at these big doors laughing my head off when next thing I know the doors open and my two mates come flying out, now my heads completely gone and I decide to do an impression of a rhino and charge doors down, now these doors are about 15ft high but after three good hits I've actually got them shaking, my mates are trying to pull me away, then the doors open and there are about five bouncers standing there, so I said 'who is the big hard man doing all the damage inside earlier, I heard one of you say if you don't calm down your going to kill him', I wanted him, but none of them would say who it was.

60

The next thing I know one of them makes a remark, and I've gone for him, completely missed him and nearly fell over, all of a sudden their all on me again, the more their hurting me the more I'm laughing like a psycho, ones sitting on top of me strangling me and I'm still laughing whilst choking, they then drag him off, and all go back inside, me and my mates then left, I'd had enough, we didn't have a chance, we then went down the road laughing, there had been five bouncers and there wasn't a mark on me, I did feel it the next day when the drink had worn off, and I ended up black and blue.

Anyway, I ended up with a one-year ban from the club for that incident, a couple of weeks later I had gone to this other club in Merthyr and I'd only been in there ten minutes and one of my mates had got chucked out, so the bouncers wanted us to leave as well, I was going to leave quietly but just wanted my money back, next thing I know a couple more bouncers from upstairs come down and one of them says 'fuck off out of here or we will do you, like we did the other day', now I weren't quite sure who the ones who did me last time were, but he had proved he was one of them, up it went again, we did a lot better than last time though, but they wouldn't come outside with us, ended up with another year ban from there now as well.

I did find out who the bouncers were in the end and have even worked with most of them later in life, I was a complete prick at the time but at the time didn't realise it.

This one night, I was back in one of the pubs in towns after a year ban after the place now had new owners. I was drinking with a few mates when one of my mate's spot's this man who had broken into his dad's car a few days earlier. So, my mate bets me a fiver he's going to knock him out, now I knew my mate wouldn't do it, and he ends up bottling it. In the end I got into an argument with the man and hit him straight in the face, he drops to his knees, my heads gone and I'm hitting him, and he's no longer moving, and there's blood pissing from him, I don't know if you have ever had a feeling you've killed someone, but it's terrible. Then this big bald bloke comes running out at me, and I've hit him to in a temper and said, 'I'll fucking kill you as well', my head had now completely gone, my mate then comes out, and I says to him 'you owe me a fiver', he just looked at me and said 'c'mon we got to get out of here'. I heard the next day that a gang of his mates had machetes and were looking for me for days. I'll be honest and tell you I was fucking scared and didn't go out for a few weeks, I later caught up with one of his mates out drinking one night, and he shit himself and said it 'wasn't true' about the machetes.

A couple of weeks later, I was spiked in a nightclub; I'd never taken a drug in my life except weed. One minute I remember drinking, then next thing I know, I'm 2 miles away and nearly being knocked down. I'd wake up in the middle of roads with cars beeping their horns at me, this was one of the worst experiences in my life, and it was like one long nightmare. I finally come around after going in and out of consciousness, and noticed I had no trainers on which still puzzles me to this day, someone out there knows the truth, but I doubt they are ever going to tell me. My mate, who was with me that night, also got spiked, and he finally comes around on top of a viaduct miles from where he lived, very dangerous as we can't even remember taking anything.

I finally got back into the Zone nightclub and all of a sudden I'm getting problems in the toilets, now I swear to you I hadn't done a fucking thing and this pricks still having a go at me, I even thought my mates had set me up for a laugh, but they knew nothing, I tell him to leave it and he's coming towards me so I've hit him straight in the face and he's dropped to his knees, there's blood squirting out through this really deep cut, some boys then grab me and tell me to fuck off before the bouncers come, I then left before they could catch me. A week later and me and about ten boys had gone there and the bouncers could see we were all pissed and if they kept me out, all of my mates would stay with me and go to, so Bernard who runs the door's there gave me this ban for a month for hitting the boy a week earlier, they knew it was me, they told me the boy needed stitches and an ambulance had taken him away, but fuck him, he started his nonsense with me; he was just another bully who got his comeuppance. Anyway, I took the ban on the chin and walked away.

About two months later I ended up with my comeuppance with the police, it was rugby international day and we had been out all day and I had had some speed off my mates to help me last the night out, it was the first time I'd taken it, and I was bouncing around all over the place. Later, I was outside the zone nightclub, having been a good boy and not got into trouble, when suddenly a fight broke out with about five boys kicking fuck out of this other pair. Now, instead of minding my own business, I decided to put the cape on and do my batman impression, and I'm putting them all away with shots all over the place.

It was just so easy; I felt invincible, and it was all over in minutes. I watched on as the people that were there carried the others onto a minibus, I saw a jacket on the floor, and I don't know for the life of me what made me do it, but after beating fuck into about four of them, I went and handed them their jacket back. One of them immediately started shouting abuse at me from inside the bus, and that's it; my head goes again as I jumped into this minibus fighting like a lunatic. As I pulled the boy with all the mouth out onto the road, I immediately found myself on my stomach on the floor being handcuffed by some copper.

With that, they put me in and this other boy into the Police van, and the fucker then starts laughing at me, so I tried head butting him with the cuffs on, but the coppers stepped up and battered the two of us on the floor. There I was, ten minutes later in the cell; speeding my tits off, I thought I was going to crack, but I finally ended up going to sleep a few hours later. The next morning, I was charged, and this cocky fucking copper, who no one liked in the town, was acting the hard man again and reckoned I was going down for a stretch on a section 18. My solicitor wanted to take the police on who battered us as they were from out of town and were apparently were well known for their heavy-handed approach. However, it wasn't worth the hassle, and the one who had arrested me didn't turn up in court to give evidence for some reason. In the end, the other boy and I pleaded guilty and ended up getting a slap on the wrist and even shook hands outside the court and laughed it off. Nevertheless, I now had a criminal conviction.

While sitting in that police cell as the drink and drugs wore off I remember realising that I was totally off the fucking rails and possibly looking at a prison sentence, my parents hadn't brought me up to be like this, and it was at that moment that I knew I had to change. I know some people say it's all part of growing up, but I was a fool and for what, a laugh and a fucking joke – it was juvenile, and I needed to man up.

At one stage, I'd been banned from the town's two most popular nightclubs, two restaurants and nearly every pub in Merthyr, I didn't venture into town for a while; to be brutally honest, I think they all deserved a rest from me, and it was now time for a change.

CHAPTER FOUR

(The Journey Begins)

I remember one rugby international day in the Belle Vue a little while before they hired bouncers. The boys and I had been out all day when a fight broke out over by the pool table, and it was spilling over in our direction.

Now, there were about eight of us in total, so I said to my mate Phillip, 'if this gets any closer, we'll jump in!' At which point every fucker was joining in, so I said to Phillip, 'c'mon then, let's get in there' as I pushed him to start running, with that Phil goes steaming in hitting everyone while the rest of us jumped back laughing; watching him in action. Looking back, it was a bit of a bad thing to do, but don't worry; I joined in the end - I'm not that much of a bastard. Anyway, we ended up fighting, and the pub was turned upside down; all the windows were smashed to bits, and I guess this was the reason why bouncers were brought in just a few months later.

So, it's 1995, and time to calm down before I wind up in Jail. I'd been lucky enough so far, having got away with murder throughout the years. I bumped into an old schoolmate named Mark (Jolly), who mentioned that he had started Boxing training in a gym they called The Slaughterhouse. The Slaughterhouse was a proper gym full of hard men, known characters from the area; let me explain a little. This place had featured on a TV documentary for the BBC with a few local hard men training there as well as woman, and from the first day I stepped over its threshold, it became like my second home, from that moment and for the next few years. The gym was run by another Champion boxer from the area called Jason Howell's, and from the moment we met, we hit-it-off and became good friends. The slaughterhouse was aptly named as such because back in the 1930's it had been exactly that – an abattoir. However, by this time, it was set up as a garage in the day, but come 5 o clock, it was transformed into a boxing gym, and as time went, a corner of the gym was turned into an area for sparring. A floor was made, and rumours that local lamp posts had been cut down (I'm saying nothing) and used for corner posts and roped off accordingly. My brother Barry painted our logo on the floor, and immediately we had a ring like no other. It was a proper old school gym, like something out of the Rocky films, that I eventually painted and postered up; it looked the fucking business, and at this point, I acquired my own key and trained in there every weekend.

Over a period of time, people came and went, and I helped train a whole host of up and coming talent, as well as putting the gloves on myself. Since the gym had opened it was just for training and keeping fit, but after a year the owner Jason wanted me to fight, only thing was we weren't a proper club, but Jason's old trainer Gareth Donovan had a gym five minutes away, so I then went on to fight for that club Merthyr Ex-serviceman's boxing club. So basically, anyone then training in the Slaughterhouse would go on to fight for Merthyr Ex. I had started the ball rolling, and before we knew it, my trainer, Jason, was back as well as a few others. Our first show in our local Leisure Centre drew over 1000 people, which for an amateur show was amazing. In the next few year's we had over ten senior fighters come out of the slaughterhouse and fight for Merthyr; we also had a sparring partner of mine Gary Turner who went on to win the UK Hardman Tournament

in Cardiff. I came to the end of my boxing career, I got lazy and kept missing training sessions; I still got my arse down there now and again to take people on the pad's and watch over the sparring, but my heart just wasn't in it. Not long after, we received bad news that the gym was about to close and was being turned into a carpet place. This spelled the end of an era, but we weren't too
downhearted because we had certainly put Merthyr back on the map in the seniors for a few years.

I'd always fancied having a go at the boxing and rugby was starting to piss me off, I was still in and out of the Dowlais RFC 1st team but most games found me on the bench and the superstar's who didn't even train would be playing when they hadn't even trained, nevertheless, I didn't dwell on it because every club have their little clicks'. I finally plucked up enough courage, and Mark picked me up if I'm honest I was shitting bricks going in but was then made to feel at home by the owner Jason Howell's an ex skinhead and very talented boxer. Jason took to me straight away and come rain or shine I wouldn't miss a night, I even turned up one night in 2ft of snow, and he knew I wanted it and we became inseparable and good friends. After a couple of months, I no longer felt the need to be fighting all the time, I was still playing rugby and fighting on the field, but that's rugby for you.

I was now doing all the fighting in the boxing ring, night after night Id spar and get battered pillar to post by boys lighter and faster than me, but I was getting better and stronger by the day until the battering's stopped.

It was also in the boxing gym I met Julian Davies, who was nicknamed 'Juggy Tank.' I'd seen him bouncing in the Gurnos shop's and heard of his reputation for years and heard stories of how he had run over the top of a car like a tank in one fight. I then get told by my trainer Jason he's bringing him into spar with me for my first fight. I was bricking it, and we met and had a war for a few rounds. We then became training partners and good friends right up until this day.

One night then in the gym, this well-known and respected Karate champion named Nigel Cleaver asked me if I fancied working on the door's with him the Friday coming and of all places The Belle Vue, which I'd been fighting in a few months earlier. I got to be honest, my stomach dropped, and I came up with all these different excuses that I wasn't available, but he said I'll ask you in two days, and It's there if you want it. I don't know what it was but I just didn't feel confident enough, don't get me wrong my punching power was now second to none and Id had countless fight's in pub's and on rugby field's, but this was a new different ball game has now I could come up against the proper hard men of the town, names Id only heard about growing up, and I just didn't fancy the job. I then returned to the gym two days later and after a good talk with my trainer Jason he gave me some confidence saying, 'there are not many who are going to stop you in this town the way you are hitting the pads,' this persuaded me to change my mind. In addition to that, it would save me going out every weekend and blowing all my money on drink and getting into trouble, and as they say, the rest is history.

The boss of the security company, Clyde, who I was working for was another Karate Master and a well-respected name in the town. I later went on to become good friends with Clyde, but at the time, we didn't even see him for months as he was working elsewhere with other boys from his firm.

So, the time had come, 7 o'clock start until 11, and I've done it, only four hours, but by fuck, it felt like the longest four hours of my life. I was a bit nervous to start with and drank all night to build up a bit of Dutch courage. After a couple of weeks, I realized that I was spending all my wages on the booze, so I knocked the drink on the head. Going back to Nigel, a kickboxing black belt with so much energy you wouldn't believe, who would smile and joke from the start of the night to the finish. Trouble was scarce there because of his reputation, not to mention the fact that he knew everyone, and there weren't many who would fuck about with him. Nigel showed me the ropes and taught me a lot in those first few months. Phil, another boxer and mate of Nigel's who'd just started at the gym, worked with us on busier evenings too, but he ended up getting the sack for head butting someone who had robbed his shed a few days earlier.

One funny story me and Nigel had 2 stools we sat on most of the night inside the doors. Now, it had been a quiet night, and we had been sitting on a pair of Stools for about 2 hours, and due to the fact that I had been training, my legs were aching quite badly, and just then a fight kicked off over by the pool table. Nigel's off his stool and straight at them; I've stood up, and my right leg was dead, which dropped me to one knee. I stood up, and my leg was more or less paralyzed, and I'm punching at it furiously trying to get some life into it, while all of the time, what was going round in my head was that it looked like my bottle had gone. As I glanced over, I could see Nigel breaking the rabble up, and at that point, my leg finally started to come back to life; I guess I must have stopped the blood going to it while it was bent up. I walk in fast but still limping and grabbed one up of the fuckers putting him up against a wall, and from there, we managed to get them out slowly, and our job was done. I explained to Nigel what had happened, and he said that he just thought I had slipped, and we laughed about it for the rest of the night.

After about 2 month's I then had the big fuck off from the boss Clyde who I'd only met once since I started for him. Clyde had lost a venue he was running, so because I was new, I got laid off, and his older experienced good doormen had my job. I was absolutely gutted but has Nigel explained it was out of his hands. Clyde then ended up getting his venue back, so Nigel was on his own again, but Clyde had told him if I came back, the job was mine permanent. Clyde had also started to train in our boxing gym as well, and I was getting to know him really well, so I agreed to go back.

It was around this time the work in the gym had paid off, and Jason had sorted me a fight out with Merthyr Ex Boxing Club. We took it on short notice, and I didn't even have any kit and wore a pair of training short's, a vest, and a pair of trainer's, I looked like I'd been dragged off the street, but the night came, and a load of boy's from the gym and my family turned up. I was fighting this Boy Named Clinton, who had one fight under his belt, which he had won. Clinton was a right lump, and really looked the part when he was kitted up. Now I'd always been used to knocking people out, but now this was different, with the gloves on, and we had a right battle. In my head, I thought I was pretty fit, especially from playing rugby. However, by the end of the fight, I was dead on my feet, and Clinton

71

picked up the win, although his nose was bleeding badly, so I obviously hurt him. And even though I'd lost, everyone was proud of me, and I remember my dad saying, 'well done, now get that belly off! Your fitness left you down there Son.' I went to work the following night with Nigel, I was busted up, but felt a lot more confident, especially with the idea in my head that I was now a boxer. I ended up working with Nigel for about a year, and we hardly had any trouble, nothing too heavy that sticks in my mind anyway. Nigel and I got on like a house on fire and just had a laugh all of the time.

Not long after, I came into work one Friday night and noticed Nigel wasn't himself; he hardly spoke to me all night, whenever I made conversation, he just kept smiling, I could see that something was wrong and was wondering if I did anything to upset him. We finished the shift, and we walked home together, but all wasn't well, because unbeknown to me, that was the very last time I'd see him.

The following night he didn't turn up for work, which wasn't like him because most of the time, he was early. Two hours later, a mate of mine Peter turned up and said, 'Will you be ok to do the door on your own, Nigel's in a bad way.' He went into detail a little, and by the sound of it, Nigel had had a breakdown. Peter then told me that even though Nigel was in a bad way, all he was worried about was leaving Big Shirl on his own and that he wanted to make sure that I was ok. I told Peter that I was fine and to tell Nigel not to worry about it, and I'd see him back on the door the following Friday.

But our union that following Friday wasn't to come because I received a phone call on a Monday saying that Nigel had taken his own life and that his son had found him hanging in his basement. I immediately broke down and cried all day. I didn't see it coming and racked my brain over every word I could remember from the previous Friday night, but all that was coming back to me was him smiling, and for the sake of my sanity, that is the way I will always remember him – having a laugh - smiling.

That evening we all turned up at the boxing class like normal, not knowing what to say to each other. Everyone was gob-smacked, but we still managed to tell each other stories about our pal Nigel, with a smile even though he was no longer with us.

Also, at the time, a few of my mates were living in Las Vegas, and I had to ring them and break the news. A week later, Nigel had probably one of the biggest ever send offs seen in the town, and it was a hard-fucking day for everyone involved. The following day after the funeral I put the Teletext on and saw an advert for a cheap flight to Vegas, which was leaving in two days' time. With my head blitzed I needed to get away from it all, and unbeknown to me, a few of the others had been thinking exactly the same. In the past year working, I'd saved up a good bit of money from the door's, so we booked the flights, and 2 days later, we turned up at our mate's front door in Las Vegas, and to say they were surprised would be an understatement.

While I was across the pond, my boss Clyde kindly kept my job, but to be honest, I actually thought long and hard about packing it all in for the simple fact that Nigel and I were a unit, and we'd been together nearly every weekend for the last year. However, I stuck at it, fueled by the idea that it would have been what Nigel would've wanted from me. Soon after, with Nigel gone the trouble started again, and I started hearing whispers of: 'Things like this wouldn't happen if Nigel was still about,' and although it hit me hard: they were right, it wouldn't have happened, because in the past I'd relied on Nigel a lot, but those days were a distant memory, because today I was on my own, and had to step-it-up a gear.

Clyde employed a new boy to second me called Paul (Boris), he was only there a week, and these two boys wanted to fight a couple of the locals, so we went out the back, and I refereed a bare-knuckle fight between them. There was blood everywhere, and in the end, I had to stop it when one of the clowns bit the other one's face, then one of the other boys turned on Boris, but thinking on his feet, Boris asked him to meet him the next day down the gym. The next day they arrived at the gym, put the gloves on, and Boris got the better of him, and it was all over. They ended up doing the gentlemanly thing and shaking hands in a show of respect for one another.

Then that night, I was talking to my mate on the door when this boy starts on me for no reason at all, so without thinking, I hit him onto this car bonnet and proceeded to smash his head through the window. I was out of control, I had totally flipped, but never mind, he was another fucking bully. Next thing you know, I got dragged off him by another bouncer named Mad Lee Morris who was working close by in another pub. After the mayhem calmed down, the drunken, battered, and bleeding bully promptly got in his car and fucked off. Moments later the police turned up and said they had seen it all on the towns CCTV cameras, and as luck would have it, they had been looking for him all day because they had got his car license plate number from a bit of aggro, he'd been involved in earlier that day. So, everything worked out in my favour in the end, and I heard no more about it. Boris moved onto another job elsewhere, so there I was, back on my own again.

I then had my second fight in which I had lost a few stones and bought proper boxing gear, and I picked up my first win over the Rhondda at a dinner show. By this time, I was making the papers regular through rugby and boxing, and I'd stopped going out drinking and had calmed myself right down. A year had flown by, and my nightclub ban was dropped, and when I did go out my mate Ross and Murdoch, the head doorman of the club gave me free passes into the nightclub so hey, I must have been doing something right. Things were on the up; I was earning a few quid chucking people out nearly every week. To be fair, the money was shit, I was only pocketing £25 a night - but it all helped.

Clyde then stepped in after he had put a few boys in there for try-outs but none of them had lasted and had started new jobs elsewhere. As for us, we weren't taking shit anymore, and we cleaned the place right up; trouble was scarce in that place for a long while. Until the international rugby day came: the bouncer's nightmare; England vs. Wales…

Just ask any bouncer in the country about the international day, the day should be banned, it's just an excuse for people who only go out at Christmas drink excessively and be a nuisance. Now, don't get me wrong, years before I was one of the part-time boozers, with my all-day drinking that went on deep into the night, and trouble would ensue. To be honest, I actually only stopped doing it after I started the bouncing.

Clyde and I arrived early, and within minutes of being there, trouble started. This was the first time I'd seen it go up like this, 'cos I would usually be the one in there drunk causing the grief.

Anyway, I grabbed hold of this one bloke from behind and dragged him to the door – so that's him out on his ear, I quickly made my way back in to grab another. Clyde passed me with another one, and I grab another round the neck and drag him outside too. Then, all of a sudden, we slipped over two men who were rolling around on the floor, and we almost ended up on top of 'em. I then noticed boots coming for my face when all of a sudden Clyde's hand grabs me on the back of my shirt and lifts me straight up in the air; it was like something out of a film, then Clyde asks me are I alright, I felt I was on my second life and went fucking nuts, we launched about eight of these lunatics out in minutes. A boy we also knew named Rob had two boys in neck locks at the same time, it looked funny as fuck, and he was drunk shouting to us: 'Take these fuckers off me, will you?' While laughing his head off. They all ended up fighting on the road outside, it got that messy the police had to close the street down.

About an hour later a couple of girls have started fighting, now girls are harder to break up than men because of their hair grip, but usually, a good tap to the knuckles does the trick and breaks their grip; police arrived again and moved the girls on.

I thanked Clyde for the rest of the night, and we laughed it off. Clyde gave me a bit of a bonus that night, simply because we had had so much trouble, and he thought we had well and truly earned it.

A few weeks later, Clyde smashed a pisshead up who started on him; apparently Clyde had had enough. He worked the following night with me and then finished.

The boxing wasn't going to plan, and after my first win over the Rhondda, a rematch was booked for the man, I lost my first fight too. On the night there was show's going on elsewhere, and we only had one judge who was really old. It was another war, and I almost managed to stop him in the first round with an eight count. Roles reversed, and he did the same to me in the second round and come to the end of the fight (round 3) I honestly thought I'd won. However, I was, in fact, wrong, 'cos, unfortunately, my opponent was given the decision. I met him later on in life, and he said: 'honestly Shirl you won that fight we had,' but at the time I just thought it was pointless making a fuss - it was just one of those things.'

Then a fight came in with a boy from Cardiff, but because he was only 17 years old, they asked could they make it an exhibition bout. We agreed, but I turned up half-hearted with no bad feelings, I even got a bollocking off my trainer for not taking the time to warm up and taking it seriously.

So, this boy weighed in, he must have been about 6ft 7in tall, and he was in real good shape. The bell goes for the first round, and he flew out of his corner and was trying to take my head off, lucky for me 'cos I had nothing left in the tank when the bell rang for the end of round one. *Fucking hell*, I thought to myself, *This is no exhibition!* As he flew out of his corner for round 2, much the same as the first. I tried, and he caught me with a beautiful one-two that dropped me to one knee. And that was that the fight was stopped.

Due to the poor account of myself I went on a total downer, but then my trainer Jason got me an exhibition with this boy named Sean Pritchard who had just become Welsh Champion; Sean was a total professional and held back a bit, it was a good experience for me, and I ended up with a massive trophy which certainly perked me up a bit.

Two weeks later, Joe Calzaghe's dad Enzo was taking a Welsh team over to Sardinia in Italy, and for some reason, the Welsh Heavyweight champion Sean wasn't available, and I was immediately asked to take Sean's place, so I must have impressed them in that exhibition.

So, there we were, off on our way to Sardinia in a minibus. We arrived 2 days later, and due to the fact that we couldn't see anyone, we all ended up burning down some beach. Come the evening, Enzo finally caught up with us, but he was far from happy because he really wanted us all training for the event. The next morning, we were all up early, kitted out in Enzo's boxing club clobber, he wanted us all in uniform for a press conference as the fights were going on some TV channel. So, we made our way to the Porto Tore's Arena, where all of the fighters were waiting in the ring, and I was the one chosen to bring out the Welsh flag for opening. Which was a bit strange as I was the only man who wasn't a champion, but one of the champs called Sean lent me his vest, and I must say it was a proud moment when our anthem came on.

It was just five fights into my career, and I was up against a police sergeant and multi-time champion named Mauro Salvatore, who had over 105 fights and was well experienced. The same has before I got back at the end of round 1 and say to Enzo, 'I thought this is an exhibition?' And with that, he slapped me across the face and said, 'are you a man or a mouse Shirly?' Well, it must have wound me up, 'cos I went hell for leather, and by the end of round five, I was fucked.

The other man won, but it had been one hell of a fight; the worst part was that we had to do it all again the following night in a different town.

The next day came, and everyone who had been to the beach two days before had all come out in really bad sunburn - we were full of blisters. A few of the fighters were so bad their flights had to be cancelled, and after traveling two hours on a bus, and waiting all night, I was back on last again for yet another little war. My opponent got the decision again, and into the bargain, I'd ripped every blister off my back.

The next day I was in fucking agony with a long drive home to look forward to; I couldn't even sit back tidy. Enzo and his son Joe took the plane back, and we continued our 27-hour journey. Soon after arriving home, I was constantly itching and so went to the doctor's; it turns out I'd taken a few layers of skin off my back. I was in agony for years, but it had been one hell of an experience having fought with and alongside a few future champions like Bradley Price, and Gavin Rees (Rock) as well as top 'sport artist' Patrick Killian.

Around this time Dowlais RFC had taken on a new coach, this man was a local hard nut in our town – a legend called, Peter Morgan. Peter had gone all the way with his rugby and played rugby league at top levels and brought his

"Rugby League" wealth of experience into our training sessions. From that moment forward, the training was a lot more fun, and everyone got a lot fitter. Now Peter was one big man - most people were terrified of him! And after seeing him going off his head after a game one day at a different club, it was clear to see why. I was doing really well in the training sessions, so much so that one of the other town legends, Gary Animal's nicknamed me "the marauding wildebeest." This was because when I had the ball, it was hard to stop as I was smashing people all over the field week-in, week-out. Furthermore, I was picked by Peter for the 1st team and was having a good few games scoring tries most weeks and if a penalty was awarded 10 yards from the line, my name was immediately called to run at them, because 9 times out of 10, 'cos the size I was, no fucker was going to ever stop me.

One Saturday, we were in a cup game against Aberfan at home, and this big prop forward was throwing his weight around, so I went at him a few times to show him whose boss. So anyway, it's half time and I'm wound right up waiting to get back on when Peter says, 'you're coming off Shirl!' I was totally confused, and said to him, 'I'm not coming off!' And he looked at me and said, 'don't argue Shirl, ya' coming off!' Now, I'd heard of being subbed later in a game but never at half time. I could see Pete's colour draining from his face, but because there were hundreds of people around, I simply accepted it. Unfortunately, our boys went on to lose the second half, and afterward, people were coming up to me saying: 'are you real Shirl, speaking back to him like that?' Anyway, we went back to the changing room. So there we sat quietly while Peter gave the team the biggest bollocking ever, I was stood wondering if he might single me out for what had gone on, then, all of a sudden, he glanced over at me and said: 'Oh, and Shirl, if you ever speak to me like that again in front of people...' However, I didn't give him the chance to finish and said, 'well, I hadn't done anything wrong!' All the boys' were trying to keep me quiet, going, 'Come on Shirl, leave it.' So, that was that I bit my lip and accepted it once and for all. To be honest, I could see Pete's point because we were a man down, and I could've got sent off – I was far too wound up. Everyone went back into the club; I think they all thought I would have gone home just in case Pete kicked off again, but like I said earlier, in my eyes, I'd done nothing at all wrong.

A few nights later, we were back in training again, and Peter called me into one of the changing rooms for a chat on my own, 'that's me fucked!' I thought to myself, but he said, 'Right, I've been chatting with a few people Shirl, so how do you fancy playing on the wing next weekend?' And I said, 'yeah, I'd love to have a go at it mate, and not one word was said about the incident a few days earlier. I finished the rest of the season with 27 tries, runner to my mate Pie who had 29. From that day on, Peter and I got on great, until his move to another club. I did play the following season but seemed to be picking up too many injuries, so at that point, I made the decision to pack the rugby in and get stuck into the boxing.

Also, around this time we lost a good friend and brilliant rugby player named Steve Fealey; he was a first-class player and had been coaching us at the time. The day he past, a big dark cloud came over the club and the funeral was the biggest I had ever seen in the town. On the day, a whole load of us walked miles to lay him to rest. Also, a few years later we lost second row player's, Reesy, Steve Lew and last but not least one of the funniest guy's, another true gentleman, Keith Winstone.

Back on the doors, Clyde started a mate of his named Chris Chapman, who had worked the pubs and club's down the valleys. Chris, who I later nicknamed "The Crazy Man" for various reasons, initially came across cocky; a bodybuilder with the arm's the size of Hulk Hogan, who loved himself, and wasn't afraid to show anybody around his muscles every night. I remember laughing when he used to say to me, *Did you see her looking at me then?* I like a windup too and would egg him on. I won't lie to you, the first couple of weeks were hard with him, and I'd see Clyde in the gym, and he'd ask me was I alright with Chris, I'd lie through the back my teeth and say, 'Yeah it's all ok, he's a sound guy,' which to be honest, he was.

After a few weeks he met this girl named Amber, and it totally changed him; he wouldn't as much as look at another woman. All of a sudden, the bragging stopped, and Chris and I became really good mates - in and out of the pub - he even joined our boxing gym.

I remember one night, there were two gangs of boys arguing. Chris and I chucked the local boys out. The gang from another town were shitting themselves inside the pub, they all looked like big rugby players who could do a bit, but they were outnumbered. So, I had a word with the local gang outside as I knew some of them, and there were some right tasty boys, but they said they weren't going nowhere till the other gang came out, so I had to think fast! Now, call me a bastard if you want, but this really worked well. I went up to the rugby players inside and said that I knew the boys outside and that they were all wankers who couldn't fight, and that you boys would kill them. I could see their confidence growing, and within seconds, they said, 'Let's go and do the bastards!' They went flying out of the pub straight into them; we closed the doors straight behind them so they couldn't get back, and we were inside laughing our heads off. Minutes later, as we were watching from the windows, there were blue lights flashing everywhere; the police ended up closing the street down again, but we didn't give a fuck as we had done our job by getting them out of the pub with no damage whatsoever.

Another night Chris and I had just chucked this boy out for fighting, and he decided to have a pop at me; he was an ex bouncer who had done a fair bit of time inside for running someone over, and he was known as a right bully. Apparently, he had nearly killed some other bouncer a couple of years earlier by punching him in the windpipe and leaving him for dead in a nightclub incident down the valleys. He looked a right psycho, with lunatic eyes to go with it. I just blanked him as he gave me all the usual rubbish about biting my face off etc. Then he mentioned something about my house and family, which was a red rag to a bull. I said, 'Right, come on then, round the back,' so as we are walking, I can see the sneaky fuckers going to go for me, so I hit him with a right hook as he grabbed me. I'm pulling him to the ground, and he's trying to bite me, I get him down and start stamping and kicking him in the head and face, his eyes have gone back in his head, and he's pissing blood from his mouth and face. Chris and a couple of boys grab me off him and hold me back, they then take me back inside the pub. I hate to think what would've happened if they hadn't been there, and where I'd be right now if I'd gone right off it. This one woman who didn't know what it was about is screaming at me for stamping on him. Now, most people say it's out of order when somebody is down and you kick or stamp on them, but this is a man who's threatened my family, almost killed a doorman and is trying to bite me, this is not a, shake hands and go for a pint together crap, I wanted to make sure this person would never want to clap eyes on me again! So, if that seems out of order, I can live with it.

About 10 minutes later, I was starting to calm down when Chris calls me, apparently the boy was stood at a Police Van pointing at the pub: turns out he's trying to do me for assault. The police came and have a word, but I think they knew what he was like and that he usually started the trouble. I saw him again in town a couple of weeks later, and he put his head down when I started laughing at him; I think he realized his fighting days were finally over. Another fucking bully laid to rest.

Another night a few of my cousins were fighting outside and were outnumbered by this other gang, so Chris and I went in to even up the score. Chris has hit one, and he's landed about 3ft away in a heap on the floor; I've smashed another, and they are all dropping like flies. My cousins who also trained in Boxing weren't shy either as they stepped in, suffice to say there was a right mess out there. There were police everywhere, and about 10 people got locked up; Chris and I were alright, though, as it looked like we were breaking it all up.

84

Later that night, I went home and was just about to go into my house when I saw three boys near my brother's car. Next thing I know one of them starts kicking the window in, so I shoot across, and he starts choppsing (being leary) to me, so I just hit him straight in the face, and he was out cold on his feet; he must have been out cold for at least ten minutes, I honestly thought I'd killed the fucker. Just a few seconds later, he started to wriggle and move, and his mates carried him away. That'll teach him not to steal cars again.

We were now into November 1997, and I'd been asked would I spar with this young kid who was making a comeback into the boxing world. The kid had won every title he could have as a kid and was about to enter into senior boxing. This young kid just happened to be one, Enzo Maccarinelli from Bonymaen ABC. I travelled with my trainer Jason down to his gym, and we hit it off from the start.

I was then offered to start training in Dai Gardener's gym in Gelligaer and would travel there two times a week to spar with Enzo. The funny part was we were both into WWF wrestling at the time, I'd be in my Stone-Cold Steve Austin T-shirt and he'd be in his Rock T-shirt, we'd smash lumps into each other and then go back into the changing room and talk about what had happened on the wrestling show on TV.

The next few year's he knocked out whatever was put in front of him, and by this time, he was getting bigger, and we both knew the time was coming when he would enter the super heavyweight division. As for me, I just wasn't dedicated enough, and I never had my own personal trainer like Enzo. Nor did I have his speed and skill levels, and the fight never came off. We remained good friends for years, and he went on to become a professional and would later hold various titles, not to mention his WBO cruiserweight title. Meanwhile, I went on to become a wrestler, which I'd always wanted to do from a young age, another off the bucket list.

Not long after this, my mate Juggy offered me a start at a new nightclub in town. It was a bit of a shirt and tie place called RM's, a venue that Juggy's boss, Rob Megson, was opening. I didn't really fancy it, 'cos it was a far cry from the jeans and baseball cap attire night's down at the Belle Vue. Chris, however, decided differently and jumped at the chance of more money, so he moved on and was now working with Clyde again, and I was left without a partner once again.

I was now working with this boy from down the valley's named Paul Curtis. So, Paul's first night came to work with me, it was the opening of the rugby world cup. All night I'd been telling him how quiet the pub was and that we didn't get much trouble. Anyway, a couple of hours later, the place has gone wild, and as we were getting these boys and girls out, one of the girls scratched Paul's face to bits, and the police ended up locking them all up. I wound Paul up on the way home about his face being in tatters on his first night, and we had a good old laugh as I had told him it was so quiet. The two of us hit it off from the first minute we met, and he was even picking me up for work due to me not having a license at the time.

The following week came and yet another rugby game. The street had been closed down *again,* and trouble had spilled out from a pub opposite where these two boys were hitting this old bloke that I knew from my local rugby club. These fuckers had belts wrapped around their hands and had really opened him up; the poor bloke was bleeding like a pig from the cuts to his face. Anyway, I'd seen enough, so, I ran in and flattened one of them knocking him out. The other one ran off like a baby back into the pub before the police turned up; they locked the boys up later that evening, for fighting again.

I was now back training hard and Picking a few wins up on the way, including a Welsh youth champion from Cardiff in my hometown. I entered the Welsh Championship's in Ebbw Vale and got a pass straight to the final where I was up against Multi Time champion Brendan McCormack who had had over 113 fights. I gave my all the first two rounds and nearly stopped him, but then he boxed my head off for the win. Mind you, it was still a hell of an experience on my journey. I didn't let it get to me because at least I had gone the full five rounds with the champion of Wales. So, another fight was lined up with another bouncer from Cardiff, and I smashed him right up. He tried hitting me in the balls to get disqualified before I finally won it on points. Then a fight came in with another Merthyr Boxer who had joined a Cardiff club just to fight me, I was wound right up for this and stopped him in the first round, and the local paper had the headlines 'Fired up Thomas is the Merthyr Champion.'

Now, remember the 17-year-old giant I mentioned who had stopped me in an exhibition, well it was now two years later when who do I draw in the first round of the Welsh championships but none other than him Peter Rideout.

The fight was in my hometown with nearly 1000 people there, and we were the last fight of the night. The crowd was drunk and loud by now, and I knew how hard he could hit, but I was focused on going flat out from the first bell, shit or bust. We squared up, and I had to look up into his eyes, he was huge and looked even bigger than last time. The bell goes, and we are off, I'm swinging with big hook's just hoping I can get up at him, he's smashing me back, and I've caught him with a lovely uppercut right on the button, I flew in with a combination of punches, and he holds on. I'm thinking there's no way can I keep this pace up for the rest of the fight when all of a sudden, the referee moves me to a corner and goes to check him out. The thousand-strong crowd was cheering my name, and I start jumping up and down ready to go for it again when the fight his stopped, the crowd go nut's, and it turns out I'd split his mouth open bad, and In amateur Boxing there is no cut's, I walked up to him and gives him a hug and then took it all in when they announced my name has the winner. We left the venue, and people were still cheering my name, it was one surreal moment that's always stayed with me.

After picking a win up In the semi-final, I was now in my second final in Ebbw Vale against a new boy called Darren Morgan from Swansea, who went on to earn the nickname 'The Beast from Bonymaen.' Now, this boy was big, and by fuck was he fast; in the first minute, he caught me with a right hook, and I saw stars, I stayed away from him the rest of the round and the second round. My trainer Jason then

88

started to slap me in a temper 'cos he knew I could do better, and I woke up a bit, and for the next three round's it was close, but he ended up getting a majority decision to become the new super heavyweight champion of Wales.

The following night I was back on the door, and after a few week's Clyde decided to finish in RM's, and yet again, I turned it down, so Paul took the opportunity of more money for less hours, free food and less trouble.

RM's had really taken off, and they were now looking for a third doorman. Chris and Paul came to see me, nagging me to go with them. I was still getting partnered with different people week in week out and finally thought fuck it, I would be earning double the money, that I was getting after three years in the Belle Vue, it was now time for a change. After three years without a scratch, I'd had a good run, but it was time to move on...

CHAPTER FIVE

(Time for a Change)

The club was previously called Hamilton's until a Swansea man named Rob Megson brought it out, hence the name RM's. An interview was arranged, and two nights later, I was doing a police function with about 100 cops all by myself. There were some right arseholes in there, and I couldn't do nothing more than turn a blind eye to some of the stuff that was going on, *I'm sure you know what I mean?'* Anyway, the following night it was the first Christmas party where all three of us were working together, it was the first chance to show the owner if I was any good, he'd only heard about me up until then from my mate Julian (Juggy) who worked in a factory called, Hitachi for him in the days.

After about two hours, the bar staff was being abused by this drunk man, not only that, but he was Irish, and he had a right temper on him. So, I went up behind him so he couldn't clock me, and immediately he starts effin' and blindin' at one of the girls behind the bar, so I stick a headlock on him and choke him out and dragged him through the back door - job done. Nice one, within two hours, I'm off and running, having said that this place had a nice atmosphere which eased us in well for a trouble-free Christmas.

One night over Christmas, after being there most of the day and getting bored, Paul came up with an idea for a laugh. He said, 'let's all put money in a pot and see who can kiss the oldest woman?' Well, about an hour later, this woman comes in who must have been pushing 75. Paul looked at

Chris and me and said, 'get your money out lad's, I'll take this!' And true to his word he won, with tongues too.

Having gotten through Christmas, some bad news reared its ugly head. Apparently from now on you had to have a council license to work as a door supervisor (bouncer), and to get one you must not have been in trouble with the police in the previous 5 years, but the thing was, I had that court appearance on my record and had half a year left to apply. So that was that I was out of a job. Soon after, I appealed, and a meeting was set up in front of an informal jury. I had references from the Belle Vue, and the new owner of RM's came with me to speak up for me. Shortly after, we were called in, and I defended myself, explaining how it was just 'one stupid moment in drink,' and since then, I'd started Bouncing for a living and had built up a good name. On the panel, I noticed one of the regular's from the Belle Vue, who smiled at me. Within an hour, I was called back in and granted my license early; I couldn't believe it; I was over the moon that I still had my job at RM's.

Within a couple of months, RM's really took off, partly due to the fact that the other two Clubs that were close by had to shut down for a few months for refurbishment, so obviously, every fucker within a five-mile radius was trying to get into our club. We were ramming about five hundred people in a night, which was fantastic, but this also meant that the place was getting rougher, and the scum of the town had made its way over to us - the cues would be down the street - let the fun commence.

I then had an argument with this bloke over the entry fee, we had no change and he was supposed to have brought it back for me from the bar, then when I asked him for it, he said he had paid. Now this bloke was a horrible bastard who used to be a bit of a bully years ago, and he still thought he could do the business. The blokes then started getting a bit mouthy with me, so I thought I would wind the other bouncers up, and I'll pretend the bloke is right, and it will look like I am bottling it. The plan worked a treat, but the bloke got more confident and started abusing me and wanting an apology, by now the other bouncers faces were a picture, then all of a sudden, I thought I can't keep a straight face any longer and just went bonkers, screaming at him and grabbing the fucker, I dragged him by his legs down about 20 steps with his head hitting each step and then launched him down another 5 steps outside landing on his face, I then went back into the club laughing my head off, the other bouncers were laughing and called me rotten and thought my bottle had gone.

The following week the same man came back and apologized, so I let him in, he was alright at first, but after about two hours he'd change and turning again into the cocky, arrogant prick he was before. All of a sudden, he comes over to me and says, 'who's the fucking bouncer who chucked me out last week?' I thought you cheeky fucker, I let you back in, and now you're having a go again, he knows it's me and came at me, so I launched into him with a head-butt and knocked him out cold on his feet. Fortunately for him, he fell straight into the arms of the other two bouncers who were with me, and they carried him out of the place. There was blood up the walls everywhere, and the bouncers were covered; funny thing was I didn't have a drop of his blood on me. Anyway, he never came back for the third week: I wonder why?

A week later, the owner of the club was having a bit of trouble with this boy and his girlfriend; I was late coming into work as I had just got back from Swansea doing a boxing exhibition with Enzo Maccarinelli. Thing is not a soul would fight him on his home shows, so I was offered money because everybody wanted to see Enzo doing his stuff. The five-round exhibition went well, and I was still pumping with adrenalin by the time I got into work. On my arrival, it appeared that this boy had been playing up earlier, starting fights and had been warned. So, come the end of the night, he's performing again, (he was a spit of the singer George Michael) and fucking loved himself to bits, with not a hair out of place and massive Bee Gee style sparkling white teeth. His misses, was now arguing with the club owner, so I tells her to fuck off out of the club in a polite way, next thing I know the "Wham lookalike" comes running at me fists flying; I could see it coming a mile off and threw a straight right into his face, the other bouncers said they had never seen someone rushing forward to land a punch and fall back so quickly. And there he was, out on his feet with blood up the walls and over everyone in close proximity. The boys drag him out, when all of a sudden one of the bar staff pointed down at the floor, and would you believe it, there on the floor lay a couple of the *Wham-Boys gnashers.*

The police turned up, took a statement from me, and tried doing me for assault. About a month later, I saw a policewoman in town, and she told me that the charges had been dropped; I bet it was killing him that his teeth were gone, considering he loved himself so much. However, at the end of the day, he would have done the same to me if he'd have got the chance.

It wasn't always about violence on the doors though, you had to try and have a laugh as well, or you'd crack up. Like one particular night, we threw some bloke out for fighting, and he offered me out! Now he was half my size, and I'm outside by the door when he started doing all these martial arts moves, trying his best to sound like Bruce Lee. The doormen are looking at me laughing as I'm nearly pissing myself laughing. Next thing ya' know the twat spat at me, so I just ran at him and slapped him a few times while still laughing. And again, two minutes later there he was talking to the police trying to do me for assault. And yet again, I'm being questioned over this drunken idiot.

The time of the Welsh Championship came around again, and with injuries, not dieting properly, I was having second thoughts whether or not to enter, but with just a week left to go, I bit the bullet and went for it. So, I hadn't trained properly and was drawn against this boy called Russ Higg's in the semi-final. I didn't know much about him, and I smashed him everywhere for five rounds; his nose couldn't stop bleeding, and by round five, I was hitting him at will with every shot I threw. Then the referee only went and raised this Russ boy's arm, the winner? Now, you know when you've lost a fight, you also know when you've won, and everyone in the room knows it too, well I was gob smacked, just standing there while everyone booed and hollered at the judge's decision. My coaches played hell with the judges, and downhearted, there was fuck all I could do other than change into my work gear and head back to work. Higg's went to the final and got knocked out first round by the Beast from Bonymaen, Darren Morgan.

I lost all heart for the sport at this point, and for that reason, never trained properly, but 2 months later, Darren's got a show in his hometown, and his opponents have pulled out once again. We received a phone call asking if I fancied fighting him, but my trainer turned it down and said he's not in the gym at the moment. After a few days have passed, they began to get a little desperate, offered me a few quid to do an exhibition match - I agreed. Anyway, we turn up on the night of the fight, and my trainer Gareth want's to call it off saying he had a bad feeling about it; I said no way we are here now, and at the end of the day it was only an exhibition match. So, I entered the ring and his music kicked in. Now, I'd never seen music in an amateur fight before, and the crowd was erupting as he was bouncing down to the ring. He entered the ring and throws this really fast combination; he's got his welsh vest on and look's ready to kill someone. Ding… ding… and we're off…

After a few second's I'm thinking, fuck me, he's hitting a bit hard for an exhibition, and as we get in close, he hit me with a body shot (that was meant to drop me.) You could hear it at the back of the venue, I now knew I was in some serious trouble, and for the next minute, the pace was nonstop. We got into an exchange, and he's hit me with an uppercut, fuck knows how my head didn't come off. With that, I managed to smash a few hook's into him as he's backing off; the ref shout's for us to break, and he throws a leary punch, so I've thrown a punch back, and he's jumped out of the way. I was not happy, and the referee jumped in to stop it. The crowd was going nuts, and I'm being pulled back by my trainer and referee. I've immediately told the crowd to fuck off, and I'm screaming at my trainer to get my gloves off just in case anyone runs into the ring. Just as quick as it had started, it all calmed down; suffice to say they announce that the bout had been cancelled. I don't know if the crowd had got to him that night and if him fighting on his own turf had had something to do with it, but the way he came out for that exhibition match was way off the scale. In honorary boxing style, we went to the middle of the ring, shook hands, and went to a neutral corner for a trophy and picture. He then said to me, 'pop up to the bar, and we'll have a drink.' I got back to the changing room, and my trainer's said, 'right hurry up, we are out of here,' and we left straight away in case there was trouble after it. But if I'm honest, I actually wanted to stay as Darren, and I got on well.

The following year The Welsh championships were on me again, and I hadn't done a stroke because of the injuries and doing the house up. Nevertheless, I said to my trainer, 'fuck it, I'll give it a go!' The matches were drawn, and I drew Darren again in the semi-final; we had a cracking fight, and he beat me on points, but I was happy I'd done the 4 rounds as he had been knocking everyone out since becoming champion. A couple of days after the fight my bad knee came back, and I had to go to the hospital to have it drained.

Here's a funny little story for you: When I was boxing, I was in a fight in Barry Leisure centre against some boy named Martin, who was some kickboxing champion. Anyway, I've hit him all around the ring, and he'd managed to survive two eight counts, then suddenly he started to get dirty. He kept holding and holding, but I knew he was closed to getting stopped, when, 'BANG,' I caught him with a peach of a hook, he's kicked me and gone down and was immediately disqualified. In my opinion, it was just a reflex after being hit so hard, or he was just some nutter.

After a while the other nightclub's reopened, and we went through a quiet patch, some nights the boss just wanted two of us working, and me being last one in meant that I had to look elsewhere, fucking great I thought, I'd left the Belle to come here, and now I'm out of work.

Paul mentioned to me that Bernard Driscoll's Doorman security was looking for boys. Now, like I had mentioned, I'd made Bernard's life hell for years and thought I'd be the last person he'd have working for him, but I was wrong, so we put the past behind us, and I jumped at it – I was desperate for the extra cash.

So, I started working in a place called The Castle Hotel or as I called it at the time "Roadhouse." There were two doors on the front, which were bottle proof because it was common practice to throw people out, and they'd kick, punch and throw bottles at the door. However, after just a few weeks there, we started to clean the place right up.

This one night, Paul and I had to chuck this bloke out for touching women up. So, I went off to find him, and he was in the toilets, a right dirty looking bastard who's on crutches and says, 'you'll have to take me out', so we get him out, and he's outside hitting the door with his crutches, so I tell him to 'fuck off' has he's scaring people coming in, he then takes a swing at me with the crutch and I duck it and push him over, he hits the ground and he looks unconscious. I thought I had killed the fucker, then all of a sudden, everyone's calling me a bully and saying I knocked him out. The fuckers not moving, and the police arrive; I'm Fucked, I thought to myself, they look at him and come straight over and ask what has happened. All of a sudden, he starts laughing like some lunatic as they are trying to pick him up, and he's punching and kicking them; it turned out he was known for touching women up and had escaped from the local nuthouse. Paul and I even helped the police put him in the Moriah van.

An hour later we threw this man out for fighting, he starts giving us a load of shit like usual then goes away. It turns out he was banned from most places in town. An hour later we threw these girls out for fighting, then I was outside trying to stop some other girls fighting, and I can now see this boy walking towards me in a change of top; he thinks I haven't seen him, but I have, and I also spotted his clenched fist. So, as soon as he's near me, I've smashed him in the face, he goes backward and gets wrapped around a lamp post and drops to the floor. He was in a right mess, so I fucked off back into the pub. I did see him the following week, and he just put his head down as he passed by me.

A couple of weeks later, Paul and I got the sack for reasons which were complete bollocks; apparently, we were not getting involved in certain fights and letting people get away with murders. A complete load of shit, but we took it on the chin and moved on from there. I just went back to the one night in RM's again, and some work came in down the valleys, this would now take me out of my comfort zone and into a different territory down the valleys where I didn't know anyone.

CHAPTER SIX

(The Fist Fighting Rugby Club)

So, I was just getting used to working on a Sunday night in a place called the Taff Trail, and then the landlord of the pub lost his entertainment license. It was only a week or two later when I got a phone call asking me to go somewhere else. So, I started work down the valleys in Treharris rugby club, another rough fucking place, it had only been open a week, and people would come from everywhere to get in; most of them would go back out the same way, flying through the doors.

The first night we took over the club, a bunch of bikers turned up, so we ask them for the entry fee, and they tell us that they are working there, they had worked there the previous week and just turned up with their girlfriends to work. Then they inform us that they are not going anywhere, phone their boss, so we stand our ground and stay on the door taking money while they wait for their boss to turn up in the club. Their boss, who is one big fucker, arrives and walks past us but nods over at Paul. My adrenaline was rushing, I thought we have got a fight on our hands here, five minutes later, and the big man walks out of the club and says to Paul 'I'll have that fucker, he reckons he left a message saying we weren't needed for tonight!' And promptly steams off. After their boss had paid them, the rest of the bikers left and wished us all the best on their way out. The DJ who we were working for "Mad Al" pop's his head around the corner laughing and says, 'have they gone yet?' Anyway, Paul starts giving him hassle saying that it could have turned nasty, while Mad Al is just laughing his head off and says to Paul, 'you lot are still here, ain't you?' As he goes back into the club laughing. It was clear to see now why they call him "MAD AL!" 'Cos straight away, I thought, *what the fuck am I letting myself in for with this mad bastard.*

Week by week, the place was getting fuller; buses were coming from everywhere because not many places opened on a Sunday, and Mad Al had a good following. After about 4 weeks we were cleaning the place right up, I got into an argument this one night with this big gold wearing pikey, he'd supposed to have hit someone, and when I goes to take him out, he started having a go at me, so I offered to fight him outside, but his bottle had gone, a bit more on him later.

This one night I was on the door with Paul when a big 6ft 4inch rugby player takes a disliking to me and starts giving me shit. This continued over a few weeks, and because I'm so quiet, he's finding his feet and getting more confident as time goes on. One evening he turns up sober on his own, and I warn him I've had enough! He apologizes, so I let him back in the club. Then, just a couple of drinks later, he's off again! Now, Paul, the other bouncer and I had a code where they get 3 warnings, and then that's it, so out he comes, an hour later, and he's calling me a wanker. So, I turn to Paul and say 'TWO!' Paul warned him again, but the drink is now in him, and he's brave. Paul's now laughing as he knows what's coming, so it's the end of the night, and most of the people have left, I see him coming, and I turn away not to make eye contact, next thing I hear is the prick abusing me with insults, he walks straight up to me and gives me the middle finger, right in my face. I was thinking, he's a big one and planning what combinations I was going

100

to do after the first punch. I then hit's him with a straight right in the face, before I could follow it up his eyes rolled back in his head and he crashes to the floor really hard. There was blood coming from his nose and mouth, and the big fucker wasn't moving. Now, I don't know if you've ever had a feeling when you think you have killed someone, but I shit myself. Five minutes later and he still hasn't moved, so I go into the hall and says to the other bouncer, Terry 'I think I've killed this fucker!' Now, Terry's laughing because he doesn't give a fuck. Terry then goes into the foyer and starts yelling at the boy unconscious on the floor, 'I told you not to wind him up!' Terry then turns to me and says, 'I think you have killed the fucker...' laughing his head off. Another ten minutes later and he still hasn't moved, then Paul looks up at me and winks because he's finally coming round. I've never been more relieved in my life to think I could have done time because of this prick. Anyway, they had to carry him to a car and take him to a local hospital. I saw him a couple of months later, and he wouldn't stop apologizing - shaking my hand like a lunatic, and from that day on, I never heard a murmur out of him again.

Another night there's a fight on the dance floor, so the other bouncer and I go running in to break it up. I turn around to see where Terry is, and he's only in a corner with his jeans around his ankles with some girl. So, the other boy and I sort it out, and when I got to tell Terry later, he just laughed it off and said he didn't see it. The big one finally came to the rugby club. I had collected a thousand pounds on the door that night because it was Boxing Day, and we had been selling tickets for a fiver. It was a decent night in the end 'cos we all had a cut of the final takings at closing. The place was rammed to the rafters, and we had thrown a boy out earlier for fighting with another rugby boy, nothing unusual, or so we thought at the time. An hour later, Paul and I are on the door when about twelve boys turn up, the first five pay to go in when all of a sudden Paul notices the boy, we put out earlier hiding behind the rest. This fucker has only brought the rugby team back with him. So, Paul goes to slam the doors shut, at which point they decide to run at us. So, about five of them are in already and have gone off on one. We launched the ones out in the foyer back out through the doors, and I run back into the hall, now one of the bouncers named H, a martial arts instructor has a boy in a headlock choking him out, and there's a boy who I swear was about 6' 4" tall, weighing about 25 stone has H in a headlock too. With that, I jumped straight up and tried getting a headlock on him, too, but he's a big fucker, and I'm struggling. I eventually get the lock on, and eh, it must have been a sight to see three headlocks in a row. As I choked him out, I dragged him down into the foyer, and as he was on his hands and knees, I was hooking him with punches to the face dragging him out of there like a rag doll. His mates looked shocked and backed off as I was screaming at them. It calmed down, and we got most of them to the door, but the rest were still inside, so Paul went to help the boys inside and left me on the door on my own to stop the other's coming back in.

They then tell me they got no grief with the bouncers and they just want the boy from earlier, when all of a sudden, the fuckers rush me, but I made sure I dropped the first fucker and backed myself up against a wall so they couldn't get me down and then I just went for it. There's a couple of them, and they can't put me away, another bouncer named Flynny who was a mate of mine comes running in and drops one of the pricks, they then decide to drag him outside and turn on him. I could see about six of them on him pummeling him, and for a second, I froze and was watching it in what seemed like slow motion. I don't know if I was dazed or what, but suddenly, I just clicked on and went running at them like a bull hitting whatever was in my way. A girl came out to help us and hit one over the head with a chair, so I dragged her back inside to safety! Things finally calmed down, and they were finally all outside; the boys in the club were black and blue, I checked myself out in the mirror, and all I had was a bit of a busted lip. Now, my adrenalin was pumping, and I felt like I could fight all night, so I went outside on my own and offers anyone of them to fight me one at a time. Not one of these cowards would take me up on my offer, so the other bouncer, Flynny, just dragged me back inside. The police turn up about twenty minutes too late when every fucker had gone home. We ended up in the hospital as Flynny had glass in his eye and one of MAD AL's DJ's had got hit with a glass ashtray, which apparently was meant for me.

After all the commotion, Mad Al comes up to me and says, 'right your all walking, your all in one piece, and please tell me you've got the money?' So, I opened my bomber jacket pocket and pulls out over a thousand pounds. Al had a massive smile on his face and thanked me for thinking on my feet and hiding it before the fight went off. We all went out the next day, black and blue, laughing about how much money we had made.

We worked the following week, but no one turned up. The club ended up losing its license, and we all moved further on down the valley to a place called the 'Taff Trail,' where I had done a few weeks before it lost its license.

CHAPTER SEVEN

(A Night to Remember)

So, I was now heading back down the valley's every Sunday night to a place in Treharris called The Taff Trail. A nice-looking pub with a hall on the side where they would hold a disco with about 200 people. They would travel from everywhere to get to this venue, and we would have to turn people away regularly.

I was with the same crew working there, but H and Flynny had now finished so we had recruited two new boys to our Sunday night crew. Neil (Beast), a 19-year-old youngster who was one of my sparring partners in the gym (who could hit like a mule) and was also a very good rugby player. And then there was Peters, another rugby player from a rival team who had just got back from Australia.

Paul and Terry were still with us after the rugby club incident, so a couple of weeks later, we were cleaning the place back up. The problem is we would ban someone on a Sunday night, and they would go back in the week because the landlord would be on his own, and there wasn't much he could do but let them drink again. So, when they came back on a Sunday, they would say, 'but I've been drinking here in the week,' and we would ask the landlord, and they just ended up getting back in again. There was not a lot we could do, so we always ended up back to square one.

The DJ Mad AL would start his night off with an explosives show which looked really wicked. I would stand by the stage with another bouncer stopping people going near has he left them off every week. So, on Beast's first night with us, I asked him did he want to do the explosives part with me, he jumped at the chance. So we are standing one of us each side, by the stage facing all the people with our backs to the explosives, now ten times out of ten the explosive goes straight up, not this time though, I hear the bang and next thing you know the shell has landed on Beasts neck still on fire, he's screaming as I run and hit it off him and stamp on it, we then take him to the toilet to put water on his neck, by now the other bouncers are crying laughing and Beasts got a burn mark on his neck as well as a burn mark on his shirt, he's fuckin and blinding that that's his last explosives show, we couldn't stop taking the piss out of him all night.

Week after week we would throw people out regularly, but what would happen is come 10.30 lights on and everybody out, then everyone would enter into the car park and for no reason whatsoever start fighting with each other, but we didn't mind 'cos we had done our job protecting the club inside, it would look like the ok coral every Sunday until the police arrived. The place was a ticking time bomb just waiting to go off.

Now, I mentioned the Pikey boy with Gold chain earlier, well he was now coming to here as well, and I'd put him out one week for fighting. So, he turns up the following week, and I had a few words with him on the door when I wouldn't let him in. He then goes across the car park and takes it out on his girlfriend. This night one of the boys was off, and a boy named Payne had covered him and was standing on the door with me watching this man now hitting his girlfriend. Terry then comes out, winding Payney up, saying, 'you'll never knock him out, but Shirly will, he's a boxer, I bet you a pound, you couldn't knock him out,' and he then goes back into the club.

So, the big pikey comes up and starts giving Payne abuse, next thing you know Payne smashes him straight in the face knocking the prick unconscious, he's hit the floor, and he's looked in the same state as the rugby player I mentioned earlier, Payne goes into the club and says to Terry, *you owe me a pound*, Terry laughed his head off as normal and he flips a pound over to Payne. As we left 20 minutes later, we noticed the pikey was just coming round, and hadn't got a clue what has happened, Payne ends up in hospital as he had split his knuckle on the pricks teeth and has to have a jab in the ass, I couldn't stop laughing all the way to casualty.

The rugby club incident a few months earlier had been the biggest fight I had ever been in until the night of June 7, 2000. This date I will never forget for the rest of my life.

It was going to be my last night down the valley 'cos some work had come up in a club in my area. I was picked up as normal by the Beast who had been up his mother's for dinner in Merthyr, and with it being my last night there, I sensed something was going to happen 'cos there had been fighting there for the last couple of weeks, my luck couldn't be that good with it being my last night and oh fuck was I right.

We arrive at 7 o'clock and Beasts misses Kirsty drops us off, you wouldn't dare leave your car there with all the fighting outside. Paul and Peters then arrive, and we go inside and have our normal pint of squash before we go into the hall. We then receive a phone call from Terry saying he cannot make it tonight, as he has to pick a few birds up (the feathered kind). So, we ring around to get cover, but everyone's out, so we have no option but to do it with four of us. What starts out has a good night turns out to be a nightmare. At the beginning of the night, it was one of the DJ's roadies birthday, and we have him on the dance floor with the usual kissogram. The whole club was buzzing from this, and there was a good atmosphere.

I was then back on the door, taking money off the people as they come in, and the night's going well with no trouble. Paul's misses was having a night out with a few of her friends when all of a sudden one of these scumbags starts chatting her up, and she then tells him that she's seeing one of the doormen on the door, he then takes it on himself to abuse her, this upsets her and she comes to see Paul, this boy had been banned 2 weeks earlier but because of the landlord he was back in. Paul goes flying across the room and grabs the boy, by this time it was only Paul and me on the front door has the other boys were in various corners of the room and didn't see anything.

Now I could see that Paul's heads gone because it was personal and his misses his crying, so he got this boy, and he's coming flying towards the door with him. Now I know he's going to hurt this boy, but I also know he's awaiting a big court case, and if he lays one hand on this boy, he's going down bigtime. The police would throw a fucking party. So, I grab the boy off Paul by the doorway and chuck him down the two steps on the entrance, so Paul's still in the hall, and I go outside to tell the boy to fuck off before he gets hurt, he looks at me in shock and says fuck all.

As I turn my back to walk back into the club, I get pushed by this small, stocky boy who says to me, 'who do you think you are pushing' now I look at him and laugh, and he starts abusing me with all the usual rubbish.

So I thought this fucker is having it and has he came at me I put one on him, now I'll give him his due, he's moved pretty fast, and I haven't caught him full-on, he's bleeding from the mouth, so I go at him, and he's a strong little fucker, very awkward, we both go flying over this bonnet of a car, and as I roll off, old clumsy fuckers only slipped and can't stop himself falling, up until now I had been half-hearted because of the size of this boy, and you'd expect to chuck him around like a rag doll but when the drugs are in someone it's a different ball game altogether, So I'm falling and thinking to myself there's a few boots coming by here.

I thought if this fucker gets a couple into me, I won't hear the last of it, all of a sudden, I just clicked on and thought that's it. I could hear Paul shouting 'stay out of it, it's one on one' to the other scumbags, there must have now been around ten people by us watching. Has he went to put the boot in as I was getting up, I rugby tackled him to the ground, held him down and got up, I then pummeled him with ferocious right hooks and uppercuts until he was nearly crying, I heard him whimpering 'I've had enough, you've done me, you've done me'. So, I thought 'ok, he's had enough,' like I said he was only small, so I stopped, but just as I was about to turn around, bang, I've taken one on the jaw; another one of the scumbags had joined in and hit me from behind, Paul went flying at him, and within seconds the fucker was laid on the floor curled up in a ball, Paul's stamping on him and then all of a sudden, I'm hit again, it now happens that all of the scumbags that are outside want a pop at us because two of their friends are fucked on the floor. So, I'm hitting whatever comes at me, when all of a sudden I get into a bit of a wrestling match with one of them, as I said we are in a carpark and I've finally gone off it, Iv grabbed the fucker by the head and rammed him straight through this car window a couple of times till the glass broke, he's gone down and the next thing I remember as I get blackouts when I go off it is me and Paul going back to back into the club and a couple of body's lying around us, I remember thinking with a smile on my face we fucking done you well, two of us did the fucking lot of you. So, I get back into the club, and the other two bouncers come to the door, no one in the club knew what was happening outside. My shirts hanging on by a thread, and then suddenly I realized I couldn't close my hand, I couldn't even make a fist with it. Turns out, I'd gone through all that fighting outside without noticing, but hey, that's adrenalin for you, I had broken my thumb, and it was dislocated and was locked out. I went to the bar and get a glass of water, it was now 10.30, and people were starting to leave, the scumbags that were in the club didn't know what had happened earlier to the other scumbags, and they were now outside getting rowdy and the gang was now getting bigger by the minute. Paul had gone to make sure that the police had been called, they had been phoned at 10.00 but didn't make it there till 10.50, not bad, nearly an hour, for one mile. People now wanted to leave, but the scumbags had decided to camp by the door and abuse us, and one boy was winding them back up, he just loved causing trouble, Peters the doorman was trying to calm them down as well as the landlord, but they were having none of it. Then suddenly, the stocky man I'd stopped hitting minutes ago sticks his head round the door and starts blowing me kisses and offering me outside, I thought to myself you cheeky fucker, I did you earlier, and now you think you're the hard boy in front of your mates. I turned to Beast and said, 'I'm dying to go out there, but I can't close my fucking hand.' They were all going nuts, throwing punches and kicks at us on the door. It looked like I was bottling it to the scumbags, then some local rugby boy said to me, 'fucking hell mate, you done them earlier on, don't worry about it,' he'd seen the whole incident outside and was bragging us up to his mates. But the stocky boy kept on saying 'c'mon, c'mon out here.' Then all of a sudden, I don't know what made me do it, I squeezed my hand so hard, grabbed my thumb and I put it back into place, the pain was phenomenal, but the smile came back to my face, I turned to Beast quietly and said 'Beast, my hands back', he just looked at me and never said a word - he knew what was coming.

I then made my way to the door and lunged at them, bit of a stupid thing to do really especially with a broken thumb, I was throwing punches at all angles, but there were too many of them, another blackout and the next thing I know I'm being dragged back in the club by the other bouncer, I remember him saying 'fucking hell Shirl, you're going to get killed, there's too many of them' the landlord had also got dragged outside while this was happening and the Beast had dragged him back into the club to.

By now, there wasn't many people left in the club, and it seemed like everyone who was leaving the club was joining them, and to make matters worse, some girl is shouting she's been hit by one of the bouncers, this was winding them right up. The crowd were by now ripping drainpipes of walls, smashing car windows and screaming at us, it was like a scene out of a film, but this was a reality. Then one boy starts screaming at me, he wants me outside, as if I didn't have enough on my plate. He's' totally off it on drugs. Now, the crowd love this boy and egg him on, he's screaming at me like a psycho and then punches his hand straight through a car window. Now I don't know if it's me, but to do something like that, I must have done something really bad to upset him, but for the life of me, I didn't have a fucking clue. I may have hit him earlier in one of my blackouts, but like I said, I didn't have a fucking clue. He was in the clubs most weeks, big, quiet rugby lad, but for some reason probably drugs he had lost the plot that night.

There was now 6 of us on the main door and all in a row stopping the fuckers coming back in, we were now joined by two local bouncers, One of the boys just about managed to close the door before an onslaught of bottles coming steaming at us, they were then trying to hit us with pipes, plastic chair legs and anything they could get a hold of, but as soon as we got the doors shut they would pull them open from the outside, By now there had to be about 20 strong at the door, but no one would come past that step as you had six men in a row waiting for them. One or two tried, but they were met with the boot of the Beast and the punches of one of the other bouncers and me. Now the one who had it in for me makes his way to the front, and I can see he's

112

going to go for it, at this stage, with a broken thumb after two rounds of fighting, I find myself laughing at them like a psycho, the pains gone in my hand and the adrenaline kicked in, *which is a marvelous tool for when you're fighting in these situations.* I then called the boy on, who probably thinks I'm just another useless fat fucker, how he was in for a shock, he comes at me, and I've hit him bang in the fucking face, only the other people behind him keep him from dropping, his eyes are in his head, and I start waving at him 'cos he couldn't move and was fucked, just bobbing about in the crowd with them holding him up.

By now, some man who used to be a bit handy in his day joins us in the row, so we are now up to 7 in the row, and to be honest, we are fucking winning, and they can't get past the threshold. Then suddenly, the last bloke who joined us and incidentally he had been drinking all day rips his top off and goes running out into them, what a stupid fucker, but the beers in and he probably thought he was unbeatable. They put him away in seconds, and he is out cold on the floor, now they have left the threshold, and all turned on him, the thing is he was only about ten stone soaking wet. I did pause for a second to think, what shall I do, they are going to kill this man, but by the time I finished thinking I was steaming into them, they seemed to scatter as I was hitting them, but I had hold of one of them and had him on the floor and all of a sudden he starts crying 'I haven't done nothing, it wasn't me', I was then hit from the side and from what I gather from bar staff watching out of the window I was hit over the head by some youngster with those green, thick gin bottles. The rest I have no memory

113

of has apparently a few were stamping on my head and kicking me. I wish there was a better end to this story like in the movies, and I come out some sort of superman but not this time. The next thing I remember is coming round in the pub, and everyone staring at me and some woman holding a towel wrapped around my arm, I then felt quite ill and ran to the toilet and started spewing blood, police eventually turned up as well as an ambulance, the ambulance man covered my arm up in a bandage. I was joined in the ambulance by two others who I did not know who had also been beaten up by the scumbags. The pain I was in, I knew I had broken my thumb, and I thought I had also broken my arm. Paul and Beast followed me to the hospital, and I still didn't know what was going on. It was in casualty an hour later when they took the bandage off, I realized I had a massive fucking hole in my arm, and the muscle was hanging out. The boys knew but had not told me in case I freaked out. Not a very pleasant sight when you think that all you have done is broken your arm.

An operation was planned for the next day to cut the muscle out and clean the arm and to put the dislocated thumb back into position when I was in theatre. I also had stitches above my eye and all over my body where I had cuts everywhere.

I never did find out how it got like this or who stabbed me as I was unconscious throughout the whole incident at the end, people later told me that they saw me getting hit with bottles, drainpipes, chair legs, and even one of them jumping on my head like a balloon and that I owe it to Paul and Beast for perhaps even saving my life and getting me back in to the hall through an onslaught of bottles and punches. I would have loved to have seen the CCTV cameras for that night, but for some strange reason, they weren't taping, which totally went against us in court months later has it looked like we had wiped it all to protect ourselves. An hour before the operation, police turned up to take a statement off me. They wanted these men locked up as soon as possible. I was visited by my family and mates who all said I should finish on the door's as it was just too dangerous. I was also labouring at the time for three brickie's' who told me to get myself better, and my job was safe, I knew they were just saying that has someone else then had my job.

On getting out of the hospital two days later, my mate Julian (Juggy) picked me up, because he wanted to go down there. I'm stitched up everywhere, arm in a sling and plastered up, and we are sitting in a car above the pub watching a few of them sitting on a wall by the pub. I wasn't really in any fit state to do anything, but Julian just wanted to see who they were. I'd lost my day job as well as the bouncing now because of my hand and just finally decided to take things easy for a couple of weeks to see how things went, at the end of the day I was still alive to tell the tale. I ended up with a nice scar and had a lot of problems with the thumb, but if you think of what I put it through that night, it did eventually heal up, and I continued to box with it a couple of months later, but it was never right again.

CHAPTER EIGHT

(Aftermath)

After the "Taff Trail" incident, there was two things I could have done: one was to just curl up in a ball and pack the bouncing in, but I chose the other route and bounced right back into it, don't get me wrong it took a lot out of me, I never had a stitch-up until that night, and I weren't one to feel sorry for myself. I think after that night, it made me stronger and a hell of a lot nastier. The injury knocked my training, and I was fucked for work in the days, and after nearly 6 weeks in plaster, I was going fucking mad and decided to do some light training. So, I started running and even went back to the bouncing with a plaster cast on, which was a fucking stupid idea, but the boss of RM's just wanted me there 'cos he knew of my reputation.

I was working one Friday night, and this boy comes there, he's a right fucking nuisance, a local town idiot and he's winding me and the other bouncers up. Anyway, I kept myself out of the way because of the plaster on my arm and because it's almost the end of the night. Five minutes to go and the old town idiot decides to get up on the table, dancing. He spills drink everywhere, so the crazy man Chapman goes across and gets him down. Then the nuisance starts choppsing, so Chapman lifts him in a bear hug and carries him out through the doors into the foyer. Paul's inside calming the others down who have had drink tipped on them and want to kill him. Now I'm at the top of the stairs in the foyer, and Chapman comes past me with the boy, and he's ranting and raving as Chaps is taking him down the stairs. Suddenly, I got the urge to hit him over the head with my plaster, not once but about five times! I'm laughing like a psycho, and Chapman is looking at me with a shock on his face. With that, he gives in and starts laughing as well. I suppose you had to be there really, but strangely enough, the boy never came back for a few months. Although he did come back, apologised, and we all laughed it off.

I had just had the plaster off a couple of days when I got asked to work a rave on a Sunday night. I was told there wouldn't be much trouble 'cos they were all good friends, but let's face it, I've heard that fucker a million times before. So I strapped on a crepe bandage to strengthen my hand, there were four of us working there, myself, Paul and Beast who I had mentioned earlier and another bloke by the name of Payne, who was 6 ft 4 and 22 stone; a man-mountain of a bloke who we used to call Queenie because he had worked a couple of times in a gay club in Cardiff. Right, so back to the rave…

After a couple of hours this boy turns up who's been fighting over another pub in town, so I let him in simply because I knew him, but the bloke who's pub he's been fighting in was inside the club as well which I didn't know, so the emergency buttons went off, and I just happened to be the first on the scene. These two loons were stuck together on the floor, and there was blood everywhere. I get the one who was on top in a headlock (strong little fucker) but I had the lock on tight. By now, there were about five men fighting, so much for friends, first night back out of plaster and I've done my hand in already, so we all got one each and we are taking them out of the club at the top of the stairs, when all of a sudden Beast is only trying to chuck his troublemaker down the stairs headfirst; I just about grabbed hold of the boy and stopped him from having flying lessons. Anyway, we eventually got them all out of the club, and they all ended up fighting outside, and one of them ending up in the hospital for a few days. My hand was not right for a couple of weeks after, and yet again, the rave nights got less popular and ended up finishing after just a month or two.

I started going to the hospital with my hand, but it just wasn't getting right. I was doing light punching with it, but then all of a sudden, I would get shooting pains in it. Finally, I received some good news about the Taff Trail, that the police were taking six of them on for violent disorder offences and that the other bouncers and I would be witnesses in court against them. Well, the months dragged while we were waiting for the court case to come around. I was still doing some light sparring ready for the Welsh Boxing Championships, which were coming up the same month as the case; however, my hand was nowhere near ready.

So, we finally got round to getting the trial on, they were still intimidating our witnesses and even put one of their sons in hospital. Mind you, it was nice turning up in court and seeing some of their faces again, it brought back some memories of who they were. Within an hour of being there, it nearly kicked off. What you need to remember is that these are the most arrogant, narcissistic, show-offs you would ever have the misfortune to meet. Run into these clowns, one-on-one, and you wouldn't hear a fucking murmur out of them; however, put them together and… It's just one big game to these idiots, the madder they are, the more respect they get from their so-called mates. Now, don't get me wrong I was no angel when I was their age, but my mates and I were different like I said these were scumbags.

So, the trial finally started, and their barristers start to rip the fuck out of us; you could swear we were up for murder. I held my own with the barristers for three hours, but I still felt like they had beat me. And after a couple of days of ripping us apart, it was our barrister's turn, but by now, they had only gone and found seven witnesses, and our barrister was able to rip them and the scumbags apart. The trial went on for about seven days until it was verdict day and after 7 days of sitting in the court with my mother, uncle, and girlfriend, it was obvious to us all that these fuckers are going down big time. Then all of a sudden, the jury, and I must say must be the most incompetent bunch of fuckers I've seen in my life, decide to go and give these bastards a clean sheet - straight across the board - six not guilty's, I couldn't fucking believe it. Had this lot been in the same room as me for a whole week or what; they couldn't have been that fucking stupid, could they? But that's a jury for you, everything looks different when you have a suit on in the dock, and your barrister makes you out to be some kind of fucking angel. A few things had let us down like the apparent no CCTV; our own witnesses getting confused and the bombshell CCTV footage of Paul Curtis chasing one from a garage two days before the trial which he hadn't told us about didn't help. I felt the colour drain from me, and I just felt deflated. I couldn't fucking believe it, don't get me wrong two of them got a section 4, but what's that, a hundred pound fine, a slap on the wrist and a, be a nice boy for a year Son. I'd heard enough, and so I got up and burst out of there, I was filling up, not to cry but in anger, I wanted to kill some fucker, which was strange how no one said a word or even looked at me. So, there's the 'Great-British' judicial system for ya, the main two who had been witnessed brandishing pipes walked away from that courtroom totally free. I went to work for my night shift thinking to myself I'm working, and these bastards are out somewhere celebrating and probably laughing at us while bragging up and bigging up their pathetic little tales.

The Boxing Championships came around and low and behold I've fucked up again; I've rebroken my thumb in the first round and let the fight slip from my fingertips. Two or three rounds up beating him with a left jab and a hook, and I've just given the man a win, so who do I blame fitness? Busted thumb again? I don't know, but it was the worst I had felt after any fight. I felt like I'd let a lot of people down. Although everyone said to me how well I had done, I personally just felt terrible and to rub it all in with them six getting not guilty's, it was a pretty bad month, bad enough to bring on my depression. The only good thing keeping me going was my girlfriend and family, so I had a fucking bad month, big deal, life goes on.

The following week I had gone out on my mate's stag party, now, he was in the police force and had made a few enemies in our town. This one prick starts giving him shit, and we just walk off. I'd drunk a few beers and thought fuck this; he might not be able to do anything, but I can, so I ran around the block and comes up behind him. All the boys thought I'd walked off in front, so he's still yelling at all the boys when they notice I'm behind him, he turned around and noticed me, but it's too late, and I've levelled the fucker, and he's out cold on the floor, with me standing over him laughing. I then made a quick dash and caught up with my mates. My mate thanked me, but I told him not to worry about it, as I didn't like the fucker, anyway I got a free beer into the bargain.

Talking about stag parties, I'd gone to Amsterdam a few months earlier on a stag-do, and hey, that was an experience, a couple of my mates and five policemen! My mates and I were worried about going with five coppers, but it turned out they were fucking madder than us. And on the last night, we were lucky to get out of this bar in one piece; there was only four out of ten of us left at about two in the morning, when one of the boys decided to start chucking pickled eggs out of a jar across the room at people. With that the owner went nuts and pulls a big machete out at us, I started screaming at him like a psycho ordering him to put the knife away, and the boys then bolted for the door while I apologised to the machete-wielding madman. To be honest, I think if I weren't so drunk, I would have pissed myself right on the spot. Mind you, I will say he looked a little bit worried when I laughed at him, and the following day the boys could hardly remember what happened.

Soon after this little jaunt, I was offered another operation on my thumb, but they told me that I would never be able to box again, so I turned it down and waited for it to come back the best it could. I even started dreaming about those bastards, and the things that were surging through my agitated mind when I was staring them straight in the eyes in that courtroom, would be enough to get me sectioned: bad, bad thoughts. I'll leave them to your imagination.

I knew I'd catch up with them all in time, and I was patiently prepared for the wait!

CHAPTER NINE

(The Ball Starts Rolling)

Things started to get back on track, I put the loss behind me and carried on training, going back on the weights and get back up to 20 stone. A few months after the court case, I was in my local gym known as Active bodies, and it was here that I caught up with the first of the scumbags...

I'd been to the hospital to pick my mate Julian up, who'd been in with heart problems. As strange as it may sound, we headed straight down to the gym to have a bite to eat, and as we were eating our food, one of the old troublemakers walked in with another taller boy. Now, this scumbag didn't see me, so I put my head down and hid behind my baseball cap. I briefly mentioned to Julian who he was, and he said, 'leave it, Shirl!' And then he went over and asks them to leave. Now, I'm thinking, hang on, this fucker has just come into our gym; was this a coincidence or did he know I was there?

Anyway, after Julian's talk, this idiot was just leaving, so I go after him and call on to him. Julian is trying to hold me back, but I wasn't having none of it. The idiot starts babbling like a baby that he is sorry and that it is all over, but the tall boy who is with him starts choppsing at me, so I belted him first and then went at the scumbag knocking him to the floor. By now, the idiot was curled up in a ball as I lean down and inform him that this is nothing compared to what they are all going to have. He's now nearly crying, and the next thing I know, I'm pummeling him with fists and boots until I'm pulled off by a couple of boys from the gym, and then I took myself back in and continued to eat my pasta as if nothing had happened. The boys in the gym inform me that, apparently, he got up and fell down a few times until he was carried away to a car. I felt great as a lot of pressure had been lifted from me.

The events at the gym sent a message to the others that this fucking thing wasn't over, and rumours were coming back that the boy was in such a state he was telling everybody four of us from the gym had jumped him with bats as well - the boys in the gym loved that fucker. I met up with one of the girl witnesses while I was working on the door in a particular venue and I banned her for lying her tits off in court. I don't think she liked it, but that may have had something to do with me calling her a few names too, and again, it made me feel really good.

While in Rm's a few months earlier, I started speaking to this girl named Anne Marie; she was doing promotion flyers for another club, and I'd spoken to her a few times a year earlier when I was working in the Belle Vue. We went out together soon after, and the rest is history! After just a short while, we decided to get a flat together. Now, because I was a builder and had some money saved up, I knew I could do a house like new if we got a bargain, and after looking for a few months, a house came up in Swansea road. All my mates and our family helped for months on end to get the place ready for us to live in.

We also received some good news of a little one on the way and finding out we were going to have a baby was one of the best days of my life; seeing my baby's heartbeat on a screen while looking at my girlfriend and holding her hand at the same time sent shivers down my spine - fucking mental.

Regarding the troublemakers and my need for retribution, I was getting grief from my family but mostly from my Anna to leave it. But it was killing me inside, knowing they had got off. Apparently, a few reports were coming back to me that a few of their cars got smashed up, so I'm guessing they must have upset other people too.

After four months of working on the house every day, it was finally ready for us, only to find it had been burgled two days prior to us moving in - they took the fucking lot - everything we had. However, what hurt most was knowing those fuckers had been in my house. Ok, we weren't living in it, but they had still been in it, and I wanted to kill some fucker that night. I also threatened a few boys who I thought might have done it, but I couldn't prove anything. Nevertheless, later, I actually found out that it was them; I'll explain that in more detail later.

So, I put the Taff Trail incident behind me, and once again, the house was nearly finished. I'd stopped training completely and had gotten really unfit but was still working the doors. Anna also ended up working on the doors with us for a few months, she'd always wanted to do some door work, so we gave her a go, that was until we found out she was pregnant.

This one night, the emergency button goes off, so I run up the stairs and went fucking flying not once but twice on some drink on the floor. By now I'm laughing to myself when I enter the hall, it turns out this big punk girl with an entire face of piercings was sitting on top of her boyfriend punching his face in, until Anna got her in a headlock and wrestled her out of the club; the punk girl was going nuts trying to bite Anna, so she smashes the girls head into the wall and dragged her down the stairs, while I got the girls

125

boyfriend in a headlock and launched him out not far behind her. Ten minutes later, I'm stood on the front door quietly, drinking a bottle of water, then the door is being kicked in. With that, I opened it, only to find the boy screaming at me, wanting to know who had hit his misses. Now, ten minutes earlier she was punching his face in, so I thought, you cheeky fucker, how fucking dare you, but what he didn't realise was that I was seeing Anna, so I then launched the full bottle of water at him and it hit him straight in the face, knocking him senseless. I thought to myself, cracking shot Shirl, while the boy fucked off a bit quick staggering up the road.

Come June, almost a year to the day of the Taff Trail incident, Anna, and I got engaged, and because we both worked there, we decided to have our party in RM's. I was really thinking of calling it a day as it was getting to my misses, I suppose she was sick of hearing of the fuckers, so I didn't want to lose her, so I was just about to put it all behind me when I went to town the next day after the party to get the photos developed and as I was waiting on the corner for my brother to pick me up I spots one of the scumbags walking towards me with 2 boys, now I didn't know If he had seen me at first, but as he drew closer he started smirking so we go straight at each other. Immediately, punches were thrown, and he goes flying into a car, and with that, I grab him and chuck him to the floor, and the next thing you know, he's back up and running away. He won't come near me and walks off, people have stopped and are looking over, just as my brother pulls up, and we drive off.

I went to my mate Julian's house tamping (angry) and within an hour, he gets a phone call off one of his police mates asking had he seen me because apparently, the police were all out looking for me. The little shit had only gone and reported me for assault and was now saying that I'd ripped his gold curb chain off his neck, so it turns out I was now about to be done for robbery as well. So, I get dropped off down the police station, and they bang me up for the day, the only thing was I was going for a meal with the misses at 7 o clock, and fortunately, I was released with an hour to go. I just made it to the meal, which was lucky 'cos if I hadn't, I think it would have been game over for Anna and me.

Three months later, after answering my bail twice, I received a letter stating that they were dropping all charges against me; apparently there was no CCTV footage of the incident, which meant I was a free man again. I bet the little shit was as sick as a dog, but I felt good - another scumbag to cross off the hit list. I started picking up injuries really easy with my feet and knees, and I even ended up in the hospital, having one of my knees drained. The doctors reckoned it was arthritis; at almost 30 years of age my knees were fucked, probably from all the years of playing rugby. I had an offer of £65 compensation: 65 measly fucking quid for a stab wound, there was no way I was taking that. Being a bit broke, to get us through Christmas, a good mate of mine lent me some money.

I was now down to working just one night a week in RM's and finding it all hard to come to terms with. I had bills to pay, and one night a week just wasn't cutting it. The only good thing that came out of it was that I had more time to spend with my pregnant girlfriend to settle us down in the new house. It didn't take long, and I was back in a place called Bessemer's, which was a little function hall that held about 200 people; the money was shit, but you could eat all you wanted at the end of the night from the buffets. I spent a month there with a Dicky bow on and had to bite my lip at a lot of the people there at the party's, 'cos it was a bit more upmarket than my usual pubs. I was then told there was no more work, which I later found out to be a complete lie, perhaps my face didn't fit, I don't know, but if I knew I was going to be laid off after just 4 weeks, there would have been a few more broken noses, and that's a fact.

So, there I was back to one night a week again, so I went back and started doing a bit of plastering in the days for this local builder with my dad. I had also gotten a tip-off that some of my stuff from the burglary was in hiding just up the street, so me and my boxing trainer Jason went up there one Sunday afternoon. We went around the back of this flat, and exactly where I got told was my cement mixer, which I had borrowed off one of my mates. Anyway, we carried it through this garden and took it back down to my house. With that, people who have clocked us with the mixer are now running in our direction. Anyway, I've got my knuckleduster on with my hands in my pocket, and within a few minutes there's about 12 of them tooled up, and my mate and I are arguing like fuck with them, they all start swearing on people's lives that it wasn't them that robbed me, and one of the oldest one's then noticed my boxing

Mam
and Dad

Mam and
Brothers

The Family

Me and My Girls

The Family Man

The Dowlais RFC Years

Trainer Jason Howells

Ready for Action

Sparring Partner Enzo Maccarinelli

Welsh Boxing Team Italy

The Slaughterhouse Boxing Club

Slaughterhouse End of Year Awards

Book Author
Julian Davies

Merthyr's Malcolm Price

On the Doors in
London with Stilks

Boxing Legend
Roy Shaw

2 of My Comedy Shows
on YouTube

JUGGY & SHIRL SHOW

The Merthyr Tydfil Metal Detecting Club

Wrestling
Charity Show

CW Heavyweight
Champion with Manager
Aron Blanhchard

Another Win in the
Gurnos Club

Celtic Wrestling Heavyweight
Champion

More Titles To My Collection

The Bassey Brothers

The Basseys Take It To England

Flying High to Victory

trainer and said, 'are you that champion boxer in the papers!' Suddenly, I think he realised the boys I were knocking around with, and everything settled down. My trainer told them that I wanted a quiet life and if anything happened to me, there would be a war, and in the end, we all shook hands. I knew they had done it, but for a quiet life, I thought I'd let it go, 'cos it was evident to me that they would all end up in jail or moving on in time anyway.

I went out and brought a Rottweiler named Cloudy and chained her to the front gate where they all passed, this was another deterrent and would make them think twice about coming back. I had her for a while and the misses decided to get a boy one to keep her company. I had a big garden and run, so we started looking and came across one in the Rhondda, he was a few years old, and one of the biggest one's I'd seen, so we went over and brought him. Now they got on great for four days and looked happy and then one day we came home on a Saturday and next thing you know they are going for it, the misses is screaming and the new dog who was almost twice the size of the girl one is ripping her apart, god knows what had happened but this is nasty, I try and part them by the collar but it ain't working, the misses is screaming he's killing her, so I smashed some punches into him, but he's not budging and throwing her around everywhere, I then catch him with a hook to the rib's, and he yelped, I then smashed a few in and he's turning on me too, I then grabbed his lead and whipped him and nothing, this was a dog from hell. I then smashed him with a punch to the side again, and he buckled and left her, I then grabbed him into the garden outside away from her, she's whimpering and my kitchen's full of blood. It all calm's down, and we phone the Rhondda explaining what's happened, and they say bring him back, and we'll give you the money. We take him back into their house and all of a sudden, the woman's son comes down and says, 'we had the same problem has he killed our Terrier a few weeks ago', I looked at my misses, and my colour's going has he's obviously dropped his mother in it, the misses start's giving her a mouthful as we steam out of there with our money. We couldn't fucking believe it and rushed home to see how our girl dog was doing as she had calmed down by now, he had ripped her apart everywhere, and I then took her to the vet's to be stitched back up with the money back from the other animal.

RM's was dying a death, and the owner was looking for new ideas to keep the club going. So, a few of us came up with an idea about having a punk rock night on a Thursday, and the owner jumped at the idea. We knocked some flyers and posters up everywhere, and Paul and I agreed to work for nothing, and the owner gave us a free bar.

The first night had over 100 people in there, and we drunk until about 7 in the morning. We were fucking hammered and opened the doors, and it was daylight. The owner had gone home early, and I was to lock up, so we made one of the chefs who was working behind the bar that night go down into the kitchens and cook us food or we were going to tie him up from the rafters, he shit himself and sneaked down there and made us the biggest fry up you could imagine, if the owner had found out we would have all been sacked.

The night grew and grew, and we were up to 200 people in there, the owner then thought it would be cheaper to pay us than to have all we could drink each night and the punk club was born and a start of a new era there.

This one night and we had chucked this English boy, and his girlfriend out, about an hour later we see the boy coming down the street with a drainpipe about 10ft long shouting he's going to kill us, so Paul turns to me and say let's run him, Paul jumps the wall, and I jump down the steps and go fucking flying splitting my jean's underneath, I'm lying on the floor watching Paul chase this boy up the street laughing my head off, Paul's belting him with the money bag as he ran off. I tried this later but didn't have much luck when the bag split open, and the money went everywhere.

Some of these kids in the punk club would wind you up so much, but you couldn't hit them as they were so small, I dragged one boy out for fighting and hung him over a wall, I don't know what stopped me but I was going to let the fucker go head-first, he was screaming, and I finally come round and just let him go. Another one who wound me up; I just tightened his tie until he was choking, and he was throffing at the mouth and couldn't breathe, but I loosened it up and he shut the fuck up.

Another time I caught this punk smoking drugs in the club, so I walked him out, he then turns to me and puts his finger down his throat and pukes all over the floor, now my head totally goes, and I drag the prick down the stairs, now the door needs two hands to open, so I smash his head into the door to daze him, open the door and then launch him out, five minutes later and he's sitting on the floor waiting for his friends outside, by now one of the bar staff had a mop bucket getting the spew off the floor, so I said to the boy

131

mopping open the door for me, I then went and chucked the whole puke filled slop bucket all over the prick, his face was a picture, I went back into the club laughing my head off, and the boy soon fucked off and never came back again.

One night this boy was working with us standing in for one of the boys; some tart had offered to take him in the cubicles in the toilets so in he goes. So, Paul says to me watch this, he gives him a couple of minutes and then rings his mobile phone, as we are standing by the toilets, we can hear it ringing. He actually answered and says, 'I can't speak now. I'm busy and hangs upon us,' he then comes out later with a stinking look on his face and calls us all the bastards going. The same time a mate of mine Andrew was also in the cubicle next to him with another tart, mad times.

Another night some of the cast of the TV program Nuts and Bolts came to the club and started chucking their weigh around, they ended up fighting the regulars, and we chucked them out, there was about seven of them offering us out to fight them, so me and one of the regulars at the time run straight at them and they scattered and got away, two of us, and they shit their selves, I did catch up with a few of them and they just apologized.

It was also around this time that I landed a part in the TV Program Nut's and Bolt's as well playing the role of 'The Tank,' an Unlicensed boxer who knocks out the star of the show with a head butt. I'd got called in when the fighter had pulled out, and it was a good payday and experience working on set.

We then started a Battle of the Band's competition over a few weeks. Now the first competition, Jolly the DJ and my brother Steven started a band and got quite far, getting to the final. The drummer and guitarist went on in the future to be a part of The Blackout and toured worldwide. The following year Jolly was replaced by of all people my other brother Barry, now Barry was known for his drawing and a fantastic artist, but I didn't have a clue he could sing. I was in for the shock of my life when they got through the first round and had some outstanding songs.

I've seen some unfortunate accidents in clubs in my time as well, we had a foam party one night and this boy had slipped and snapped his two fingers completely the opposite way, people were spewing just looking at them but I managed to cover them up until the ambulance came, I did offer to put them back for him but for some reason he wouldn't let me. I don't know if he had heard of my past experiences, especially what had happened one day on a rugby field, my mate had broken a finger and I offered to put his finger back into position, he then continued the rest of the game but was in agony later in club. I then seen him a few days later in training and he was telling me I'd only put his finger back wrong.

Also one night a girl got a bit close to one of the live bands guitars, she comes screaming out of the hall holding her head, her face red with blood as if she had painted it, the floor was dripping with blood and after taking a closer look I realized that she had a hole in her head, I wouldn't swear it but I think I could see part of her brain; I held the cut together with a towel and then passed her to my girlfriend Anna who was working on the doors with us at the time until the ambulance came.

Another time some prick was launching pint glasses through the hall with about 200 people in it, we couldn't catch who was doing it and when we would run in no one would have seen a thing, anyway one pint lands straight on this girls head shattering on impact, again she comes screaming out into the foyer, another hole in the head but this time there was about a 3 inch piece of glass wedged in her head, now I'd always been pretty good with situations like this and knew not to pull it out, a couple of girls start puking and fainting who was with her on looking at it, but I calmed her down until the ambulance came.

Another night it wasn't far off closing time, and people were leaving, when all of a sudden this man walks in with a Labrador, so I shouts down the stairs, 'we are closed now, mate', he then starts fuckin and blinding at me, turns out he was gay, so I started to walk down the stairs to chuck him out when he leaves the dog off the lead and shouts 'kill, kill' next thing you know this fucking Labrador is coming for me, I turned around and bolted up the stairs in to the nightclub. I couldn't stop laughing even though I was shitting it. The dogs running around the nightclub and Paul got the dog out, and I chuck the boy out after calling him some harsh words. The next day I found out he'd been to the police and the club and he wanted me sacked, I also found out he was on day release from the hospital, where he got the dog from fuck knows.

I mentioned before it takes two hands to open the club doors, and one day, I saw one of the doormen almost lose his finger after opening it fast and jamming it.

This one night, this girl is leaving and tries pushing the handle down with one hand, her finger got wedged in the side of the door, and it can't open out or in.

She's screaming in pain and thinks her fingers hanging off. I ran and gets a crowbar from downstairs while the other bouncers are trying to calm her down, we try and crowbar it open, but it only makes the matter worse, and she starts screaming worst, by now there's a crowd about 20 watching and next thing I know the girl began to faint with the pain. One of the bouncers holds her up and my mates there drunk, and he starts to talk to her like a doctor giving her instructions on how to breathe, I thought for fuck sake you swear she's having a baby, I couldn't help but laugh at him, anyway the owner of the club Rob comes up with an idea and to get some butter from the kitchens, so me and him go outside, and I've got a pool cue jammed in the door and he's buttering her hand up from the outside, this is now 20minutes later, and we are all drenched in sweat, we are just about to phone the fire brigade has I thought she's got to lose the finger when the door goes flying open and everyone starts cheering has her finger slips out. They take her downstairs until she comes round. I'd never had such a hard night at work in my life, ten minutes later, and she's back on her toes and goes back into the club dancing.

This one night this girl had gone into the toilets and hadn't come out for a while, so someone goes and check on her for us, and it turns out she's passed out on the floor, spewing all over her, and she's unconscious, so I goes and phones an ambulance and gets a towel for her, while Paul and his brother Anthony are looking after her, anyway she's gone off to hospital and about an hour later this woman turns up ranting and raving, turns out the girl was only sixteen, Paul gives it right back to the mother as she used to drop her off and she calms down, her daughter was telling her it was an under 18s disco every week ,the girl ended up on a drip all weekend, the hospital said she had been given a pill, we pulled a few people in but came up with no answers. The girl stayed away for a while, but the mother then asked us would we leave her back in to watch the band's if she promised not to drink.

Also, this one night we had put some pissheads out earlier in the night, and we are on the front door, and Paul said to me, 'what the fuck is that?', I looked at the wall, and there was this red laser beam light on us, Iv dived to the floor in panic, and he's laughing, I wasn't taking any chances, and he can see someone up in the bushes pointing it at us. It must have been one of those handheld pen ones, Paul then shout's, 'c'mon if you got a problem' a voice then start's shouting 'we were dead men', nothing came of it though until a week later when we are standing on the door, and I heard a shot sound and then something whizzing past us, we looked at each other, and next thing you know a pellet hit's the door inch's from our face, we slammed the door shut and made our way out of a different exit running up the hill in the direction it came from but by then whoever was shooting at us had run off, thank fuck they were a lousy aim and no hitman.

Now Paul was a fucker for his wind up's and having a laugh. Around this time, I had a video camera and was always filming. This one-day, Paul comes in, and his misses Ceri was having a baby in a few months. He then said to me, 'I've been speaking to my misses, and we want you to film the birth' has you can imagine my face was a fucking picture. In the end, he even had his misses in on it. He kept this going right up until the birth of his daughter Alex. We were in work one night, and he received a phone call saying his misses had gone into labour, he comes running into me and says, 'Shirl I've got to go! Ceri's in

Labour! Can you shoot and get the video camera?' Then with that he burst out laughing, and was gone.

Another day I had gone to the club to watch the rugby. I was off duty but usually sorted the trouble out if it kicked off. So, I was there with a few mates and an old school friend named Andrew (Biggie) who had now started drinking there and chatting to us. The games just finished and I'm eating my food quietly when I noticed a good couple of pricks on a table who had been getting rowdier by the minute, so all of a sudden its kicked off, there's about 10 men fighting each other, so I run in and try and part them, but because I didn't have my uniform on they just thought I was jumping in, there's tables and glass going everywhere, but like I said people are swinging for me now, so I go off it and start knocking a few out, they are dropping like flies, then this big bloke who I didn't know joins in and helps me to get nearly all of them into the foyer at the top of the stairs at the entrance to the club, I then put my head down like in a rugby scrum and run into about five of them pushing them down the stairs, but there's this one big fucker with a big moustache who had knocked a few out inside and he was still causing hell, so I go back in and go straight for the fucker getting him in a choke hold, I drag him into the foyer, I then begin to let him go, and the fucker goes straight for me, he puts up one hell of a fight for a couple of seconds I thought the choke weren't working but then you could see the life zap out of the fucker, next thing I know I'm getting hit with a stiletto shoe over the head by his misses who's screaming at me to let him go, I then start laughing at her and screaming for her to hit me harder as I applied the grip even harder, by now he's gone blue and his legs have gone, she's now crying and I thought I'd better loosen this hold or I'll be

137

doing a bit of time inside, I then dragged him down the stairs, by now everyone had left the club before the police arrived, I then went back into the hall to finish my food off and the owners of the club thanked me with an extra curry and chips, I then went home, had a quick shower and was back down the club working as if nothing had happened.

Talking about Andrew (Biggie), he must have been about 6ft5 and had the voice of an angel, and he started singing there. I hadn't seen him since school, and he was now mad as a hatter. He then went on to make his own comedy videos and self-publish over twenty of his own books. He may as well been bouncing there, because he was there more than us.

The Punk-Rock Club really took off, and the owner and his new girlfriend Mel really made a go at it, I had some good laughs with them all, and we really got on well. Then one night both owners were away down Swansea, and this boy who we thought was dealing in the club had kicked off, and he's stamping on this boy's head, so Paul goes at him and tries to get a choke on him, but he was so tall he couldn't get it on, so I came in from the side and drags him out, he's putting up a fight as I drag him down the stairs, I got him outside and just pushes him to the floor and tells him to fuck off.

An hour later, the owner's misses return's from Swansea on her own, and she's screaming at me like I'm a little kid and calling me a bully, it turns out she had the boy's number has he was going to do a night DJing there. She's still screaming, so I told her to fuck off and stick the job up her arse, and I walked out of there. The following day I hear the police are looking for me again and are going to do me for assault. I then caught up with the boy in town and found out it was a load of shit. The following day the owner Rob rung me up and said just ignore her, they'd argued in Swansea, and I caught the back end of it. I was as stubborn as her and wouldn't go back and all over a stupid fucking argument, but that's life. I waited for a phone call has the bouncer Lyn who was working there kept telling me that they were going to phone me and offer my job back, but after a couple of weeks, nothing came of it, so I thought it was time to start looking elsewhere. I'd been there for two years, and it was now time for a change.

It was around this time Anna had given birth to our first baby called Abigail. Anna had gone through a lot of problems with pre-eclampsia and was in and out of the hospital for a few weeks with her blood pressure, and soon after, our little angel popped out and changed our lives forever.

Rob had asked me to pop to the pub 'cos Mel wanted to see the baby too. I went there one day, and she wasn't there, and I was gutted we had missed her. Not long after I found out that Mel was dying of cancer and never got round to going to see her which was something that I regretted quite a while; within a few months she had passed away, I was gutted, and I went to her funeral to pay my final respect to her.

Every year I was getting lazier and putting more and more weight on and just wasn't fighting fit. I was now 34 and in a young man's sport. I then get offered to fight some African man who must have been 6ft 7 yet again. Only the money made me take it, and when he got in the ring, he looked like a young Anthony Joshua and fucking hit like him to. I gave my all for two rounds', but every punch I saw star's and I'd never had that before, he then stopped me in the second round and I went back to the changing room and said to my trainer Jason, 'I'm done with it all', Jason didn't even argue and knew my time was up; it had been a great experience on my journey of life, but it was time to move on to my next challenge and become a Wrestler, Yeah you heard that right, a wrestler.

CHAPTER TEN

(On Top of the Hill)

I was offered a Friday night permanent in a place called Baverstocks, and in the first year, you could count the amount of trouble on one hand that went on but all of a sudden it was the place to be and was rammed every Friday with nearly 300 people, and as we know booze, fueled with drugs and numbers is a recipe for disaster – and it was! The place was situated right on top of a hill in between two towns, it was a large hotel with a vast central hall. It was a singles club, but that didn't stop the married people coming in; basically, it was a knocking shop. The place was owned by an Englishman named John and his son Conrad, and they had previously been funeral directors. Conrad's wife Sally was on the door taking the money, and we all became good friends; they'd even feed us before work, which was a bonus. I worked with two top boys, Lee Callaghan and Paul Curtis, and we went on to do a few years there, having some mental times.

One night it kicked off really early, and this bloke named Big John (who was easy 6ft 4 and about 21 stone) had started fighting. Now, he used to be a bouncer in London and had worked for Geoff Capes security firm. Anyway, a few months prior to this he had tried being the big man with us, but we put him in his place, but this time him and this other bloke are going at each other on the dance floor, so I ran straight in between them, punches are whizzing past me as I'm holding them apart, so I told big John he's got to go, but he just ignored me, so I start to lose it! I began yelling at him, and he starts to back off, walking out. I had a few words with him, and it all calmed down, and to be honest, he wouldn't stop shaking my hand after that. Then one-night Lee, who we call "3 amp," simply because he had a short fuse, starts getting abuse from this man, we had put out earlier. The man then pushes Lee, next thing you know Lee's slapped him to the floor; I'm thinking he's just knocked the man out with a slap, lucky he didn't punch him, or he would be a gonna! Anyway, Lee's jumped on top of him, screaming things at him, so I go out and pull Lee off him. With that, a couple of minutes later, the man gets up but falls straight back down again; Lee goes back into the club as the man staggers away. The police were involved, but nothing came of it.

Now, Lee is only about 5' 8", but he's built like a fucking tank due to him training for Mr. Wales at the time - so was quite a handful. Anyway, one night this real big man comes in and start's taking the piss out of Lee's size. Now Lee's one of these quiet guy's until he's poked, and this big fucker ain't letting up The big man then drop's to his knees, taking the piss 'cos he's still taller than Lee, but I knew what was coming next because this prick had crossed a line. Immediately, Lee start's smashing hooks into him, and the man went flying back, and he's spark out cold. We drag him through the door and put him outside on a bit of grass; a few minutes later, the man came round and walked off without a clue what had happened to him – just another wannabe bully who met his match that night.

An hour or so later it's gone off again, this big boy is punching fuck into this other man, so we go running in and grab him from behind. They'd already smashed into some innocent people near them, and there was chaos everywhere. I'm dragging the man out into the foyer, and Paul has another one in a headlock. I pull the big one to the floor, he's still screaming at us with threats, and the next thing I know, Lee has gone to his knees and has some "Spock-like-death-grip" on the man's neck. So, I dragged him to the door, but the boy wasn't saying anything! We reach the door, and his head has smashed into it shattering the glass, the door usually swung open, but Paul had forgotten to take the bolt off; we then drag him the rest of the way to the main entrance and he's screaming like a fucking baby, pleading with us to not hit him. A few minutes later, the man he was fighting with is outside, and they start hugging each other; we thought you bunch of pricks; we've just smashed this door to bits, and this pair are nearly kissing each other. We called Conrad the manager over because this wasn't the first time, we had smashed the door glass, and we expected the worst, but he said laughing, *damn, I wish I'd seen that,* and promptly walked off, still giggling.

The DJ for the place at that time was "MAD AL" who I'd worked with quite a few times in the past; his DJ booth was about 20ft above the whole hall, and I was placed up there with the mad bastard most of the time. This man (as his name suggests) was nuts, you just didn't know what he was going to do next. There would be 300 people in the hall dancing in front of him, and he'd have a laptop on behind his counter with porn films on laughing his fucking head off. Baverstock's was unlike any other venue I'd worked in; we even had a suit and tie. Trouble only occurred now and again, and we had a lot of tribute acts on as well.

This one night, these two men who were bouncers from another town were in there, the big one always used to talk to Lee and Paul but looked at me like a piece of shit. Anyway, it's gone off inside, and the big one has knocked this man out, and he's screaming at anyone to fight him. The boys and I grabbed him and took him out. He leaves the club, and he and his mate go around the front of the building, to the hotel's reception to try and get back in; immediately, we were called on the radio, and Lee and Paul shoot around there to stop him at reception. As soon as they approach him, he goes off on one again, and while Lee and Paul are now around the front, he steams off and makes his way back to the nightclub. The boys quickly radio through to me saying he's coming back - so that I can be alert and ready. Then I hear the idiot outside shouting, 'open the fucking door?' And then he bangs it, I opened it, and he started swearing at me, so I smash him once, and he's gone down. A split second later his brother, (who I hadn't seen at the door) comes flying at me from the side, so I've smashed him as well. And both men are now lying on the floor 'knocked out,' when Paul came running out. After a while, both men get up and leave; two weeks later, they turned up and apologised saying, they were off it on cocaine because a family member had died. We told them they were banned for a few months, and the two of them returned and thankfully never played up again.

Around about this time Front magazine was doing a few pages article on bouncers for their magazine, they took thousands of pictures from all over Merthyr that night, and we ended up in Baverstock's with them; they just couldn't believe how mad Merthyr was. I made the final magazine, which came out a few months later.

144

Now when it came to jokes, I'd be right up there in the thick of it. I'd been involved in so many with the boys having strippers for their birthdays, but I never really thought I'd get caught out myself. Every birthday no one on our firm was safe 'cos goading Bernard would throw money at the stripper's straight out of his own pocket. I've even seen some of the boys' take nights off thinking they'd got away with it. Now, my birthday had been on a Saturday in July, and I'd booked the night off to go to town with my misses, also thinking I'd get away with another year without Bernard getting me.

I got a phone call a few days later off Bernard saying he had the local Merthyr express photographer's coming down the Crown pub at the bottom of town where we used to all meet up the following Friday night. He had just changed the name of his company and said, 'the more boys you can get there, the better it will be for a picture.' Well, at this point, I'm sure you can see where this is going? So, I'm ringing round telling all these doormen not to miss out and said that this would be a cracking photo opportunity for us all; however, basically, unbeknown to me, I was simply setting myself up for a fall - very smart Bern. Come Friday night, Paul picked' me up, and we headed down there. Masses of doormen are all talking when Bernard said: 'apparently, they're running late, but are definitely on their way.' Now, at the time, I was always taking photos of myself and other doormen, and being aware of this Bernard then says, 'Shirl jump in the pub and see where you think is best for this picture?' Still clueless, off I go, and as I'm chatting to Paul, I heard someone saying, 'something's up, the police are here!' So, I turned around, and there's this blond policewoman, she walked straight up to me and said: 'Anthony Thomas, I'm arresting you!' With that, the stripper music hit the speakers, and I'm stuck to the spot. In a split second, I eye up all my exits, and there's a doorman at each entrance laughing, shaking their head as if to say, 'no chance Big Lad.' I'm surrounded by 20 doormen and Bernard, with a look that could kill, and he's laughing. You can imagine the rest, I'm whipped, stripped, creamed and then given a bottle of champagne. I said to all the doormen laughing, I will have every fucking last one of you back! Paul had to take me back home and explain to my misses what had happened, and she eventually found the funny side of it.

Around this time, the SIA License came in force, and our boss hired Baverstock's to do the course. There were about thirty doormen on this course, and they were showing us different scenarios. One trainer tried telling us that if there was trouble to offer to buy them a drink, they obviously weren't from Merthyr because thirty men were just stood looking and laughing. Then I got picked out to do a scenario up on stage, and I had to choose a partner to go with me, so I picked Paul because we worked together. Then another doorman was called up to play the part of a drunken punter causing trouble. So, one of the boys goes into character and acting drunk has Paul's dealing with him, and I'm standing at the side of Paul all quiet like normal. The drunken punter is getting worse, pushing Paul for a fight, with all the doormen watching and laughing. I then come in from the side around the punter and put him in a chokehold - he's kicking everywhere, probably 'cos I've put it on a bit too tight and his legs are going. I quickly loosen my grip as the 2 trainers are shouting: 'That's enough!' The trainer's faces were a picture, I apologised to my mate and said to them, 'well, that's the way we do it here boys!' They didn't have a clue what to say - everyone else just laughed.

After a few years, the number's started dropping every Friday night in Baverstocks, and I ended up finishing and jumped straight into a job in a different town. Paul finished too and came with me to the Aberdare Con Club. This was another rough place with functions upstairs; the hardest part was getting people down the stairs. I don't know how many times I almost broke my neck falling down them fucking stairs while ejecting people. Then one-night, Paul picked me up for work and tells me he's finishing because he's had enough of working the door and was looking for a career change: every weekend for five years is enough for anyone. So, Paul quit, and I worked on my own for a couple of weeks with a few different faces. Shortly after, I was asked to work on a Sunday in a pub in town called 'The Vulcan,' or, as my misses calls it "The Titty Twister!" If you have ever seen the film From 'Dusk Till Dawn,' then I'm sure you'll know what she means.

Now, as I've always said, The Vulcan was the roughest pub in town, I'd grown up in there and had many scraps myself when I was younger. There's isn't a week goes by without trouble there - right up to this day. Soon after, there are three night's going at the place; I needed the money desperately and jumped at the chance of the extra work. Apparently, the previous firm of bouncers that were employed there had been turning their eyes away from the trouble, letting drug dealer's deal in the place, so it was our job to go in and clean it up.

147

CHAPTER ELEVEN

(Full Steam Ahead)

I was now in the Vulcan, partnered up with a bloke called Wayne Price from Mountain Ash. Wayne had been bouncing over 22 years. I'd worked with him a few times in the past, and a lot of the boys called him psycho, to be honest, he had the eyes for it.

After three weeks of chucking someone out every night, you could see the place getting quieter, and we had cleaned it right up, and the owner was over the moon and was well impressed with us. The dealers had calmed right down and had to fuck off elsewhere to make their money.

One particular night when Wayne was on a night off, there was this boy having murders with his misses, so we ask him to leave, and he smashes a glass bottle and makes a few gestures at us. His mates then make him put the bottle down and soon as he does, we rushed him and chuck him out, and a couple of his mates follow him and started to have a go at us. He then goes running past me back into the club, so I push him back, he then comes at me punching, so I grab him at the back of the neck with my left hand pulling him down while I uppercut him with right hooks in the face, I then wrestle him onto the street, and I was pulled down to the floor by some of his mates, the boy with me then pulls them off me and I'm back up hitting whoever's near me, all of a sudden there's police everywhere,, and the boy who started it all want's to press charges and get me done. The police end up moving them on, I go back into the pub doorway, and there's blood everywhere, up the walls, on the floor has his nose was smashed to bits.

The following day these men were ringing my boss asking who I was, and he pretty much warned them that I was no pushover and to leave it. A week later, the boy comes back and wants to shake my hand and doesn't stop apologising, a couple of weeks later he ended up fighting again, but this time, the other person wasn't so lucky and ended up having his nose sewn back on. We got off to a bad start, and I got to know all the men years later.

Another night two girls were fighting, so I grabbed hold of one but her boyfriend pushed me flying. So, I jumped straight on the steroid monkey and put him in a neck hold as his girlfriend was also trying to hit me, Wayne's got the other boy locked up and the boy I got hold of put up a good fight, but I had a good arm lock on him, my other arms gripped to his chain choking him. I got him to the door and threw him out, he goes up in the air and lands in the middle of the road, and a taxi misses him by seconds. I then chucked his misses out and runs back in, by the time Wayne as choked this man out, and we carried him out through the door. I go back out where the steroid monkey and his misses were, but he had disappeared out of sight, it would appear his bottle had gone. Wayne turn's to me laughing and says, 'you made a meal out of that Shirl, he was only tiny,' I looked at him and rolled my eyes as we were laughing.

This one night and these men are arguing with some others, and there is this really tall man there. One man gets hit to the floor as I've run in, and the next thing you know, the tall man hangs onto this TV, which was on a bracket by the bar and pulls the TV down onto the top of the man. Now this tall man was usually quiet, but he looks in shock and puts his hands up and walked out. He apologised and said he couldn't work out why he had done it, and walked off while talking to himself.

An hour later and it has gone up big time up the back of the pub. I ran in, and pool cues are going over people's head's and glasses are being thrown and smashed, it was absolute chaos, so I go to work choking one man who's got a cue in his hand, and I'm dragging him out holding onto the pool cue which is choking him. He's out of the way, and I'm back in for the next, IV grabbed these two men and gone over pool team with them, and both have landed on top of me, I managed to get back up and get one of them out. I then go back in, and Iv grabbed this skinny fucker who's bleeding and push him against a wall, then he spat the biggest mouthful of spit and blood into my face and eyes, I literally seen red grabbing him and he's trying to scram my eyes out, I then manage to grab his hand and I snapped every finger the opposite way, he's now screaming like a baby has I ram him through pub and out the door. Police are there to welcome him as he's screaming that Id snapped them. I then told the police Id lifted him up off the floor, and he spat in my face, and police asked me did I want to do him for assault for spitting at me, but it was pointless and part of the job.

The following night it's gone off again and early, this man's knocked out cold on the floor and as we get in there this man's getting off him. We take the man out, and I noticed he was a copper who was on a night off. We then get told the man had asked for it. Police turned up later and asked what happened, and we could not tell them it was one of their own because he could have made our life hell.

Then toward the end of the night, this man kicks off and his arguing with his misses, so I warned him, and he looks at me like a piece of shit. Not long after he is arguing again and really loud, so I grabbed him from behind and put him outside; I then got all the usual threats. The following day I am over my daughter's school; I had not passed my driving test by then, so I was just walking over for her when he passed by me in a jeep. He laughs at me, I laughed back and then he did a complete circle and his coming straight at me in the jeep. He's picking up speed, and I'm calling him on, he's getting faster and nearer, and I'm looking at the bank ready to dive out of the way when all of a sudden, he pulls away from me and back onto the road and drives off. It was a game of chicken, and I won by not moving, bit silly thing to do but you couldn't show these people any fear. I see him a few times after that, but nothing was said.

The following week there was a rugby international; Wales had won in the day, so it was always going to be a mad night. Wayne had the night off, and I was working with a boy called Dean Pitt. We both walk-in bang on 7 o'clock and as I was just about to put my phone behind the bar, we get called over by the bar staff; they tell us that four girls are fighting at the back of the pub. So, off we go and throw them out of the pub, these lunatic girls were hitting us with their stilettos and everything! Lucky for us the police turned up and arrested two of them. It so difficult dealing with the female of the species, 'cos let's face it, you can't, and wouldn't ever want to hurt them.

Hours later more girls are fighting, and we end up closing the doors 'cos the pub was too packed with just two of us working it. It was nonstop chaos all night, and one of the women we put out went straight on the phone to her husband hollering over to us that we were dead men walking…

The following night I was working, and these two big men turned up, and one asks could he have a word. Turns out, It was the husband of the woman I'd put out the previous evening. So, I explained everything to him, and he said: 'you did right! Woman are nuisances with drink in 'em.' And we shook hands and went about our business. I can't remember how it came about but, Wayne had to take a few weeks off, so I had a different doorman to second me on a nightly basis.

One night I was working with my boss Bernard when this bloke came running out of the pub and keels over in pain up against a wall. Bernard and I went over to see if he's alright because he was looking terrible. Bernard got on his phone to call an ambulance, and after a couple of minutes of talking to the people on the phone Bernard starts to lose his rag and shouts, 'fucking hell, he'll be dead by the time you get here!' The boy in pain looks at Bernard and yet again slips into some sort of unconscious state. Bernard looks at me with a look saying, those weren't the words he was hoping for, what with the boy in such a state. Then, all of a sudden, we found the funny side of it and couldn't stop laughing. And every time I looked at him, I just started laughing while trying to keep the boy awake. Finally, the ambulance arrived, checked the boy out, noticing that his abdomen was ripped, and immediately took him away to Hospital. To be honest, Bernard and I laughed for the rest of the night 'cos I was branding Bernard, a cruel fucker!

Another night I was partnered with this man called Daryl (Stevo.) Now, he and I had worked together in the past in Brecon, and so I knew that Stevo was a right handful. After a while this fucking knob-head was playing up, thinking he was something special. Stevo was quiet and kept to himself, but the bloke's then got in Stevo's face taking the piss of the scar he had on his face. I said to him, 'look, mate, leave it there now, or you'll end up getting hurt…' But the cocky fucker just continued, and it was quite evident from Stevo's face what was coming next. Anyway, to cut it short, together, we carried the troublemaker out, and he was out cold as we dropped him around the corner up the side lane. Ten minutes later he's out on the main road with people trying to hold him up, he didn't know where the fuck he was.

By this point there was only about 10 minutes of the night left to go, and it was only that one prick we'd had trouble with. Then one of the women who was a regular collapsed on the floor. Now, this woman must have been 20 stone, but she was a bit of a drama queen and used to act up all the time. So, we thought she was acting again, I said to Stevo, 'you'll have to give her the kiss of life?' He laughed and said, 'You can fuck off Shirl, you can do it!' We then try and lift her up off the floor as Stevo's pulls his back; I'm thinking to myself; he's winding me up, but he wasn't, he was in pain. Finally, we get her up, but momentarily she goes down again. The ambulance turns up, and she's screaming, but again, we still did not know if it was all an act or real. Stevo finished on the door's and ended up evicting travelers all over the UK. Sadly, two years ago I received a phone call saying that he had passed away; I was gutted because I'd only
spoken to him in the pub I was working in the week before. Another good doorman taken from us at a young age.

Back to the Vulcan…

This one night this alcoholic is walking up towards the pub, and he's got his dog on a lead with him. Anyway, he

153

goes to enter the pub which is packed so I said to him, 'that the dog can't go in!' And he starts arguing that the dogs not banned and that the dog has never caused any trouble in the pub in his life; he was so fucking serious; the other bouncers and I were pissing ourselves laughing. So, he tells his dog to sit while he goes in for a drink and he's by the bar staring at his dog and the dogs just sitting there. I actually felt that sorry for the dog, I nearly let the fucker in.

When the man left, he asked us how long his dog had left before he would be allowed back in. I couldn't look him in the face and just walked off laughing to myself. A week later he's walking past eating a burger and puts it in my face saying, 'I bet you'd love this you fat bastard?' I pushed him in the face, and he threw the burger at me, I don't know why but he took a disliking to me.

Now the following week I have taken the misses out for the night around town; I'd told her all the stories about this man, and we go to the Vulcan for a few drinks. As we were leaving, I notice the man up the back by the pool table, and he's up by a wall. Now, I've had a few drinks and says to the misses, 'I'll meet you outside babe!' With that, I go up to the man and says, 'remember me?' And without warning, he then goes to throw a punch, so I've smashed him over this table and start hitting him. I grab him by both ears, and I've lifted him full off the floor. The doormen manage to pull me off him, so I apologise and walk out. I went outside, and one of the doormen said, 'your misses has gone on up town.' So, I ran to catch her up, and when I approach her, I noticed that she's only gone and pinched his fucking dog; I'm pissing myself laughing. Anyway, under some duress, she let the dog go and watched as it walked back down the street to the pub. The lunatic came past the following night while we were at work, and strangely enough, he talked to the doorman quite tidy (nicely.) and me to be truthful, I think he sometimes got himself in such a state and could never remember anything.

The first bank holiday of the year came round, and all weekend it was packed to the rafters but with no trouble whatsoever. It's Sunday night and about half an hour to go, and we get asked by the landlord to take this girl out of the pub. After asking her a couple of times, her brother decided to pick her up and carry her out for us; she apologised to Wayne and I outside and went on her way. Ten minutes later, her husband came steaming into the pub with a couple of other men. Now, this man was known as one of the hardest men in town; an ex-boxer and rugby player who was rumoured to have had bare-knuckle fights for money. I had played against him in the past, and he had trained in our boxing gym for a few months. I had also taken him on the pads once or twice, and he was one of the hardest hitting men I'd ever taken. To be honest, I thought I knew him well, I was obviously wrong. So, he goes steaming past us while I tried reasoning with him but he as tunnel vision mode and heading for the landlord who, (I might add,) was also an ex-boxer but the man jumps straight on top of the gaffa and begins pummeling him on the floor. Wayne goes in first and tries to pull him off the owner in the corner, but the two men with him grab Wayne from behind in defense. So, I grabbed the two of them from behind by their shirts and try and pull them out of the door. With that, while I'm holding the other man, the taller one of the two swung a punch at me and smashed me straight in

the face; I later found out it was the man's brother. I let go
of the other man and smashed the one who's hit me with a
few hook's, Wayne's grabbed the other and threw him over
a table. The tall one who I just hit dropped to the floor and
I drag him outside when suddenly, someone pulled my
jacket over my head, so I aggressively rip it off. The taller
one then comes running at me, now, I very rarely ever head
butt someone, but I had no option, after which he dropped
to the floor, and he's pissing blood from his nose. The
woman then jumped in, and they are both attacking me, but
I'm just thinking to myself, 'Shirl, you've got to get back
in there and help Wayne.' I run back into mayhem! It looked
like every fucker in there was fighting. The landlord's fucked
on the floor, and the man is on his way out, 'cos he's just
found out about his brother. He comes running at me shouting,
'who's hit my brother?' And I thought to myself, 'I'm not
going to lie to you.' So, I screamed at him, 'I fucking hit him!'
He's now in full rage mode and were going at each other as I
smash a few into him, but everyone's in the way trying to part
us. Wayne's pushing him out of the door, and he's still
screaming while I'm laughing at him. With that the police
turned up and threatened to arrest them all if they don't go
away; his tall brother who by this time was across the road
with a face was full of blood is ranting saying that he'll have
me when I'm finished work. I just let him do all the talking
and glared at him from where I'm stood. With my shirt ripped
to pieces, I got myself back into the pub noticing that there
was blood all over my face; a lot of people ask if I'm alright,
but what they didn't realise was that the blood wasn't mine. I
finished work that night, but no one showed up, a bit of a let-
down really 'cos I had wound myself right up. I saw the man a
couple of weeks

later, and he just gave me a little stare and walked off; maybe he got the full truth of what happened and realised that I wasn't the one in the wrong and that it was his brother had hit me first.

A month or so later the pub next door was reopening, and you wouldn't believe who was going to be in charge, yes, you've guessed it. Although we were right next door to one, another nothing ever came of it. I spoke with my boxing trainer the next day because he was good friends with the two of us and he couldn't believe it, it was a bit gutting in a way, 'cos I liked the man.

A week later Wayne had taken the night off and was passing the pub to get some food. So, he pulls up for a chat for five minutes when all of a sudden, it's gone off inside, and boys are fighting everywhere. I'm launching them out, and the other boy who's with me gets dropped, so Wayne's is watching my back and has a boy in a headlock, then suddenly, he gets hit from behind and ends up losing his glasses and having his rugby shirt ripped off. Unexpectedly, the DJ Mark turns on a blue flashing light like the ones on top of police cars and starts playing the BILL music from the TV show; everyone in the whole pub had paused and were looking at each other expecting the police to be standing there. Wayne and I are now back to back screaming at them all, they bottle it, and we manage to get them all out. At which point, the police turn up, and we are laughing 'cos Wayne said he had only come for a chat. Just then a boy came out asking: 'whose are these glasses?' Wayne puts them on and says, 'fuck me these are a better fit than earlier!' The glasses had loosened up after he got hit; Wayne then gets back in his jeep, with his ripped shirt and drives off down the road - with his usual psycho laugh fading as he goes.

So, it's the evening after, and with only a couple of minutes left of the night, I popped into 'Hing Hong's,' the Chinese restaurant next door. Now if there was ever any trouble in there, the owner May would call on us, and we'd get them out for her, and while as pleased as punch she'd give us extra food with our orders. Anyway, I was about to order my food when I hear Wayne calling me, 'it's gone off!' So, we run back in and throw a man out. Immediately things then calm down, so I go off and carry on ordering my food.

The man we put out was now outside starting fights, and I'm watching him start on these men while his brother is trying to stop him by pushing him away. The police turn up and thinking they are fighting together; they sprayed both men in the eyes with CS gas. They then arrest one brother and leave the other, who walks passed me calling his brother a nuisance. Anyway, I go back in to get my Chinese and realise my eyes are watering; I must have caught some gas in the wind, the woman in the restaurant asks if I'm ok. For some reason, I was in fits of laughter, and then Wayne was as well when he noticed the state, I was in.

We'd gone in one Sunday night, and the pub is full again when we notice smoke coming from the back of the room and people are screaming. I honestly thought we had had a fire, 'cos you could hardly see in front of you. Nevertheless, we had a job to do. Suddenly, women are running past us screaming trying to get out of the pub, and the smell is foul. Next thing you know there's these series of bang's, and we are all diving for cover; turns out some stupid fucker had only left some fireworks off and run out of the backdoor. The smoke didn't clear for a while, and we had to try and open the doors to get rid of the smell; fortunately, no one was injured.

I'd taken the Saturday night off from the Vulcan and gone out with the misses starting in a pub called the Alpha Bar at the bottom of town. At the time, our door firm also ran the place, and they were having problems with this man week in, week out; apparently, they had thrown him out for doing cocaine, and he was giving them hell and was off his face every week. We'd had a few problems with him in the Vulcan, so he was banned from there and a few other places to, simply because he always wanted to fight the doormen. Now, the night we were out, Merthyr FC had played Cardiff in a friendly in the day, and this boy who's playing hell used to play for Cardiff as a kid; he had a good following and knew a lot of the Cardiff fans. So, knowing Cardiff fans were in Merthyr most venue's upped their doormen including the Alpha Bar who had four men on. Anyway, we popped into the pub for an hour and are chatting to the boys on the door. As we leave to go up town onto the next pub through the market stalls as they're packing up, we spot about 20 boys walking towards us chanting football song's, and right in the middle of the crowd was the man I mentioned previously. We quickly step into a shop doorway while I lit up a fag with my back to them and started talking to the misses. They are all pissed, laughing and we heard them say, 'they're going to have it!' They walk straight past us without batting an eyelid at me, probably because we had never really had any trouble before.

159

Immediately I tried ringing the boy's at the Alpha Bar to warn them, but unfortunately, no one's answering. Time was running out 'cos they were getting nearer to the actual venue. Now, the last thing I want is to be fighting 'cos I'm out with the misses, and I obviously thought she'd play up about it. Then what apparently happened was they sent 10 of the men in 'all nice' who the boys didn't know, while the rest of the men hid round the corner; then with an element of surprise they came out from around the corner and started on the doormen while the rest attacked them from behind - an old trick but a good one – although cheap and sly as fuck. A couple of the bouncers' girlfriends were drinking in the pub and ran straight to the police station screaming, in shock, but due to most of the police being out around the town, there was no one available. With some urgency my misses, Anna, turned to me and said, 'you better get back down there and help the boy's' At that moment I was a bit unsure about leaving her and spoiling her night, but she then started shouting at me to go and help my pals; which was strange 'cos let's face it, most women would have told their fella to stay out of it – thankfully, my Anna isn't like most women, she knew they were good mates and that they would have done the same for me.

So, I'm let off the leash and its game on! I started jogging down slowly, and by this time, all the boys from the market were running down to watch it, egging me on as I'm flying past them. Honestly, I still didn't know if it had kicked off 'cos the pub was out of view, around the corner. Nevertheless, I had a good feeling it had gone off, due to the noise and all the commotion.

As I come around the corner, I could see that the doormen were holding their own, but were totally outnumbered, and were desperately trying to make their way back inside the pub. Now, in much the same way that our boys didn't expect the attack from behind earlier, this lot was about to get the same treatment 'cos every one of them was on the street screaming abuse, throwing bottles and trying to hit the boys with me coming up behind. With an almighty flurry of aggression, I go at them from behind like a bull in a china shop; smashing them as I go, and they're hitting the pavement without a clue who had done it. I didn't stop for one second, straight onto the nearest one to me with a hook and then onto the next. I then had the usual blackout when I go off on one, but the boys would tell me later they were dropping like flies and bleeding badly. A couple of them started throwing bottles at us, and as I turned my back, one of them almost took a doorman's finger off. Another doorman had a lump on his head like an egg, where one had chucked a glass ashtray at him, but because I'd taken a few of them out, it had undoubtedly evened up the odds, and it was clear to see that the fight had gone out of them. I began screaming, walking up to them, telling them they were all fucking wankers, and not one of these prats would say a word in retaliation. Some of them were walking off, and some started to run away from the pub; either their bottle had gone, or perhaps they could hear the police sirens. I walked up to this tall skinhead who seconds before had been making threats and didn't say a word to him, I then smashed him in the mouth, I had to do it 'cos, he was one of the leaders throwing things minutes earlier. There were another 2 boys behind him, and they were pissing out blood from their mouths, it looked like something from a film. A Police Van turned up, and most of them legged it up to the railway track. A couple got locked up, and again, one of them wanted to do me for assault, but I'd hidden in the pub by the time. Just then, my misses turned up; apparently, she had been watching it from a distance with the market boys while they were all cheering me on.

After everything had settled down, Anna and I went and had a few free drinks in the pub courtesy of the landlord. The doormen thanked me no end when I was leaving, and by the way, they were explaining it Anna said they thought I was like a lunatic and that I had smashed a good lot of the "cheap-shotting" twats up. Big Payney turn's to me and said, 'I thought we were holding our own when all of a sudden this big rhino looking thing came from around the corner like a fucking lunatic. But thank fuck it was just you coming to help us. Shirl.' Even the DJ shook my hand on the way out and said he had never seen anything like it.

We left the pub after a good drink two hours later and went into another pub where I recognised a few faces from the fight - but it was really dark in there to be conclusive. Then we were by the bar, and the DJ announced over the mic: 'We'd like to welcome our Cardiff fan's in tonight, let's make them feel welcome!' Every fucker was cheering, so I joined in laughing my head off knowing what had happened earlier. I think they recognised me, but they didn't want to know! We left soon after and found out later they tore the pub down and was fighting with the locals. I went to work the next night expecting trouble 'cos the boy

162

knew where I worked, and I thought he may have brought some boys back, however, nothing came of it.

The following week and I'm on the door in the pub, and he's coming up the street on the opposite side of the road, so I start shouting at him and offer him up the back lane just him and me; he didn't know where to look and just put his head down and walked off. I thought he would have at least given me a mouthful back - coward. Then the following night, he turned up and asked if he could have a word with me and starts telling me that he has no problem with me and it's between him and the other bouncers. And even though I told him he was out of order taking some of the Cardiff fan's down there, we end up shaking hands and putting it behind us.

Around about this time, my dad had become ill after they found a shadow on his lung. He was in and out of the hospital but admitted back in one Saturday night. Bernard had been short in the Vulcan, so my younger brother Steven was going to work with me after we came from the hospital. Treatment for the Cancer was going to start the following week, and we left the hospital that night with Dad smiling. We had a quiet, trouble-free night in the Vulcan and then I received a phone call about six in the morning; to be honest, I knew what it was before I even answered it. And I was right, my dad had passed away with a heart attack through the night. This hit me for six, I can't remember much of what went on for month's as we managed to get a spot for his funeral on Christmas Eve. I don't even know If I went to work on the door's, something's telling me I did to get my mind off it, but I don't really know, it was terribly hard times for everyone, and a massive bout of depression kicked in.

Now, working the doors most night's you get the threat's and comeback's and most of the time it's all just 'piss 'n' wind.' Except for this one night when I was working, and this boy had threatened to go and smash my house window's in. Like I mentioned earlier about when I had been burgled, well this was the day before and just as we were about to move in. It seemed that everything was sorted with the gang, all except this one boy who had taken a disliking to me and only lived a few doors up the street in a flat, and because of this, he knew where I lived.

I can see him walking up the road, so I moved from the door when he came in, so he didn't see me. Twenty minutes later, the landlord called me and tells me that he's dealing drugs in the toilet and that he wants him out. So, rather than me putting him out, I went over and told Wayne who was straight on him and put him out. Then as I'm by the door talking to Wayne a few minutes later, he's clocked me and start's shouting abuse, wanting to fight me etc. Now, this boy was half my weight, and I just didn't need the hassle as I'd only just moved into the street. He then goes off, and I ring the misses who was on her own to let her know just in case. With that, she rang her parent's and her mother Christine and thirteen-year-old brother Karl pop up until I got home two hours later. Wayne drop's me off and offer's to come in in case, but I said its ok.

When I got in, it turned out he had been true to his word because he had knocked my door and told the misses he was coming back for me. The problem was my misses was 8 months pregnant and had only just come out of the hospital with her high blood pressure. Just as the misses is explaining everything, my outside security light came on at the front of the house; my misses and her mother ordered me not to answer the door, but there was no way was I just going to sit back and hide. I opened the door, and he is at the end of my path making threats to come out and fight him. With that I walked out front, and even apologised, saying, 'look you've won your war; we just want a quiet life!' Nevertheless, he was so off his face on something, he had tunnel vision and basically just wanted to kill me. He then grabbed a baseball bat he was hiding behind the wall and runs at me swinging it. He did manage to get a shot in, but I rugby tackle him to the ground, and I am trying to grab the bat off him.

Like I said earlier, I hadn't moved in long, so didn't know the house that well, and I can see a shadow at the corner of my eye come from around some tree's and as I'm wresting him for the bat the next thing I know I've been hit over the head with a fucking iron bar. I honestly don't know how it didn't knock me out; maybe he didn't catch me right; all I know is I went flying backwards, rolled and got straight back up on my feet.

By now my mother in law was on the phone to the police, my misses his screaming, my 13-year-old brother in law is fighting my misses to get out and help me, and the Rottweiler's going nut's, and the police are recording all this conversation, but it was too dangerous to leave them outside has these boy's had weapons.

Anyway, I am up on my feet dazed and bleeding but still had my senses. I could not believe I'd fallen for the old one-man hiding behind the tree's trick and I didn't even know who he was. I am now in the middle of the road, and both men are circling me with the bat and the bar trying to hit me from different sides, and this is where the boxing had come in handy as I was ducking and diving and moving around them. The blood's pouring out of my head by now and into my eyes, and I thought to myself 'I've got to get that bat off him, or I'm fucked.' I then ran at the one with the bat taking a shot on the arm on the way in, and rugby tackles him again to the ground. I am ripping the bat off him still taking iron bar shots from behind on my back, I start smashing him in the face, and he releases the bat. It was like Christmas had come early, and it was now my turn to do some damage I started swinging it like a lunatic hitting whatever I could, I pummeled the both of them, but they were still taking shots, I think they had so much drug's in them and adrenalin that they weren't feeling the pain. I chased the one away and just clipped is legs dropping him, I then started smashing him again until his mate came at me with the bar again, I chased them both away still hitting them, but they eventually got away. I walked back into the house, and by now it's a few minutes later and my girlfriend's having trouble breathing in shock and I look like something out of a horror movie, but she could see I was still alive. Minutes later the police arrived, and I handed over the bat as evidence, and a few went out looking for them. The police then tell me to get up the hospital, so my brother Steven comes and picks me up. I then shoot down to a local nightclub and ask the doormen to go up to my house after work until I get home. Has I am talking to the doormen my father in law Gareth then ring's me and says, 'Ant, there's an ambulance up the street by the boy's flat and they are putting the two boys in the back,' and they are both screaming in pain'. The adrenalin must have worn off, and the pain had kicked in, and they both ended up in casualty before me.

So, we arrive at the hospital, and I can hear one in a room whimpering in pain lying down waiting to be seen, and one's by the counter crying his shoulder's broken, by now I'm so wound up I start screaming at them, and a few security guards get in my way. My brother then grabbed me and says, 'fucking wise up, police are here, their fucked anyway.' I listened to my brother, and we went and sat down for an hour before they glued my head back together. I went home and thanked the doormen for staying with the misses. I didn't sleep all night 'cos my head was pounding, and I was so full of adrenaline. We both talked about moving has we didn't need this shit with a new baby on the way, but we both agreed we wouldn't let them beat us.

The next morning the amount of call's I had off people was amazing, and it was nice knowing if they wanted a war, we would wipe the whole estate out, but I had to do this on my own without any help. I then went and made a statement to the police only to be told that they were trying to take me on as well. The copper read their injuries out, one had a suspected broken spleen and the other one's shoulder was fucked, as well as other stuff.

At the end of the day if they had their chance, they would have killed me that night and like I told the copper that they would have had worse if they didn't get away so if I'm getting charged then so be it. I went straight from the police station, brought some CCTV for the house and installed it straight away. I made a point of being outside the front, and people were coming to see me all day, I just had to show that I now didn't give a fuck for any of them, and it was the same with work I just had to go into work that night to prove a point, so I sent the misses up my parent's house for the night and I went in with a glued head. I then spoke to the boy's older brother that night and explained what had happened, and he said they get everything they deserve. We got a court date back within weeks, two of them were being done with a Section 18 and next thing I know I am being threatened by one of his brothers to drop the charges, or something was going to happen.

The court date came, and I, my misses and mother in law turn up. Now I don't know if they thought we wouldn't turn up, but they went not guilty all the way until the morning of case. Their barristers then ask us if they plead guilty would we accept it, they were both looking at 5 year's but rather than dragging my misses and mother in law into court I said, 'yes, well accept it', and they both ended up getting 21 months each. I suppose a bit of a result for them because if I'd have said 'No' I guarantee they would have got the five years.

A month later I saw the boy's brother again down the shops, and he starts shouting 'don't think I've forgotten about you, your windows are going through', by now we had the baby who was a few month's old and I couldn't take the risk. I ran at him and smashed him to the ground, I then stamped on his head when next thing I see is brother coming at me with a car jack handle, he then throws it at me cutting my calf open, I then pick it up and chase them down the street as they ran off. I saw the boy in town two days later with a massive bruise on his head, and I start shouting at him, telling him that he's fucked when I get hold of him. I just could not sink it into my head that these brothers were defending their brother after what he had done, Ok they ended up worst with injuries, but they had started it.

A week later and I'm working in my garden when the brother I had beat up turns up and asks for a word, I went straight at him, and he's standing there with his kid holding his hand, I knew straight away he hadn't come for trouble and he apologizes and says he no longer wants anything to do with his brother and he was out of order as well. We shake hands and off he goes on his way. I even give him a bit of work in my garden a few weeks later because he had no money.

After doing his time the brother was released and guess where he turned up a few days later? The Vulcan, and he's across the road giving me shit. Here we go again, I thought, and this went on for a few weeks of verbal attacks, and I'd just laugh at him. I was at the stage I had a new baby, and this boy was making my life hell, and I didn't know what to do next then next thing I heard he'd gone back down for another year for something, so we had a bit of piece again.

A year later I pulled up outside my house one morning, and as I'm getting out of the car, I can see him coming towards me on his own, I thought this has to be done and before I do anything, he asks me can he have a word and that he don't want no trouble.

Now I could have just smashed him up there and then with no witnesses, but I could sense he had changed. He then explained how he had got off drugs in prison and had even done courses. He could not stop apologising for what had happened, and after speaking for ten minutes, I shook his hand. He asked could he come down and talk to my misses in the night and apologise and I said to him laughing, 'look I might shake your hand, but you best off not coming to see her'. However, he turned up when I was out and apologised, it felt like a big hurdle had been jumped in one long race.

One night these two boys I knew were drinking in there when one of them decides to have a go at the owner, so the owner asks us to throw him out, so he leaves quietly offering the owner to fight him around the back, so his mate tries bringing 2 bottles out of the pub to give to him, so I said to his mate who was also a bouncer that he's banned and can't come back in and that he can't take the bottles out. He then starts fucking and blinding and pushes past us, so I pushes him so hard he knocks his mate over, now these are big boys who I have known for years but were pissed, and on drugs, the one bouncer starts kicking the window as well offering the owner out, so we move them on and they start giving me shit about how I had changed and all that crap, Then after about five minutes they were really getting on my nerves and the bouncer says 'I'm going back in, I'm not banned', so I push him back and he calls me a prick and starts to walk towards me so I gives him a right hook not catching him tidy and grabs him up against the wall, as I'm leaving him go his mate his coming at me so I smashes him in the mouth as well hitting him back, I then offer them up the lane one at a time, and they both looked in shock and the bouncer one then says to me that he's sorry and well out of order and will I shake his hand, he then says to me, that it was out of order me hitting him from behind and my head goes again, and I smash him in the face, yelling at him, well you seen that coming. I could see they were off their head's on drugs and the ones now moving his teeth with his hands as they walk off. Ten minutes later and they are still hanging about staring and mumbling so I said to them, I clock off in ten minutes if you want me then?' But as usual, they're nowhere to be seen.

A couple of days later I bumped into a taxi driver who told me that he gave them a lift home and the one was going to do me with a hammer. I see them a few weeks later both on their own, and they just nodded and said 'Hi.'

One night I was working when my mate came to see me as he was having problems with this doorman in this other club over town. He asked would me and the other doorman back him up after work while he goes in to sort this doorman out. He was totally outnumbered so we couldn't let him down, so he waited until we finished our shift. We then planned it in my car that my mate and I would wait around the corner, he goes in and then if they all throw him out and go for him, we will plough into them. So, he's gone in, and he's been gone a while, and then he comes flying out' he's then kicking the door, so me and my mate then went and dragged him away and made it look like we were just passing.

A few weeks later on a Sunday night, we were expecting trouble has it was the football derby between Man United and Liverpool and boy was I right, but this was nothing to do with football whatsoever. We do a quick tour of the pub in case anyone who has been banned is in there has there had been no doormen on in the day; about an hour later some gang from out of town were arguing with a local gang. This one gang leader had half a year, and it turns out one of the local boys in the other gang had bitten his ear off a couple of months earlier. I warn them all once and then Wayne does the same, but the atmosphere is building, and it then goes right up, glasses and tables are going everywhere, and the police have been called. This one-boy smashes this other boy over the head with a bottle, so I jump on him and then realise it was one of the bouncers who worked for us. I still threw him out and then a couple of seconds later I get belted on the back of the head by a flying chair. I had now gone totally off it and was launching whoever was in my way at the front door. I grabbed one of the main ones and run him out headfirst onto the street, I go flying back in, and by now the boy with half an ear is going nuts and is trying to pick a table up above his head to chuck at the others so I run at him like a lunatic, grabbing the table legs and pushing all the weight down straight on his head, I then rip the table off him and wrestle him out of the door as he's trying to fight back but didn't have a fucking chance, so I threw him out of the door so hard, he went fucking flying onto his arse in the road, I ran back in as Wayne was telling the others to get out of the pub, but this one big fucker won't go, so I charges straight into him and get him out too with Wayne. By this point, it was like a warzone outside with people fighting and then you could hear the police sirens, and everybody scattered like rats.

The police arrive, and my shirt is ripped open, and there is blood all over me, and the place is now calm except for one of two from the one gang who are still shouting threats from across the street, they end up arguing with the police and are locked up. The police then go, and ten minutes later Wayne comes from inside and tells me that this girl has just had a go at him inside and she was calling us all the wankers under the sun saying we could have prevented the fight happening, it turns out she and her friends had got smashed when it had gone off. The last thing Wayne needed after still being wound up from the fight was for some girl's screaming at him that he was out of order, so he's told her to fuck off. We had just chucked out about ten boys out, had ripped shirt's, blood on us and someone has the cheek to say we are this and we are that and it's our fault. About two minutes later and one of my girlfriends best mates came out fucking and blinding so has I ask her what's the matter, she then goes steaming off swearing her head off with her friend's, it was only then I realised it had been her who had gone on to Wayne. The girl's mate then came out and said to Wayne, 'you wouldn't have spoken to her like that if her boyfriend was here,' Wayne tried talking to her again tidy, but they just go off shouting stuff down the street. I then turn to Wayne and says, 'he won't be long.' I knew he was coming, but what happened next, I didn't see coming.

Now, I knew her boyfriend really well, or at least I thought I did, I'd had a run-in with him in the past, remember when I mentioned earlier about getting strangled by that bouncer in a club, well that was him, but that was years ago, and we'd patched things up since then, and his misses and mine being mates I thought we got on well, but boy was I so fucking wrong that night. The man had a reputation as one of the hardest men in the town and had also been head doorman of the biggest club in town, and I'd played against him in rugby, and he was an animal but a lot older than me. So, I am waiting for him to turn up and being a doorman himself, he will totally understand what happened and all will be sorted. Half hour goes and nothing so I'm talking to Wayne outside the front of the pub and all of sudden I hear a car screeching toward us, the brakes are slammed on and it is skidding towards us into the pub doorway over the curb, as I turn around this car clips me hitting me up against the wall, I don't know if I jumped out of the way or not as it happened, but the next thing I see is it smashing into Wayne straight on. I look into the car, and there's the girl's boyfriend screaming at me and that I'm a dead man. I then look at Wayne, and he is on the floor holding his knees, gritting his teeth in pain. Suddenly, my head just flipped, I honestly thought Wayne's legs were broken, and I just happened to have a full can of coke on window shelf by the door, I thought if they want to play psycho then I'll show them psycho. I launched the coke can at the front window and then jumped on the car trying to put my hand through the windscreen with punch's screaming at him to get out, but he wasn't stupid, no matter what drink or drugs he had taken, which I gathered was a lot, he didn't leave the car in the pub doorway because if the police had turned up then he would have gone straight down for a long time.

He then starts reversing the car as I am still punching it and he drives off down road and parks it in a proper layby down the street. I am now trying to get Wayne into the pub but the stubborn fuckers having none of it and will not leave me on my own. The man gets out of the car and comes running at me like a psycho, all the rumours of his reputation had now gone out of my head. Has he's throwing bomb's I grabs him by the throat and he's throwing punches, but he can't get near me has my arms are longer than his, and he hasn't got the reach, By now I'm laughing and then hit him with a straight right hand, then hook after hook, everyone connecting, I then pull him to the floor and stick some uppercuts into his face, I then get on top off him screaming when all of a sudden, I'm being pulled off him by some boy's I knew. His mate had also gone to hit me, and Wayne has jumped on him as well, I still didn't know how Wayne was walking, but that's adrenaline for you, Wayne then got hit with a shot from the one man who had rings on splitting his eye open.

I then managed to chuck the boy's off me and by now the blokes back up, he's breathing heavy and bleeding badly and he's screaming at me 'is that the best you got', I thought ' fuck, I haven't even started yet' and goes running at him this time, I smash him again, and we get pulled apart but this time I got a girl on my back, so off she goes over my shoulder, and I go at him again for the third time, we get broke up again, and by now I'm laughing at him and screaming at him. Now don't get me wrong he's still up for it, but he's in a mess, and he gets dragged into the pub next door.

The police showed up five minutes later as if there had been a murder and we told them there had been a fight inside, but they had all fucked off, and we did not know who they were. One copper say's to me, 'we have had a phone call 2 doormen have been knocked down by a car in a head-on attack. Wayne said laughing, 'Do we look like we have been run over,' the one copper then looked at me and said, 'I know it's true Shirl!' I just smiled and said nothing as Wayne walked off inside with a bad limp. We both knew they would have done a few years inside if we had spilt the beans, but Wayne wasn't a fan of the police and refused to talk with them. So, I was winding Wayne up calling him the terminator has he was still walking when all of a sudden, I could feel running going down my legs and a stinging feeling in my knees, the adrenalin was finally running out, so I goes into the toilets and both my knees were cut open and bleeding. Anyway we finished the shift as usual and I went home thinking of what could have happened, I then had my girlfriend cleaning my cuts on my knees and then she bandaged them both up, and I stayed up all night in case he came back to my house. All week the main topic in the town was that this bloke had been beaten and that I'd done it and he was in a mess; rumours were getting back that they were coming to get us the following week with a few more boys, but nothing came of it.

One story was I'd only beaten the man because I had slipped a knuckle duster on, now I won't lie to you, I had a duster for year's tucked away in the house, but not once did I ever use it, and the man knew that and the ones spreading the rumours did.

Two weeks later, I seen the bloke from the fight, and he stopped and shook mine and Wayne's hand and couldn't stop apologising and that it was all his fault and that he was sorry. He had been drinking and received the phone call that night and just seen red. He then walked off as I went back into the pub thinking to myself what a difference a few week's makes, one day he's a psycho trying to run us over, and now he was like a lamb and was the nice bloke I had once known. I'd speak to the man again a year later in our work do, and he apologised again and thanked me for not sending him down. I said, 'look it's in the past', and we had a drink together, and then from then on, we'd always chat when we see each other. I carried on working the Vulcan, and surprisingly we didn't have any trouble for the next few months, then Wayne goes, and finishes has he'd had enough of the door's, and I was back working with different people yet again.

Around this time my boss Bernard and I were contacted by Sky One and we ended up on their program toughest pubs in Britain filmed outside of The Vulcan. I also appeared in Charles Bronson's book Heroes, and villains as Big Tony, with a nice, write up by the late Tel Currie. I then had a lot of my stories published in another of Tel Currie's book's which he had written with my mate Julian Davies called bouncer's, so my name was getting out there, and I always knew I'd write this book one day as I always wrote stuff down.

A job then came up in the Kooler's nightclub, this was another massive step as it felt like I'd earned everyone's respect, so I jumped at the job.

CHAPTER TWELVE

(Climbing the Ranks)

Up until now, I was doing a venue here and there for
Bernard Driscoll but just hadn't met him. Until Paul told
me that there had been murders in the Kooler's nightclub
and a few of the doormen had walked out, so there was a
space going for Sunday nights. So obviously, I jumped at
the chance of working in the biggest nightclub with over
1000 people in town that most nights had 10 doormen
covering it. Also working with me was Paul and
Bernard: Bernard was the boss of the company,
Wayne who'd been bouncing more than 20 years,
Snuffer an ex-boxer and Big Payne who I mentioned
earlier, not to forget Stuart who played rugby for one
of the top teams and the boss's son Brendan.
Honestly, you couldn't get a better team if you tried,
and within a few weeks, we took control of the club.
This being the only nightclub in town, it pulled people
in from all over the place as the DJ Sean Jay was one
of the best around. There was so much scum in there,
drug dealers, car thieves, you name it they were in
there, but the thing was we all knew who they were,
and they respected us. So, for the first couple of
weeks, I was put upstairs, right in the middle of
it, and with a different partner every night, two of us
upstairs watching about five hundred people with no
radios.

The first night Paul and I were upstairs, it's nearly the end
of the night, and it's gone off, with two girls fighting on the
floor and two boys fighting right by them. Anyway, I ran in
and

pulled one boy off the other and chucked him to Paul as I grabbed the other boy in a chokehold. Now, the two girls are still going for it by the side of me, so I grabbed one of them in my other arm, and now I've got one of each in both arms at the same time; lucky the other bouncers turned up quick, or it could have turned ugly.

A couple of weeks later and we're two men down, I was upstairs with Stuart, who was a bit of a martial artist and rugby player. All of a sudden there's a fight over by the bar, so we go running in through the packed crowd to where this big bald fucker is pummeling someone by the bar, and there's two more going for it on the floor. Anyway, I grabbed this big bald one around the neck while Stuart grabs the other one. Next thing you know the bald one's brother is whacking me, so, I turned round to fight him, but it's gone up proper, so I'm just throwing punches at whoever came towards me. After taking a whack, I then punch the boy's brother to the ground and start stamping on his head, but due to drugs, he's still putting up a fight. I then dragged him across the club by his legs, and there's a big circle of local boys watching me beat the fuck out of this prick. I manage to get him to the top of the stairs while some local boys cheer me on to hit him. So, I'm still hooking him, and he's trying to bite my legs. I then dragged him down about twenty stairs, he must have done about 3 somersaults on the way down and the fuckers still going when we land at the bottom. I was exhausted and waiting for the other bouncers to come running and help; it was like some horror film 'cos I just couldn't finish the fucker off. Next thing you know he's laughing while still trying to bite my legs as he's clutching onto them, suddenly I felt all numb and couldn't feel my legs at all and

I was now praying that the boys were near me to take him off me, but it turns out they had heard about the fight and gone up the backstairs and were apparently fighting upstairs. At this point, I was only about ten yards away from the front door, and while he was still biting, I hit him with a couple of heavy hooks, putting everything I had left in the tank into running him through the door. With that, I launched him into the barriers and closed the doors behind him. The boys came flying down the stairs with the others and the next thing I know I have gone all light-headed and can hardly stand; Snuffer grabbed me quickly and takes me into the side room, the cellar, at which point I collapsed and was puking up blood; I still didn't know what was happening with the others and what was hurting me more than anything was that I couldn't do a fucking thing to help them.

Snuffer came back to see if I was alright and told me not to worry as Payne had just knocked the main one out cold, he also said that there were ambulances and a police car outside. About thirty minutes later, I'm still puking and choking, and I honestly thought it was the end for me and my bouncing days. I wasn't right for about another half an hour, and the boys tried to make me go to the hospital. I refused, putting it down to being unfit; which could have been the truth 'cos we had been fighting upstairs for quite a while. Anyway, the next night I hit the roads running and was back in work the following week as usual. This particular week, Payne finished on the door, because he had started a new job, so they needed another boy for the main door. Now, after last week's performance, I was happy to be offered it and jumped at the chance. Things were getting worse on the front door, although it appeared that the antics the week before were down to whoever it was who chucked them just went back into the club and left the two boys on the door to take all the backlash. Every night you'd be guaranteed several fights, and we would take turns on the doors. It was a bit of a nightmare because people would just not move from behind the door, so half the time you would just have to smash their heads in with the door until they moved; sounds a little heavy-handed, but these people can be c***s when fueled up with the drink.

Anyway, it must have been a week later, and we have gone in, and it's really early. This local troublemaker's off his face up the back of the club downstairs, and his trainers and jeans are off, and he's sitting there in his boxer shorts and t-shirt pulling all his jib's with his eyes closed. So Keith and Ray call me, and I goes in and just looked at him thinking what the fuck is going on in his head. So I start shouting at him, and he wakes up out of this trance and pulled his boxers off, grab's his dick and says, 'fuck you, suck this', that's it, Iv dived over the chair and grabbed his head, Ray and Keith got his legs and he's pulling this sofa with him, we drop him by front door and push him out and throw his clothes at him, we all couldn't believe what we had just seen.

Come the end of the night and there are three men refusing to leave the upstairs, they are all drunk and think they can fight the world, the eight doormen try their best, and then they call me up, I walked straight up there and said, 'c'mon you fucker's, I want to go home, now the two knew me and said we are on our way, Shirl. So, they get downstairs and get to the coatroom, the two are waiting for the big man with them who is now taking the piss, I asked him to hurry

181

up, and he just laughs at me, I then go up again as he's now winding us all up, I said, 'I've asked you twice now mate, you got to go, now this man must have been 6ft5 and I'd always seen him about the town. He then turned, looked at about 8 of us who were all around him and said, 'what you lot think you can get me out?, I just walk up to him and bang, he's down on the floor and I grab his head screaming at him, 'no, I'm getting you fucking out', I dragged him hitting him all the way to the door and threw him out, his two mates come at me and then back off and say he's had enough Shirl. We lock the door, and one of the doormen says laughing, 'why didn't you do that twenty minutes ago' but like I've said one thing I'm not is a bully, I gave him ample chance to leave until he was making us all look like fools and fancied his chances. That set of doors would take some bashing over time, 'cos every week you would be offered out to fight someone, but when you finished at the end of the night there would be no fucker there.

One night this boy offers me out and comes running at me. So, I've hit him once and dropped him. Seconds later another boy came at me, so I dropped him with a kick as well; the police turned up and moved everyone on, but five minutes later and the one I dropped with a kick was back in the queue, and he thinks I haven't clocked him. Anyway, I pretend I haven't seen him and let him in out of sight of the police outside, he now thinks he's okay then all of a sudden, I dropped him with a body shot and launch him out through the door straight into the barriers. Paul's watching, laughing his head off and I'm thinking what a cheeky bastard. I think I was put with Paul to learn the ropes about being on a club door and Bernard was with us most of the time too, and I got to know him really well.

A week later, I was doing my floor-walk, and this boy is punching his girlfriend right in front of me, then he just ran up the stairs. So, I go after him and grabs him in a neck hold lifting him completely off the floor, he was only about five feet tall and as skinny as shit, but fuck was he strong. I really had to choke him out to take the wind out of him, but he was that strong that at one stage I thought he was going to break my hold, the veins were popping out of his neck, but I had the hold locked on good and strong. With that, I dragged him out of the club and chucked him into the barriers in front of the club. I immediately closed the doors behind him, and he's kicking fuck out of the doors as I'm laughing at him; a police van turned up and attempt to lock him up; I swear to you, it must have taken eight policemen to put him in that wagon, I don't know what he had taken but fuck he was strong. He came back 4 weeks later, did the usual apologising and was back in the club with his girlfriend.

We then had a run-in with some bouncers from another area, they kept coming back, but we just kept laughing at them on the door until they finally got the message. I was also working Wednesday nights there, and with only three of us staffing it, when it was my turn on the door, we had a few arguments with different people, 'cos, strangely enough, I always ended up getting shit, even from people I knew really well. One of the boys from my own boxing gym turned on me with his mates once, and I ended up smashing him with the door, I saw them the following day, and the drink was to blame once again. This one boy who I'd known since a nipper turned on me one night and reckoned, he was going to burn my house down; I knew deep down he didn't mean it, but he was drunk and well capable of doing it. He used to be a right nutter who had been inside (prison) a few times. This one night, he was refusing to move from behind the door, and I had to let people in and out, so I rammed the door into his head a few times splitting him wide open. Nevertheless, the fucker still didn't move, so I grabbed him and launched him into the barriers, at which point he could see that I had had enough of him and moved, although he kept giving me the old, 'I'm gonna shoot you' signs with his two-finger pointing to his head. I finally finished the shift, and he was nowhere to be seen, which was a bit of a shock. A few months later I saw him in a pub in town, he just nodded at me and said: 'alright?' I made the decision not to take it any further, because at the end of the day it was just the booze talking.

This one night we had just about got everybody out, but this ex bouncer didn't want to leave and was having a go at Paul, so I grabbed him from behind and launched him out of the door; he's immediately giving Paul more shit and won't move from behind the doors. Now, the front doors have a safety bolt across them, and Paul's starting to lose it, next thing you know the safety bolts open, so I lock it quick then a couple of seconds later Paul launches a kick into the door thinking the door was going to knock the boy flying, but Paul goes flying back instead; Paul didn't know I had locked the bolt to hit the door into the boy, so I felt a right prick. However, we all had a laugh about it, and the boy came back the following week and apologised to Paul.

One Wednesday night this local hard man started chucking his head about, so I run in to chuck him out and next thing

I know the bloke he's butted as got a stool above his head coming at us. Payne then grabs the stool from behind and launches the bloke out, next thing you know the bloke who's done the butting is refusing to go. Now, up until now he'd been getting away with murder 'cos the bouncers had been turning a blind eye to him, so I had a few words and said to him, 'I don't give a fuck if it's your fault or not, you're not coming back in!' He immediately stormed off and knocked a bloke out cold outside, he then tries to get back into the club, but I told him he's banned for a month. I saw him the next day in a café and went straight over to him to see if he had a problem with me; he instantly started to apologies and asked how long he'd been banned for. A couple of weeks later he ended up fighting with one of the other doormen and landed himself a life-ban. Then one Sunday we get a phone call saying he's on his way to the club, and that no one's going to stop him coming in - he never turned up.

A couple of weeks after Payne had finished, this steroid monkey came looking for him; he'd been banned for fighting on another occasion when we weren't there to witness it. Anyway, he says to me, 'tell Payne, I'm going to kill the fucker when I get hold of him!' So, I replied, 'if you want, I'll phone him now?' He then says, 'fuck him, you'll do!' And starts offering me out, at which point he's in a full steroid rage screaming at me, so I opened the doors and offers him in, after a while he ran at me and ***BANG*** one punch, and his eyes have gone back in his head; he's gone down and hits the barrier - he's out cold. About ten minutes earlier we had chucked this boy out, so all of a sudden, he decided to help the steroid monkey and comes running at me with punches, with that I give him one kick, and it's buckled the fucker, and he goes

185

straight down. To be honest, by the way he'd fallen, I thought I'd broken his leg.

Soon after, the roider's back up fucking and blinding, and I'm now laughing at him as he's picking things up, chucking them at the door. He moves away before the police come, then I noticed the one that I had just kicked out about two minutes earlier, and he's standing in the queue again. I thought to myself, he can't be serious can he, but he had drunk a fair drop and didn't know what day it was Anyway, I let him come right up to the front of the queue, and as he's about to pass me, I shoved him back out.

The following week Paul was on the door having some right shit from these wankers. Apparently, one boy had tried to give the manageress who was with us a slap, so Paul was trying to drag him into the club to hold him there until police arrived. Suddenly he broke out, and Paul's smashed him. He then began telling everyone outside that three bouncers had beaten him up; Paul yelled at him saying, 'there's only two of us on the door you silly fucker!' However, after a while of offering us all out, finally, he fucked off.

Another night and almost the same again, different rugby team this time and we took them down the back stairs and Bernard the Boss start's shouting 'Lock and Load' now no one could go down these stairs as they were just for staff. So, the top door was locked behind us, it was like a blood bath there, this one doorman's stamping on these men, and we are dragging them downstairs and most of the time the police were outside waiting has they wouldn't come in. The police could see straight away they had started it, and most would end up getting locked up.

Then one night this man and his misses came in and I was
searching so I sent the girl to the door girl to be searched
and the man refuses, obviously he had some drug's on him,
we then start arguing, and he's swung for me, so we are
fighting, and I push him out the door. He's then going off it
when the police arrive, and he twists his leg before finally
getting arrested. Next day I heard rumours that he was
trying to get his family involved and then a month later I
gave his cousin a lift home from town, and he was telling
me the boy was offering money to do me over and that
he'd even rung the boy I was giving a lift; they knew I was
sound and wouldn't have started trouble.

Another night this man was fighting inside, he was a right
cocky fucker who had done a bit of boxing and thought he
was 'Rocky Marciano,' anyway, while I held the door open
for him, Paul took him outside when another new bouncer
(a new employee) stuck his nose in and got in Paul's way.
The boy then throws a shot straight at Paul's nose and
smashes it: it's bleeding, and his eyes are
watering as the boys outside choppsing his head off back at
Paul. Frustrated, Paul says to me, 'stay on the door for me
while I go and sort my nose out.' All the while this prick is
still offering us to fight him, outside. With that, I opened
the door and wind the fucker right up; he comes in closer
and closer, so I've hit him with a kick, then he finally
shows all of his cards, comes at me and ***BANG***
I've caught him with a shot right in his eye, he immediately
goes flying back and hits the floor with an almighty crash,
the police are there within second's and he's now
screaming at them to lock me up, apparently now, he wants
me done for assault – fucking pussy. I thought to myself,
you cheeky fucker. Anyway, he's getting louder and
louder, and the police end up locking him up for his own

good. Shortly after, Paul came back from sorting his nose out, and he was fucking furious, so I let him know that I had sorted the fucker out and that he had been carted off. I saw the boy a few weeks later and he just put his head down. Police asked Paul if he wanted to press charges, but he didn't bother.

This one Sunday night these three Swansea road boys' had started on this up and coming doorman who was out drinking. Anyway, he's knocked two of them out on the floor, and I could swear he was choking another one to death. This doorman was massive, he'd seen red and just won't stop choking this one boy out, so obviously, I had no option but to do the same to him. I've got a grip, and his neck is massive, and I'm tightening, but he's not budging. I latched on and squeezed harder and harder until I could see his grip loosening, only thing is I'm now putting him to sleep; fortunately, before this happened, he let go so I dragged him out managing to put him out through the front door. He was then hanging over the railings, getting his breath back so I stood my ground and
he apologised. I was thinking thank fuck for that 'cos it had taken all my energy to get him out. He then fucked off before the police came because the two, he had hit were in a bad way.

A bit later, we put this other man out, and he'd grown up and was my miss's age. He had now started on the weights and was finding his feet. He's giving me all the verbal's from behind these railings and then mentioned that he knows where my misses lives. With that, and while he's still giving the big one, I've seen red and grabbed him over the railing's; I got him in a headlock and put's his ear in my mouth, and I'm screaming at him that Ill bite his fucking ear off for threatening my family. I was actually nibbling it, and I was close to just biting it off. Another doorman then came and grabbed me, and the boy fucked off. I got home that night thinking to myself, 'you're supposed to be in charge of everyone and there you are biting ears off!' Best thing was, he wasn't even the biggest fella and wasn't really a threat, nevertheless, after having trouble brought to my house in the past, I had to prove that I wasn't to be fucked with.

The following week I was upstairs, and there was a man in the club drinking when suddenly this big boy comes flying over with his mate and says, 'how the fuck is he in here? He's a fucking Paedophile!' He then goes onto explain that he's from a different town and had been in the paper for it. I was working with Beast, and we said that we didn't know anything about it, so we couldn't just throw him out without any proof. Come the end of the night, and the "Paedophile" goes to walk down the big stair's; I can see the big man running in from nowhere and watch as he kicks him in the back hard and he goes flying down about fifteen steps. The man's arm's look like something out of a horror movie, they're snapped, and the big man's on top of him hitting him. I get to the bottom of the stairs and scream at the man to get off him, but he's got tunnel vision, so I put him in a chokehold; I got him to the door and threw him out. As I'm standing there he tries to get back in, so I pushed him back out, the big man then says, 'he deserved it, Shirl, he's a fucking Paedo!' to which I reply, 'Yeah, and a fucking dead one by the look of it son!' The boy soon fuck's off when I inform him the police have been called. I then went back in to see Vicki who is now working on him

189

and has him in the recovery position, and then this man ignores the bouncer's and stand's over him to get out, so, Beast grabbed him, and they end up fighting - Beast drop's him, and he's out cold. The paramedics turned up and were working on him before taking him away.

A few years later I was working in a different venue in town and this man's in there; I still had no evidence of who he was or what he'd done but get told to ask him to leave for touching woman up. A few months later I'm working this venue in town, I'm on my own covering one of the boy's and this supposed Paedo turns up again. Anyway, I refuse him entry, and he's starting to lose it. He then comes at me and grabbed me by the shirt, so I hit him with a hook dropping him, I'm then smashing him up on the floor and he's screaming like a baby, which sounds a bit funny 'cos for a big man he's got one hell of a squeaky voice – he sounds like Pinky and fucking Perky. The doormen ran from across the road and grabbed me, and he then walks off. Ten minutes later I can see him at the end of the street pulling a police van over, he's talking to them, and moments later they pull up outside the venue, but I made a point of going over to them and explain the situation; they thank me and go on their way. I'm taking it that they knew of him and his antics.

One night the radios had gone off because there was fighting upstairs. I'm on the door, and it's gone a few minutes, so the owner Vicki said, 'go up the backstairs Shirl, I'll watch the door!' I could see this new doorman, "Peanut" in the cage and he was having trouble getting this boy out. So, Beast and I grab his legs as Peanut's screaming, 'he's biting me!' He's putting up one hell of a fight, and as we get him to the top of the backstairs, he's trying to bite me as well, so I've smashed him with an uppercut splitting him open, and he's out cold. We then drag him outside; with that he gets a second wind and is kicking the door, until the police moved him on.

I worked a few more nights over Christmas, simply because I had time on my hands having been sacked from the other nightclub, RM's. Then one night one of the doormen, Paul Elliot had had word's with one of the owner's after he accused him of ignoring a fight, now I've seen a few doormen in my time who have gone missing or turned a blind eye, but not Elliot, he certainly wasn't one of them; Paul was as tough as they come. Bernard then told the owner's that we would do our last night on New Year's Eve, the following week a rival door company took over. In a way, I was glad we had lost the contract because something big was about to happen. And after an interesting six months, it was now time to move on.

Over the following few days it became clear that the door staff who worked there were bitter that we had lost our jobs, however, we all stood by Elliot and Bernard's decision. A night was then planned to go in there because this rival company had been trying to get in there for a while and were using some naughty tactic's. About ten of our doormen had planned to go in there and play hell. Now, I'd always got on with the owner Vicki, but this just wasn't my cup of tea, I could see we had a point to make but at the end of the day innocent doormen were in there working and at the best of times the job's hard enough without us nut-jobs kicking off. Come Sunday night I had promised to have a quiet night in with the misses. The following day I found out there had been murder's there and that the police had been called, and like some sort of trophy, even the owner of the security company's tie hung on our boss's office wall. I was out drinking the following week and popped in there to see if I was banned even though I was not with them on the night of the trouble, but I was welcomed with open arms.

CHAPTER THIRTEEN

(Head of The Door)

We had proved a point, however, just four months later, the firm couldn't handle the trouble in Kooler's, and the owner came running back to Bernard pleading for our team to step in again. This time though she wanted me as the head doorman, on the premises at all times, so as it turned out, my decision not to join them that night had actually paid off. So, there I am running a twelve-man team in the biggest nightclub in our town, with a few extra nights and a nice pay rise; although it was back to chaos night after night, fighting, fighting and even more fighting. I think one bank holiday the incident report log's had counted up over twenty fights in one night, and I'm not talking about little kid's fighting over some girl, no, these were big rugby players going for it.

Some people might be reading this thinking we're knocking them out every week and that we are bully's, and to be honest at one time we did have a bad name, but the only reason for that was that we only ever did proper damage when it kicked off badly. Not once have I or the boy's I worked for, ever gone looking for it. Because, there's nothing better than going home to your family after having a quiet night with no aggro, but like most doormen, we all get tarred with the same "bully boy" brush! What frequently happens is the troublemakers start it, and we finished it, Anyway, rant over.

Not long after being back in Kooler's we heard the sad news that our pal, Paul Elliot, had passed away; I had only trained with him and his mate Jamie two weeks earlier, and not a soul among us saw it coming. Every doorman in Merthyr turned up to pay their respects, to say our goodbyes to yet another hard nut and gentleman, taken way before his time.

Talking about Paul's, like I had mentioned Paul Curtis, who I worked with for years had packed the doors in and had found another job as a carer - helping people. I had not seen him much since I was back at Kooler's, and then my second baby Alicia was born which had taken the rest of my time up. I passed Paul's house one Saturday when I was doing a fifteen-mile charity walk to raise money for my mate Lyndon's kid's and knocked at his door; he answered, we had a good chat and arranged for him to come up and see the baby just a few days later. He turned up on Tuesday, held the baby and had a good chat for over two hours with me and my misses, he even said he was going to pop up on Friday night to see Bernard because he said that he might want to start back on the doors. That day he left all smiling, but unbeknown to me this would be the last time I'd ever seen him because two nights later, Paul took his own life. To be honest, it hit me really hard; it was like the other doorman Nigel all over again. I wracked my brain trying to think if there had been any clues, I just couldn't get my head around it and I broke down in tears on numerous occasions. Anyway, for this reason alone, the whole of the next month was a blur, and then we had to lay our good mate to rest. I arranged a memorial night for him at the club. The evening was crammed full of well wishes, which just went to show just how much he was liked by everyone. At this point, the depression that had left me a while ago reared its ugly head once again, but life had to go on 'cos bill's had to be paid. I will say though, I found it so fucking hard to lace them boot's up every night and try and put a smile on.

Sunday nights were getting madder by the week, we had all these different act's in from fire eaters, half-naked stilt walkers and midgets, to a man using disc cutter's that were shooting spark's onto the stage at his private part's, 'Yes you read that correctly.' The place was just mental, and my delicate head felt like It was joining them.

One night this tall man who I'd knocked out in Treharris rugby club turned up with a few of his rugby player mates. Now, I'd put this story in Julian Davies book Bouncer's a few months earlier, and he had got to see it. He was laughing and found it quite funny and was telling the other doormen how I'd knocked him out, and for how long. An hour later I'm on the front door when the owner called me into a room and said, 'we have a big problem, that tall man you were talking to is upstairs, he's fucking about, and he's got a Stanley knife on him, and the other doormen won't go anywhere near him.' Being the head doorman, I was there to sort things such as this out, so I went steaming past the crowd pushing his mates out of my way and said, 'I want a word with you!' After his near-death experience last time his face dropped a-foot, so I pulled him to one side and said, 'I've heard you've got a Stanley knife on you?' Suddenly, he began laughing and went to put his hand in his pocket, but I was watching every move he was making, getting ready to strike then, with that, he pulled out a plastic joking knife with a plastic blade, so I took it off him, and he apologised. At which point I warned him not

195

to fuck about anymore. To be honest, by the time I'd got back downstairs, I actually found it quite funny, nonetheless, at the time it was quite a scary encounter.

I knew it was only a matter of time before it would go off again with these lot and I was right, 'cos minutes later the radio's gone off! So, I made my way upstairs leaving Beast, who was part of our team to operate the door. One of our doormen Keith, was breaking some men up fighting, but the men have turned on him and managed to pull him to the floor. One of them was smashing punches into Keith, so I've hit him with an uppercut, and he was out cold. I was right by this fire exit, so I dragged this half-dazed man down the stairs; by this point, Beast was passing me as he was coming up the stairs. I leant on the door for a minute to get my wind back, but then thought, I've got to get back up there quick, and as I reached the top of the stairs Beast is fighting with this huge rugby player, so I've immediately come up behind the man and put a chokehold on him and dragged him back down the stairs. Beast then smashes him in the face which makes his nose explode, and Beast is screaming at him hitting him more. With that, we dragged him all the way out and put him out by the front door entrance. At which point the other doormen were coming down with other troublemakers; we must have put at least ten of these idiots out. The big massive one that Beast hit was hanging over the railings in a bad way. Suddenly, the police turned up, and these idiots tried telling the police that all the doormen had beaten them up. The big tall man who had the knife walked down the stairs with his hands in the air saying, 'nothing to do with me boys – nothing to do with me!' I bumped into him a few years later when he was coaching some rugby, and together we looked back at those times, laughing; turns out he's actually a nice man.

The following night we were raided, but to be honest, we knew it was coming. What happened was the owner would ram it past its capacity by a few hundred, and because we only had about ten men, we had asked for more door staff, but she just wasn't having any of it. So, I'm on the door, and opposite there was a car parked for almost the entire night, anyway we didn't think much of it because cars were always parked there. The place was packed with about a 1000 people inside and all of a sudden, there was police and all these officials slamming badges into our faces. Turns out the owner had gone over by a few hundred punters, and they had clocked everyone coming in from the carpark opposite. The manager was immediately taken into a room and arrested, but guess who else was questioned, yeah, you got it, me, and all because I was the one that had let them all in.

The following day I was called into the police station where I was met with the big sergeant who, I might add, I'd never seen before. However, it turns out that because I didn't have a clicker to count the number of people coming in, there was nothing they could do to me. Nevertheless, the gaffa of the club was fined thousands of pounds for being over the limit. The Sergeant said that from that day forward, we must always have a clicker on the front door. Because, he said, if there had been a fire or something, I would have been the one to blame, as well as the management.

Now, a few weeks before, Bernard had given us this new Pepper Spray like the police use and he told us that it was legal. So, I gave it a try on the door; however, I got so carried away. I was spraying every fucker and nearly emptied the whole bottle in one night. So now being in the station I asked the sergeant if the spray was legal for us to use, but he said, 'no, you definitely can't go using that!' And I said, 'well, we got told that it was all above board and totally legal!' But he reiterated that it most certainly was not. Whether it was one of Bernard's little wind up's again, I don't know. Nevertheless, I've just admitted to a "police sergeant" that I'd been spraying people all over the place with it. I then asked the sergeant about the use of coshes for doormen, because I said, when we had helped one of your policewomen a few weeks previously against a tooled-up rabble, we never had a single weapon between us, and yet again he just laughed.

So, after us clearing the club on the night of the raid a lot of people weren't happy, but not long after, the same thing was to happen again. We had thrown a few people out, and we were nearing closing time when the owner came to see me and said that she had just had a phone call saying that there was a bomb in the club and that we had to evacuate the place. Immediately, the music was shut off, and we were passing the word around the other doormen but telling them not to panic everyone. I then said to this one doorman, 'hang on a minute, we've been informed that there is a bomb in here and our lot are still inside the fucking place!' But we laughed it off because we knew it was a load of rubbish. Mind you, the number of people who were pissed up and just ignoring us was unbelievable; we were screaming at them in the end, until we joined them all outside while we waited for the professionals to arrive – but we weren't wrong, because nothing was found.

Another night I was working upstairs when I got called downstairs; apparently a bunch of rugby players were causing hell down there. I got myself down there, but by that time they had all gone up the other stairs, so, I asked this doorman what had happened, and he said that this team were playing up, so he sent them upstairs because he knew that Beast and I were up there and that we would sort them out. I looked at the doorman and said, 'So what the fuck are you here for? You should have got them out!' So now, Beast and I have got to get them down from upstairs.' We were not happy one bit but obviously made our way upstairs. When we got up there, we saw that the big rugby player was holding court by the bar, he was messing around, so I went up to him and said, 'right you've got to go. The owner wants you out!' With that he looked at me like I was a piece of shit and laughed, so, within a split second I spun him around and got him in a chokehold, and within ten seconds his legs have gone to sleep; so I loosened my grip as I dragged him down the stairs, and not one of his mates wanted any trouble as they looked on, in shock. By the time we reached the bottom of the stairs he had gotten a bit of life in him, so I put him to sleep again and threw him out through the front door, while Beast and the other doormen walked all of his mates down – they never uttered a word. Soon after, the rugby man tried to get back in with his girlfriend, but I just wouldn't let him in, so he called the police over and tried telling them that I didn't have a doorman's license; he looked a right prick when they came over to check, and I revealed it.

Another time this boy I'd known well had sneaked into the club and was upstairs; he'd been banned for hitting doormen a few weeks earlier, so we got him down to the front door, and he started kicking off. Anyway, I asked him nicely, and he started playing to his little crowd, who also began kicking off. He had a glass bottle in his hand, and as I've gone to grab it, the other's that were with him started to hit me, and it's gone right off. I'm kicking this big one out through the door, then his mate start's so I'm fighting with him too, one of the girls working with us had her shirt ripped off and the boy who had started it got thrown out, with a twisted leg. The police turned up, and the boy went off to the hospital. The police took statement's from all the doormen, and I thought it was all over, and that it was just another fight, and as per usual we'd run into them when they were sober, they'd apologise, and that would be the end of it. However, the owner couldn't leave it there. She nagged the police for months until they finally arrested a few of them and a court date was set. The other doormen and I didn't even want to go to court, but because we worked for the club, it would have looked bad if we didn't see it through. I was then offered a few grand to pull out, but it wasn't about the money, and us doormen weren't the ones that were in the wrong.

Come the day of court a few of us turned up, but for some reason within the first hour it was all thrown out of court and my mates, and I quickly went off for breakfast before they had time to change their minds. I bumped into them all years later, we shook hands and put it all behind us.

This one local hard man had taken a disliking to all the doormen in the club; I'd had a weekend off, and this man's friend's son was playing up; apparently the doormen had thrown him out, and the boy had been arrested. So, this hard man had started offering doormen out to fight him. Not long after I was back in work when the man came in again.

Now, I'd been butted by this man before, when I was a lot younger, and he probably didn't even remember it. He knew I was head doormen, so started talking to me explaining what had gone on; he then told me that he was going to beat up every doorman in the club for what they had done to him before, so I said to him, 'well listen, you ain't beating any fucker up while I'm here!' and with that he went on his way.

The following night I was working elsewhere in the town when I received a phone call saying that he'd made a right mess of the doorman in the club and was on his way around town doing the same to other doormen and we were next on his list. Now, I didn't mind fighting this man, but I knew it was going to be a hard fight because I'd seen him knock people out and I'd also had the pleasure of throwing him out in the past, I was up for it, but wanted to show him another side to me. So I rang my mate who was on his way down to where I was working and asked him to bring his Desert eagle gun; he'd shown us it the week before, it had blank's in it, and he let it off in the corridor of the club, and let me tell you, the noise alone was enough to drop you, it was so loud everyone came running out. So, he turned up, and I put it in the back of my trousers, with my long jacket covering it. The other doormen and I were laughing about how much of a shock this man would have if he did actually, come to fight us. Anyway, two hours later the man had not been near but then passes by us, beep's the horn and waves; for fuck sake, I thought, we had built ourselves up a right treat, and all for nothing. The man calmed down in time, and from then on, we got on well whenever we spoke.

One night after being involved in throwing some big man out, he started goading me to fight him. This boy was a right bully, and he'd apparently beaten up a youngster who had to go to the hospital. Now usually, when it came to closing time, and we were leaving, the club and its surroundings would be desolate, but not this night, turns out this bully had the hump and was waiting in the car park of the pub opposite.

Now, obviously after a hard nights graft all I wanted to do was get into my car and get home to the misses, however, not tonight 'cos suddenly, out of nowhere he's coming at me all gun's blazing, but unfortunately for him, 'in his haste' he's run himself straight into a right hander and gone flying back; in his anger he immediately ran back at me, and bang, I smashed him again, and he's out cold, and because he'd taken a bit of a liberty I sat on him and started smashing shots into him, over and over again, but something told me to stop, and I got off him, looking back as I waked away at his unconscious body with a face all battered and bloody, then I just got into my car and drove, and with this all going around my head, not knowing what to do for the best, I did a few laps round town, staying out for an hour; you see, sometimes in this job, you're still on the clock long after you've finished your shift.

With my mind racing, I popped to see my mate Julian (Juggy) washing all of the blood from my arms and knuckles while I was there. I explained to Julian what had gone on, and he immediately came up with an idea 'he's sharp like that, is Juggy.' So, the plan was that I should go down to the police station and say that this bully had been playing up and later attacked me (the truth), which in their eyes would be seen as assault. I said to Julian, 'How can I say he's assaulted me; I haven't got a fucking mark on me?' Immediately Julian looked at me with his well-known "psycho smirk," and just from this, I fucking knew what was coming next. Anyway, he says, 'right, sit on the end of the chair and close your eyes and get ready for my count of 3?' Oh' hell I thought, this isn't going to end well, 'why fucking me!' I was thinking; nevertheless, I knew I had to do it. With that, the lunatic started to count, '1… 2…' and smash, he's banged me straight in the eye. Fortunately for me (especially for situations that involve Juggy) I've always had tough skin, so he hasn't broken it, thank fuck, and then he said, 'Right, I'll have to do it again Shirl?' (is he fucking joking) I thought, but no, so, 'AGAIN' there I am sat on the edge of chair and he begins another count, 'ONE…!' And he's smashed me with a beauty, and I've gone flying back over the chair, all in a daze. He then grabs me and says, 'I'm sorry, Shirl,' and the two of us rolled around laughing. A few minutes later, I noticed my eye was now closed up, and he said, 'Right, let me have a look at it.' Which he followed up with a Julian Davies corker, 'to be quite honest Shirl, I don't know whether to take your lip out as well!' Is he fucking mental, I thought, so I said, 'you can fuck right off you nutter…? I'm off down the station; I think you've done enough damage.' With that, we left the house and laughed all the way down to the police station, and in true "Juggy style," he reckoned I'd thank him for it one day.

So, we arrived at the station, and I walked up to reception and informed them that I wanted to report an assault; they asked for my name and said that someone would be along to interview me in a few minutes. A few minutes later, the door swung open, and a policeman said, 'Anthony Thomas?' And I replied, 'Yeah, that's me.' and he said,

'Anthony Thomas, I am arresting you…' If I'm honest, I knew this was coming, and with that, I was routinely put into a cell to wait for the inevitable. I tried my best to counter charge the man, but they weren't having any of it, and all because he had gone in first. During my time there, the coppers were great and to be honest, I knew most of them anyway, and they told me that the case would probably turn to dust. However, due to the official protocol, I was locked up for the whole night and charged. A month later, it was thrown out of court, and I was a free man again. Whether there was no CCTV or witnesses to back his story, I do not know, or perhaps they put two-and-two together because of what he had done to the youngster earlier that night. But I like to think it was the damage I'd endured 'with my pool ball looking eye' at that hands of my pal Julian that had done the trick – no-pain, no-gain, 'isn't that what they say?'

A few months later, I was in almost the same situation again in the club. It had kicked off, and Beast and I had smashed some men up, and they were outside bleeding when a police van turned up. A little while later, one of the bouncers from the front door came upstairs to get Beast and me because the police had asked to see us. So, as we are heading down the backstairs, out of sight, I said to Beast, 'Beast, quick, head butt me in the face?' Beast looked at me with an all apparent look of shock across his face, and without giving him time to say, no, I wrapped my hands around the back of his head and hollered, 'fucking head butt me!' And with that, he smashed his head into my face, but it didn't do the trick, so I shouted, 'for fuck's sake Beast, harder than that.' Well, he didn't stand on ceremony that time 'cos next thing you know I've gone flying back on these stairs and I'm in a fucking daze with the birds singing; my eye was split open, and I was bleeding quite heavily. We then made our way out through the front door to speak to the police, where I immediately explained to the police how these boys' had started it and we simply reacted, and as the officers inspected my eye injury (because of how bad it looked) they even asked us if "we" wanted to press charges instead. I said: 'No, we're ok officer. But could you please move the troublemakers on…' And with that, Beast and I just nonchalantly walked back inside the club. I went to the toilet to look at my eye, and Beast said, 'Shirl, you're fucking mental!' To which I replied, 'It worked, didn't it, Son?' As we laughed and sauntered off to finish our shift.

I'd bought this new car on a Monday; it was an excellent little runner, and I was just getting used to it and popped over the school to pick my daughter up. So, I parked up and opens the door to get out when next thing I hear is this loud noise and a car coming towards me, the only way I can describe it his in slow motion and only because of the sound I could see it was coming towards me, in a split second I dived back into my car across passenger seat, and the car crushed my door slamming it into my feet, the car shook, and I was screaming waiting for something to happen, I was shaken up badly and smashed my head on ceiling, I got out of car dizzy, and my legs are numb, people are asking me am I alright and to sit down, it turns out the car was speeding and being chased by police and had bumped four cars altogether, five minutes later kids were crossing that road, they eventually caught the boy a mile away, I got offered to go to hospital but I refused, I was more shook up than hurt anyway, the police pounded my car and it was a write off, so I had to get a lift to work in the night. The boy ended up pleading guilty and admitted being on drugs, and he was made to pay me back the amount for the car. He must have known who I was has he had a mate a few months later ask me can he come and apologise, but I told his mate I didn't want to know.

One night at the bottom of the stair's I get called over, this woman's ankle had completely turned the other way after her coming down off a few stair's, it was sickening, and most of the staff couldn't even look at it, I grabbed an old coat from the cloakroom and covered it over not for the woman to see it.

Now, while working in the Kooler's for the past few year's Id noticing thing's happening there and in my own house, yes paranormal stuff which couldn't be explained. I became hooked on the subject and started a quest for the following few years.' A few of the other doormen became hooked to, and every Friday before work, we would go to different places and eventually, I started an internet site called "The Psychic Doorman." We started putting on a few investigations and even appeared in our local papers. Now a lot of people took the piss, but we were serious in what we were doing. I won't delve into it too much in this book has I already have another book coming out called The Paranormal Quest. We even had a Sky Channel interested in a documentary; they started filming, but I pulled 'cos I could see they were going to take the piss out of it all. I got into it a bit deep to the stage I thought things were following me home. I finally managed to break away from it all, but it still interest's me to this day.

Another night we had two men fighting in the club, and one of them had been thrown out, said nothing, and gone on his way. Now, this boy was known as a bit of a psycho,

So, we were surprised he had gone so quietly. An hour later the man he had been fighting with leaves the club and opposite the club is a layby and most night's car's park in there watching the trouble. Anyway, it turns out the boy we put out first had gone and pinched a car and drives it straight at the man he was fighting, the man dives out of the way and the car hit's the wall, the one man's run and the man driving gets out of the car cool as fuck, takes his t-shirt off and light's it on fire and throw's it in the car and run's off, someone had witnessed all this and run and got me and Lee Arndell from the door of the Kooler's, Lee grabbed a fire extinguisher and we run out and lee out's the burning t-shirt before the police turn up.

Another night these boys are giving us shit outside after we have thrown them out, then one of them started saying then I'm going to your houses and do this and that. Now we did not have long left, and he really pissed us off, so another three doormen came with me because I wanted to have it out with this man. So we pass him in a car and pull up around the corner. I jumped out and ran at him, chasing him down street when all of a sudden I have slipped and gone face first, I was hurt from the fall, and he thinks his Christmas has come, he stopped and ran at me to kick me but my back up was there and one of the doormen Payney's shoulder charges him flying and he ran off. I felt a right prick, and the boys didn't stop taking the piss of me all the way home. I saw him a few months later, and he apologised and said he couldn't remember anything.

Every week there was a story to tell; our time was running out, and it seemed that a "prison break" was imminent.

CHAPTER FOURTEEN

(Banged up)

I'd been banged up in the local prison cells a few times in the past, but this time was totally different because I had a wife and kids at home, and believe me there's no worse feeling than sitting in those tiny little room's pacing up and down thinking your life's over, and you won't see your family again for a while - and for what; just trying to make a living and provide for them.

I had a terrible few months and got arrested a few times, but all the time I got off with things because it was proven that the others had started it. One night it's gone off big time downstairs, as usual, so I ran in and grabbed someone, and quickly wrestle him out. But sometimes they would turn and hit you, and no fucking way was I being used as a human punch bag. So, I've given one to Lee on the door and ran back in to sort it. I can just about see Keith parting two men as this one man's gone to hit him over the head with a bottle. Immediately, I've hit his arm down and got him in a headlock, I gave him to the boy's, and his face was bleeding, they smacked the bottle away, and the police turned up, only then I was arrested the following week and taking in on a GBH charge. The boy said I'd smashed his face into a wall, which opened him up. However, you couldn't see anything on the CCTV footage. So, after a couple of times answering bail, the case was dropped.

Another time (I always found this funny) there had been a fight upstairs and I'd gone up the back stairs to help bring two boy's down. One was bleeding, and the police turned up, and that was about it. A few weeks later, Bernard, the

208

boss rang me telling me that the police wanted the two of us to go down to the station that evening to make statements. He said, we'd only be about ten minutes, in-and-out. So, he picked me up and we walk into the station, he then told the desk Sargent who was expecting us, that we were there. Next thing you know they arrested the pair of us, we were laughing to each other while Bernard was going off his head ranting and raving saying that he wanted his solicitor. The best thing was we were both on the door that night, and we had all the proof we needed; plus, it was all on CCTV. The mental thing was, he and I hadn't even been involved in the fight but when some man was questioned (because he knew our names) he pulled our names out of the hat and offered them up to the police, this quickly backfired on him though, when we were released with no further charges. So, with that out of the way, I was back in work the following Sunday night, and our local town youth rugby team had got to a final in some cup and were all out on the piss with their coaches. Now, these youth player's used to play up all the time; don't get me wrong I've been there myself and worn the proverbial t-shirt many times - it's just a part of growing up. However, the coaches should have known better seeing as they were supposed to be in control of them.

Two hours later they are throwing toilet rolls around the club and even glass bottles, so obviously, I was called upstairs. We tell them they have to go, and quite a few of them walk down with us calmly, all sorted. Now, as we get down the stairs, the place is empty, and after their drunken coaches have found out what has happened, they come running down. One of them immediately started screaming, 'you're all fucking bully's throwing kids out!' I thought to myself, have you ever seen what a bottle can do when thrown you stupid fucker? But no he's getting in my face while I'm walking towards him, and the next thing I know this other coach (who had a bit of a reputation as a bully in the town) step's in front of me, grab's both my hand's and tries bending my fingers back, I'm thinking, what the fuck's he doing, as he slammed a full head-butt straight into my face. I later found out this was a trick of his that he often used in the past,

Anyway, he caught me good, and we've started fighting, and I'm holding onto him. We then get split apart, and all these youth players have joined in; this one big player (who later went on to play for Wales at International level) grab's me over the bar, but I turn him and start butting him. At this point, a few doormen are fighting, and the whole downstairs is one mass brawl. Suddenly, my senses are back, and I can see the head butter coming towards me again, he's then gone down, and I've smashed into him, and he's shouting, 'I've had enough!' But punches are coming in from everywhere, and I'm just punching out until the doormen Kevin along with the owner, Vicki pulled me off. The fight had now gone out of them all, and they were all outside except, the head-butter who was unconscious, being carried into our side alley to be worked on. The police turn up, and ten minutes later, I was being arrested along with the other doorman, Lee. A few of the team went to the hospital and the other coach (who I'd known a long time and played on the same team with) then went and made a statement saying I had stamped on the head butter's head. And after taking my boots and clothes,

I was thrown straight into a cell. No one would tell me in the station if the man was ok, because the last thing I saw of him, he wasn't moving at all. As I sat pondering in the cold, brightly lit cell, I began thinking that my time was up and that I was probably on my way to prison. My misses and kid in the house and I'm going on a "horror-holiday," all over some bullying cunt.

It was now coming to twelve at night, the club's been shut down and knowing no one's going to talk to me for a while I get my head down. I then get a call at six in the morning from an old mate of mine, he couldn't say much but let's just say he wasn't a fan of the bully either. My boss Bernard was straight on the scene in the morning having got me a solicitor, and as usual, seventeen hours later I'm charged and released.

A few days later the bully's gone to the local paper (with his face looking like the elephant man) wanting them to run a story, detailing how a bouncer had beaten him up, the newspapers' contacted the local police who told them that they couldn't print anything until, and if, we had been convicted.

A week to the day and I'm back on the door of the club and who's walking past the club other than the man himself. He kept staring at me, I don't say a word, and he's screaming that I'm going to jail; I just smile at him as he's getting cockier by the second, thinking that my bottle's gone. What the stupid fucker didn't realise was our CCTV cameras were filming him and first thing the following morning I went down and told the police that he had come to my workplace calling me out. The police left me and went straight up to the club to see if this was true. I was bailed again for a few months, and when it came to my

211

final date where I thought it was going straight to court, but no, I got a phone call saying, everything had been dropped by the CPS. They must have taken another look at the CCTV of him starting the brawl and butting me and thought this is going nowhere. Two weeks later, after the charges had been dropped, I was arrested yet again; this time they didn't pinch me on the night of the incident, this time they waited till the following day. Anyway, what happened was…

It had been Halloween night on Wednesday, and Yuan Lozano's Elvis band was on at the club, and it was sold out and was rammed full. The upstairs was in complete darkness, and no one had been up there. There hadn't been one bit of trouble all night, and everything was wrapped up, just asking the stragglers to leave. I then walked out into the foyer, and one of my old school mates said, 'Shirl, two men just went upstairs!'

Now, I'm not a fan of the dark, 'no matter how big I am' but I thought surely, he's winding me up. So up I goes on my own, as I got to the top of the stair's, had a look around and I saw nothing. So, I shouted, 'hello, anyone here?' I now think it's a wind-up, and as I turned around to go down, I heard a bang, and fuck me I thought, 'he's right!' Anyway, a week before a polish man had tried sneaking a baseball bat into the club and it was still behind the counter, so I went and grabbed it. I then see Neil (Beast) coming from downstairs, and I said to him, 'Beast, come with me?' And so, we went up to the top of stair's and shouted, 'look if anyone's there come out now.' Still no answer, at which point Beast thought I was winding him up. Next thing you know I could see movement over the other side of the club, we walked across, then these two men go up another lot of backstairs into the woman's toilets on the third floor, it's now lighter in the toilet's and this man's standing there with a bottle in his hand; I asked him to come down but he refused, and was full of attitude, so Beast and I make our way up the stairs and rush at him, he goes to hit me with the bottle, so I swung the bat, by this point Beast has grabbed the other man, smashed him down to the floor, and is sat on top of him.

By this time, the other doorman Michael (Peanut) was with us, and I've hit the man down and peanut's sitting on top of him too, he's spitting blood up saying I'm a dead man and making threats to my family. I then said to the boys, 'are you pair alright, while I go and get the police?' And with that I ran down into the owner's office and told her that we had caught two burglars on the top floor, I still had the bat and told Vicky that I was not going to lie that I've used the bat, but Vicky then said, 'I can't cover for you, 'cos it's all on CCTV.' But I was thinking to myself, that I didn't want her to cover up anything, I was just telling the truth.

Anyway, the Police turn up within minutes, and they arrest these boys and the ones still choppsing. I told the police I had used the bat and then we all went home. The following day we are all getting pulled in, me, Neil, Peanut and even Belinda who didn't even go upstairs' and we all get charged and I was getting done on two charges.

I couldn't fucking believe it, was this really happening, self-defence after hour's and we are getting charged. Their story was, they had gone upstairs to sniff some cocaine and also when police checked CCTV it looks like Neil had a cosh running across the dancefloor when the truth of the matter was it was a wooden witch's broomstick from the Halloween night. Thing wasn't looking good then the following week me and Neil are on the door, and these two boys were banned has one had caused trouble elsewhere, the other one began making threat's, and it turns out he was the one's brother from the Halloween night, they then threaten to go over to the car park and smash all our car's up, so we laugh at them, and off they go, next thing you know a taxi pull's up and tells they had actually jumped the gates. We run over there and beast his straight over, by now the other doormen from the club are out and make chase and catch them, they had smashed one car up that didn't even belong to the bouncers. Our doormen then held them until the police arrive to take them away.

Not long after that we all received a message that our charges had been dropped; now, whether these boys and their threat's and action's had affected their brother's case, or the CPS actually had some sense and realized they were in the wrong and that they were actually trying to do the place over, I honestly do not know, all I knew was I was a free man again, which of course was another weight lifted off my shoulders.

Another strange night and quite scary for everyone involved was when one of the girls who worked the door got stabbed in the head with a knife. There had been a fight earlier on in the night, it was just a regular fight and people were put out, and that was that. It's nearly end of night, and people are leaving and the one door's open for the girl Belinda to leave people out, I'm behind the other door and Beast is there also, so we were just talking away, having a laugh when out of the blue this man ran in and stabbed

Belinda in the head, then immediately ran back out. Beast and I dive at him, but he's back out through the door as fast as lightning. We still didn't know what the fuck had happened, when Beast shouted: 'it's a knife!' With that, I've Grabbed Belinda in my arms and got my 2 hand's on her head, I'm waiting to see the blood pour out, but there's nothing except a little mark, it turns out the knife had buckled, and god was on her side that night. The owner then grabs her, and Beast and I ran out and chased him up the street, we get to these garden's and looking back now I'm glad we didn't catch him as we were both on one. Then a load of police turn up in van's, and we told them he's here somewhere, and they said we'll take it from here, he was only a few feet away from us, hiding in a shed in some garden.

A court case came up a few months later in Cardiff Crown court, and I looked at the boy and did not even know him. It was then my turn to give evidence, and the boy's barrister said, 'are you the same Anthony Thomas that in 1995 got arrested for affray? If that is correct your honour, this man's word's mean nothing!' I then turned to the judge and said, 'yes it is me, if I could explain myself to the jury' the judge asked me to continue, and I explained how that one stupid night drunk I pleaded guilty and had gone on to work on the door's for fifteen years and was head doormen', the judge then thanked me and told the barrister to continue with his questions. The boy was found guilty; however, I didn't go in for his version of events, and to this day, I still don't know why he did it.

Another Sunday night it had been the same old shit, fighting and throwing people out and we were now down to the last half hour, and things were cooling down. I was working on the front door with Neil and our mate Keith had popped in for a chat. I received a phone call from my missis, she was screaming, saying that our house was being broken into. I grabbed my keys and Neil, joined Keith and me. I got to the house, and my missus was shaking, she could hardly talk. Turned out some robbing creeper had been going through our stuff downstairs. She had left the front door unlocked (as I was due home soon) and had gone to bed.

She had heard a noise and gone down to the front door, and the scumbag decided to run back at her, but she had kept pushing the door and screaming that her boyfriend was a bouncer and that he was on his way. It all went quiet, but she knew he was still there, so she grabbed the Samurai sword we had on the wall above the TV until it went quiet and he had gone. My daughter was upstairs and luckily slept through it all. I was now mad, frothing at the mouth while she was telling me, and I jumped back in the car as she was shouting that the police were on their way. I told Keith to stay with my missis while Neil and I went off in pursuit of the creeper.

Now driving up through the estate on the way home we had clocked a scumbag and even asked him had he seen anybody, and we had felt it was him, so we headed down this rough street and caught up with him. Some youngsters then told me he had been just trying to sell them a gold ring. I then swept his legs away, and he hit's the floor hard, and I swear the gold ring popped out. By now a few people were coming out of the houses lived with him, and they got baseball bats, Neil is screaming at them, and they go back in. I then said, 'where's my video camera?' He just looked as though he hadn't a clue what I was talking about, so he got another whack. Anyway, to cut it short without going into all the detail, we had our man. A little while later the police turned up and arrested him and then I had to go on down to the local police station (with blood still on my shirt) to make a statement. It was two am, and I was thinking to myself could this night get any worse. I shot back up to the house, and all the doormen followed to see if all was ok. I then said to my misses that he had my ring, but there was no sign of the video camera, and she said, 'that's ok, 'cos I moved that earlier! It's in your drawer.' I immediately began laughing to myself.

I finally got out of the station and arrived back home at around 4am

The scumbag went straight back down the following morning and was back inside for another year. Then one day I was going to work, and who did I spot standing at the end of my street, yeah, you've got it, the same fucking scumbag, I goes across screaming at him, and he ran away, next thing I know the police have come to have a chat with me has he had said I'd made threat's on his life, I laughed at them and they told me I'd have to have an injunction put on him to stop him coming near my street. I said, 'don't bother, if he comes near the place again, I'll deal with it myself.'

All the time it always seemed to be Neil and me doing the throwing out, fighting and getting arrested. We had now gone into the red on the light's system in the club has there was so much trouble all the time and the place was close to getting shut down.

We were going to work one night, and this policeman call's us for a private chat and tells us to calm it down has

Mine and Neil's names were on their watching list, but in that job and in a shithole like that what could we do, turn a blind eye like other's or ignore bullies who were calling us rotten, it just wasn't in us and jail was on the cards.

Then that weekend it's gone off downstairs. I'm working with Keith, and a few men are going for it, so we are dragging them all out. Two Aberdare boys are on the door's called Lee and a new kid who'd been there a few month's named Tony. So we pass them to them, and Keith and I went back in for rest, we grabbed another two and did the same again. Now one boy's outside and his face his just red covered in blood. To cut it short, the police and ambulance turn up, and Tony gets arrested. It turns out when he's thrown the one out, he's slipped and smashed his head into the railing's opening his head up. A court date was set, and Tony ended up getting a guilty and sent down to Parc prison. The police had seen the CCTV on the door and said he had done it on purpose. It looked like to me though the judge had made an example of him because of all the trouble in there, that was the end of Tony's short run on the door's, but that could have been me that they used to set an example.

Not long after that, I was on the door one night when the owner let this man back in after I said he was banned; he'd taken Warren one of the doormen on a few months earlier for fighting, but the case was dropped. I found it strange how she had left him back in has Warren was also in the same building working, it was like she wanted us out of there and looking for an argument and then one of the other doormen Brendan goes up and start's arguing and there's murder's, come the end of the night 3 doormen walked out and she had enough, but we still had the one night to go to get paid, the 3 doormen refused to work and my boss asked me would I go in has it was the last night of the weekend and he hadn't been paid, we all bit our tongues who worked and the atmosphere was terrible there but we didn't let anyone down and just got on with the job.

So after 5 long years it was finally time to see the back of the shit hole, It was quite gutting has Id got to know everyone, and I would also miss the money but If I stayed in this place any longer there was only one place I was going, there was only so many times I could get off with thing's.

It was now 2010, and the timing couldn't have been better; the Vulcan was looking for new door staff and were about to open as a nightclub in the upstairs room. So, I jumped straight back in there and was head doorman yet again for the entire building, however, before I get into more detail, let me explain a little about the drug problems we had in the town.

CHAPTER FIFTEEN

(Drugs Are For Mugs)

'Like I mentioned previously, in my younger year's I smoked cannabis, this I put down to a part of growing up, and let's face it, in those days, everyone was at it.

Now, working the door's while taking something is an entirely different story to what you would imagine; I'd rather be in control and have one up on the punter's that are out of their minds. So I never found the need to take any substances even if it was just to have a laugh has some doorman told me. Anyway we had just gone into the new millennium and drugs were rife everywhere and I don't just mean the punters. No! The actual doormen were taking stuff too, and sometimes more than the punters.

One night in this venue these 2 biker's used to come in and they liked their weed but would never smoke it in the place and always go outside out of the way. Anyway me and the doormen got to know them and every week they would come in with a few joint's rolled for us, and also a few Viagra but we never took anything there in work until this one night one of our doorman was bored and went and dropped two Viagra, well an hour later you can imagine the rest, he's walking round in these tight black trousers' with what looks like a tent pole sticking out of the front, the look's he had, and he just didn't give a fuck for the next few hours, I was laughing so much and we just couldn't look at him for the rest of the night.

After a few month's I had a box with loads of joint's and by now Id stopped smoking the stuff so just gave it away to the other doormen.

Now in those day's cocaine was a lot dearer to buy, and not many people were on it, unlike today where everyone's on the stuff. The pills were flying out as well as the speed, and a lot of people were off their tits and bouncing around the town.

Then came along the date rape drug known as GHB and I first started hearing of it when doormen had been out drinking and changed into a completely different person.

I've seen one doorman so bad on it he actually thought he was a gorilla and even the local police would drive past him because they didn't know what to do with him.

It then got to the stage that the doormen were taking it to work with them just for a laugh. Now small doses you would still have your senses but take that little too much, and you didn't know what you are doing. I am speaking here as if I have taken it, but not once did I ever touch the shit but only recalling what the doormen told me. It got to the stage that half of the firm I worked for was on it, and the boss couldn't sack them, or he'd have no doormen to continue running the venues. I then got told that one of our doorman who was on a night out had taken too much and collapsed and paramedics were sent and brought him back to life. It never stopped him as he was back on it the following week.

At one stage when I was head doorman of a club, I'd say at least five out of the ten doormen was on it, putting it in their tea and in the end just chucking lumps of it in their mouth. I was in an awkward situation has how can I put it,

221

I was one of the boys and these were all mates, I couldn't tell the boss has I'd look like a grass so I'd just keep an eye on how out of control they'd become in the night, most could handle it, but then there would be one or two bouncing around the place, sweating their tit's off and wound up.

It got to the stage something had to be done so I had a kind word in their ears and even then, if i'd pulled them, they would deny they had anything.

Then this one Sunday night the owner of the club, Vicki came out into the foyer from inside and called me over, she said, 'Go and have a look in the smoking alley', so off I goes with this other doorman and I can see everyone laughing, I then go round the corner, and there's this doorman all in black, standing there with his eyes closed bobbing to the music, he looks like a fucking zombie and his stuck to the spot, I look's at the other doorman who came with me and we just laugh at each other, by now Vicki's joined us shaking her head laughing to. I then slapped him across the face, and he instantly wakes, I've done this a few times before when they were going, he looks at me, and he's almost back to normal, and I said to him, 'right off you go, your sacked,' he didn't even argue or explain himself and just left the venue.

Another night we had 2 Welsh rugby International's in the club, and everyone's making a fuss of them. One of the doormen then comes up to me telling me he had been in the toilets with the one and had given him GHB for a laugh. An hour later Vicki comes down from upstairs' and tells me the rugby player is off his face and has to go. I shot up stair's, and he's hanging from these rafter's and don't know where the fuck he is. I went over and grabbed him, the bouncer who had given him the stuff came across and whispered something in his ear. The man with him who went on to captain the Welsh team then says to me I'll take him out. He walks out, and his hanging over the railings outside, I think the bouncer had told him to go; otherwise, the owners would be getting straight onto the papers in the morning. They both apologised outside and went on their way; it wasn't long after he did finally make the papers.

The same was happening in other venue's too, and I had a phone call off my boss one night when I was in Kooler's asking me to shoot over to another pub in town 'cos a few of the doormen were off their tit's and the landlord had contacted him. With that, I jumped in the car with another doorman, parked around the back of the venue and goes down the side lane to the front of the pub. Three doormen were working, and every one of them was off it. Two of the clowns still had some senses, but the third one had turned into a gorilla and was sleeping, then immediately waking up, which had everyone laughing at him. Yet again another slap got him out of it, and I told him to go before we lose the pub totally. I spoke to the other 2 who by this point, had come round a bit, then I went back to the club. The following day the landlord said he didn't want any of them back in, and fortunately for us, he said that we still had the contract and that we had had a lucky escape.

Another night this doorman had taken some GHB, and he was off it, bouncing around the club like a lunatic, and he was playing hell with all the girls. He then comes up to me with this girl as I'm standing at the back of the room and says, 'will you take a few pictures of us?' So he gives me his camera, and he's hiding behind this wood panel, he shout's, 'we're ready now Shirl.' I knocked the camera on,

223

turned around to see that she's only got his cock out in her hand, and she's on her knees while they're both smiling at the camera - talk about not knowing what to do next. Suddenly, while I'm taking pictures, she began giving him a blowjob, the girl was laughing her head off, I mean I knew she was a bit of a nutter like him, but this was on another level. Anyway, I tossed him the camera, laughing, and said, 'I'm not getting involved in all this...' But he just didn't give a fuck. I then said, 'you're going to get sacked if the owner knows what you're up to.' Then with that, he sauntered off laughing and goes over and shows the owner. She knew how mad he was and just laughed it off.

'Another night; another close call.'

I was working in Baverstocks about 3 miles from the town. It was 9 o'clock, we had just opened, and it was all quiet when we receive a phone call from our boss Bernard again asking us to get to a pub in our local town as soon as possible because he'd just had a phone call saying that two of our doormen were dead.

So, me, Lee and Paul jump in a car and shoot straight down to the pub fearing the worst; we still didn't know what was happening but knowing that these doormen took GHB we had a rough idea. As we turn up, there were ambulances outside, and it was chaos everywhere. Turns out they had both taken too much and were what we would refer to it as KO'd. They were in a bad way, and reports were coming back that one had died earlier, and they had brought him back to life. The two ambulances took them both away, and Lee stayed on the door of the venue while Paul and I went back to work. Both men ended up in the hospital for a few nights and were sacked straight away.

Baverstock's
Team

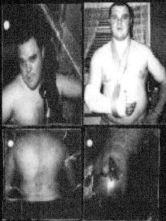

Bad Night at the Office

Me and Pricey outside Vulcan

The RM's
Crew

The Alpha Bar Team

The Play Nightclub Team

Bessemer's with Jason 'Tomo'

Me and Lee Tank in Aberdare

Beast and Peanut in the Koolers

The Koolers Team

The Koolers Lunatics

Cancer Charity Night with Keith

Me and Paul
Curtis (RIP)

Me and the Beast
in the Vulcan

Celtic Bar with
Mad Kris and
Walshy

The Celtic Bar Team

The Crown Team

Dowlais Rock At Top Team

Charity Day Team

Working Rock At
The Top

Bodyguarding
Joe Calazaghe
with the Team

Dowlais Rock
Team

The Koolers Team

Down the
Crown Pub
with the Boys

Celtic Bar with
Dynamite Dan

Bowfest with
the Boys

The Vulcan
Nightclub Team

Play Nightcub
Team

The Strikers
Team

The Strikers
Band Day Team

Another night a good doorman mate of mine had come up to Baverstock's where I worked after taking some GHB. He then left us to drive to his girlfriend's house in another town, and within an hour I got a phone call saying he had wrapped his car up and was in a bad way. As per usual, I spent the night up the hospital with Paul until the early hours of the morning, until they could take him to Cardiff for an emergency operation. His family were in tear's not knowing what drugs he had actually taken, so I went out and told the doctors what he'd had, just in case they gave him something that might negatively mix with it and kill him outright.

The next day he had an operation which was thankfully successful, and soon after he was awake in his bed. I told him that I hoped he'd learnt his lesson, and he said, 'I'll never touch it again Shirl!' Given something that serious you would think he would have learned his lesson: but did he fuck, within a year he was back on it and twice as bad.

I had a phone call one night while I was five minutes from the venue on my way to work, it was the landlord saying that there was a warrior jeep parked sideways across the road, he said, it's at a standstill but the jeep's running and my two mates were slumped in there unconscious; now if the police had seen this they would have been fucked. So, I parked up and ran over to the jeep, both men were totally KO'd on GHB again. Like I mentioned, one had even died before from an overdose on it, and the other hadn't learnt his lesson from the car crash. By now a crowd had gathered, and I had to act quickly; I dragged my mate out of the driver seat slapping him hard across face to wake him up, and I'm screaming at him, 'what the fuck are you doing?' He didn't even know what day it was. So, I opened

225

the back seat up and threw him in. I then ran around and dragged the other one out too; he was out cold, and it took a few hard slaps until he sat-up on a wall with a few people from the pub who knew him. I quickly jumped into the warrior jeep and drove off, speedily passing the police who were on their way there. I got him in his house, and he's fucked, walking around the house like a zombie. So, I locked him in and borrowed his jeep. Then a few months later and I'm on a building site when this copper turn's up. Apparently, the same boy had gone down a motorway swerving back and forth like a maniac, and the police had stopped him, and he didn't know where he was. Immediately, he was rushed to the hospital and had his stomach pumped, and they put him on machines to monitor him. He had told them he'd taken too many pain killer's 'cos he was still suffering pain in his back from the car accident. Anyway, he had this massive dog in Jeep, and the police wouldn't drive it, and as they knew where I was working they asked if I knew the dog; to cut it short the copper drove me there and I drove the jeep back to site where me and the other security guard cleaned the jeep out just in case they came back, so we were fortunate that the dog had scared them off. The Boy turned up the next day, and I said to him, 'what the fuck are these?' He apologised and flushed them all down the toilet and said for the second time, 'Honest Shirl, It won't happen again.' A week later he was back on it - addicted to the stuff.

After a while, he got his comeuppance when his house was raided, and he had pots of the stuff, but he got off without doing a prison sentence and joined rehab, and I kept an eye on him every day for months. I spoke with him recently, and he swore to me that he was off the stuff altogether, but then again who knows.

One night in this nightclub, the police had given us new head camera's to try out, and I was the "Ginny pig." So, I'm walking around the club, and all the doorman are laughing and won't come near me. I then got called into the search area downstairs, 'cos a man had been found with hundreds of pills on him. He clocked me and started pleading with me to let him go, he then says that he'll give me x amount of pounds to turn a blind eye. I knew the man and was trying to point at the camera telling him that he was being filmed, but he just kept on without noticing it. Soon after, the police arrived, and he was locked up and later sent to jail for it.

Someone will always offer you a line or two to turn the other way while you're working the door, I can guarantee it. Countless times I've been offered stuff to turn a blind eye in club's and be part of the payroll. I could have been a very wealthy man by now, but it's against everything I detest. I've seen girl's frothing from the mouth and fitting on the floor, with some even close to death, and it's not a pleasant experience. So why would I give these people that chance? After a few years, the drugs became less and less on the doors, and a lot of the doormen finished or moved on. I was now back at the Vulcan with a drug-free team of boys' working.

CHAPTER SIXTEEN

(Here we go Again)

I thought I'd seen the back of this place a few years ago, and now I'm back in the shithole, which is now on two floors – double trouble. The new owner was named Perry who was like one of the boy's and just let us do our jobs, I got on well with his wife at the time to, but every now and again she wasn't happy over something a doorman had done or this and that, quite a few times we just bit our tongue's over incident's in there.

I'm now jumping back and forth between pub and club, and one night it's gone off downstairs,' so we manage to get all these girl's and boy's out, they are still fighting outside when next thing you know some girl has taken her stiletto shoe off and stabbed a girl above her eye. Keith Taylor's back working with me and we are holding the girl down on floor who's in a hell of a mess until the police come. The cut is bad, and everyone's still fighting over her as we are covering her. The girl then goes off in an ambulance.

I was on the door another night with this doorman nicknamed Stan, and it's the end of the night, and we are clearing up. I can then see this cocky Englishman walking up, taking his time. Now, smoking had been banned by this point, but this man's got a fag in his mouth, now he and Stan had a run in before, and Stan knew he could be trouble. Stan's then walked up to him and smashed the fag out of his mouth, the man is going nuts has it turns out it was a plastic joking one which even lights up 'cos he was trying to quit. He is screaming for Stan's job, and I had to walk off has I was laughing so much.

Over Christmas, I got involved collecting for the Merthyr Cancer Aid charity, and we put a few bucket's in the nightclub. One night we had a bit of a power cut going in the nightclub, and the tills were down, so, the owner Beth said to just leave them all in. Now, thinking fast I grabbed the bucket out of the cupboard and started charging everyone the normal £2 entry; not one person moaned simply because it was for a good cause and we raised almost a grand that night alone. We also appeared in the local newspaper.

One night I was on the nightclub door, and this drink has come down all over me from the balcony. I looked up quickly and could see these boy's fucking about. So, 'cos it was eating at me, I went up ten minutes later to find these boys still fucking about, then, one of them threw a bottle out onto the floor. With that, I ran at him and grabbed him. Now, he's quite big, so I got underneath him and threatened to throw him over the balcony; his hands were holding on for dear life, and while I've got him up in the air, his mates are trying to calm me down. I finally put him down and dragged him out and down the stairs.

I was on the front door one evening because it was a Sunday and it had gone quiet. The owner's daughter was seeing this boy, and he's been over another club fighting, and when he was making his way back to the Vulcan, he'd got into another fight not far away and had his lip bitten off. Anyway, he comes into the pub and his face covered. So, next thing I know he's in the toilet being held by a doorman, and he's punching the walls. This boy was going nuts, and no one could control him, so I held him up

229

against the wall and said to him, he seriously needed to get to the hospital. After a battle, I finally talked some sense into him; thinking on my feet, I grabbed a glass full of ice from behind the bar. We jumped in the car and drive to where he'd had his lip bitten off earlier to see if we could save it. I've got my main beam on looking for it, but there's no sign of it. Anyway, I get him to hospital, and he's still going nuts, so I'm trying to calm him down. I thought, I've done all I can to help him, but the doctors won't look at him 'cos he's in a rage, so I ended up staying with him until he was seen by a doctor. With that, he says to me, 'how bad does it look, Shirl?' And me trying to be nice said, 'it doesn't look too bad!' But he clocked himself in a mirror and screams, 'not too bad, my fucking lip's gone!' A nervous laugh came over me, and I said, 'well sorry, but I was just trying to be nice.' Soon after, his girlfriend and father-in-law turned up from the pub, so I leave them to deal with him. I heard later that they managed to get some skin and he had plastic surgery to fix it, and it looked alright after that. I did see him a few years later, and he thanked me for what I did that night.

Another night, years later, I 'm looking for body parts yet again. I'd been called to a toilet in a venue where a man had his ear bitten off. The man who had done it had been thrown out but "Van Gogh" was still in shock. We all got our lights on our cameras looking for his ear when my pal, Warren spot's it. We then get a glass of ice from behind the bar, I pick the ear up and put it in. I knew the ambulance might take an hour to come and also that we had to act fast, so I offered to take the man and his girlfriend in my jeep to the local hospital. I'd had a few run-ins with the man in the past and thrown him out a few times which obviously goes to show I'd help anyone in need. The boys misses was sat in the back seat calling him rotten and holding the glass while I went into the hospital and explained what had happened, with that, I left and went back to the pub. I saw his misses the next day, and she thanked me and mentioned they hadn't been lucky enough to save the ear.

Another time, this well-known Bouncer and hardman were out with a few boys from a different town. We get called inside later that night, and this man is knocked out cold on the floor, I ask everyone who did it, but no one would say a word. Now, I'd seen this bouncer leave a minute or two before and had a feeling it may have been him. So, someone goes and does first aid on this man at the back of the club, and I go back on the door. This bouncer has now gone off it and his starting fights with everyone, innocent people who didn't want to know and he was twice the size of them. He then turned to them all and said, 'your all fucking wanker's the lot of you.' He turned around and goes to walk back in the pub as if nothing has happened, so I put my hand out and says, 'you're not coming back in mate!' And he looks at me like a piece of shit and says, 'well you won't stop me!' Then he goes to hit my hand down, and I've smashed him in the face, and he's gone backwards hitting a 3-foot road bollard that's behind him, and he's stuck there in mid-flight like a dying fly for a few seconds. He then rolls off and is out cold as I'm standing over him screaming for him to get back up. This man then ran from inside the pub saying that I was out of order, so I threw him too. Shortly after, the man comes round goes off down the road, stumbling everywhere. The mates who were with him come back into the pub, one turn's to me and says, 'we're glad you did that, he's been playing up all night long.' Strangely enough, I bumped into the man a few weeks later, and like most of them, he apologised and couldn't even remember a thing that happened.

One Sunday night while it was rammed upstairs in the club, this horrible rugby prick who we'd had trouble with before, kicks off. Warren's dragging him through the club and down the stairs and all his mates are getting involved. Beast took him from Warren and slammed him to the floor, there were a few outside having a fag, and they noticed their mate and what's happening, so it's all gone off on the door. I noticed Warren's on the floor, so I've grabbed him and helped him back up. Suddenly, this monster of a man hit's Warren from the side so I've flown in front of Warren and smashed him in the face, and he's gone flying back. The fight's gone out of him, and the police are standing 2ft away outside the door entrance watching, but for some reason, they wouldn't come inside the venue to help us. Anyway, we drag one of them outside, and they arrest him but still wouldn't step in the club. After this fracas, the owners of the club put a complaint to the station 'cos we had all the proof on CCTV.

Another night these two bullies were downstairs, they've kicked off with Warren, and he's quickly flattened the pair of them. The doormen then drag them outside, but as they're ejected, they grabbed some glass bottles and were throwing them at us. With that, Warren walk's up to a table himself, grab's two bottles and smashes the ends off them and tries making his way outside. Anyway, I've grabbed him and said, 'what the fuck are you doing?' Because only minutes before two off duty coppers were in the place drinking. However, Warren didn't give it any thought 'cos he had seen red after the bottles had nearly hit us. I was just trying to tell him to try and stay professional. Which was lucky 'cos the Police turned up seconds later and moved everyone on.

It's Christmas morning at my house, and as we now have two young girls you can only imagine the amount of wrapping paper and boxes scattered all over the place. So, I came up with an idea to burn the paper and stuff at the side of the house before we go to my mother's in the afternoon. Later, after lighting the fire, my misses said, 'have you put that fire out Tony?' and I told her yes as we drove off. Now my mam's house was about a mile away, but you could see our house from there as we were up on top of a hill. We then have food up my mam's and it's just turning dark as we leave there when I notice blue lights flashing by our house, my heart sunk and I was praying It wasn't our house in flames, however, when we turned the corner I was so wrong, 'cos there was a police van, ambulance and 2 fire engines and the whole street that ran alongside ours had been evacuated, and firemen are about to smash my doors down. Seemingly, the small fire had caught the gas main going into our house, and the fire was burning furiously. We unlocked the door to our house, and one man entered, quickly knocking off the gas; the house was a terrible sight, and my name was dirt. Fire specialists were in, and the side of our house was dug up, and they fitted a whole new lot of gas pipes. It was like a Christmas "Duff-Duff" scene from EastEnders. Not long after my father-in-law Gareth turned up and said laughing, 'only you Ant… only you!' And Anna and the girls' went to stay with him while I waited at the house. It wasn't till, 8 o clock that they finally let people back into their houses – 'Merry Christmas everybody…'

I was doing a bit of work on a building site in the town in the days, and my boss rung me and asked if I want to earn some extra cash, because there was two of us working the site in the day I left the other guard to look after the site while I went up to a car auction place with my mate Beast 'cos apparently they'd been having some trouble with a bunch of Indians' and travelers, who had been pinching car parts. All Beast and I had to do was blend into the crowd and try and catch the fucker's pinching, which was easy and after a couple of weeks we managed to eye a few culprits and quickly eject them – so, all was good – it was nice getting two wages for a while though. *Oh well, all good things...* A little while later, the auction was broken into, and a few cars had been damaged, so they put security in, full-time.

One day my mate Julian (Juggy) called me up 'cos he was expecting a bit of trouble; apparently, his other mate was living in a caravan, and while he was out one night it had got stolen, and the caravan was now near a Gypsy site called the Bogey Road. Julian and his brother and mate had looked around Merthyr all day and found the caravan, but it was now getting dark, and they thought someone was coming back to strip it, so the game plan was for us to look after the caravan until Julian's brother got a tow rope to move it. So, his brother dropped us off, and Julian and I sat in the caravan in complete darkness; just me, him and a couple of claw hammers. We were in there for about an hour when Julian said, 'don't speak, they'll hear us! Look, if anyone turn's up we will surprise 'em and jump out on them!' Another twenty minutes pass and we received a phone call; apparently Julian's brother has broken down, and he needed a hand to push his van – fuck sake, what a cock-up I thought. So, Julian says, 'right I'll go and push my brother, you stay here on guard!' Now anyone will tell you I hate the dark, especially on top of a mountain with no one around.' Fortunately, Julian was only gone two minutes, and my mind's working overtime, I heard all sorts of weird noises, 'Fuck this!' I was thinking to myself as I grabbed my hammer and started running down the hill calling to him. Julian's crying laughing calling me all the names under the sun as I'm shouting, 'fuck his caravan.'

Sometime after, Julian started doing "DVD's for pirates" (well, at least I think that's what he said.) Anyway, he asked me if I wanted to get involved with the selling of them, but I wasn't into all of that and politely declined. Now, Julian has never watched a porn film in his life, his family and friends will all vouch for this, I mean yes, he's been in a couple of Donkey porn films in the past, but nothing more. Unfortunately, a little while later, Julian was arrested on a charge of video piracy; he had a large business and was doing well until trading standards tracked him down, and to be truthful, it did him good.

During the court case, he was offered a deal where they would not charge him for the small selection of porn films he was selling if he pleaded guilty on the other counts. However, he didn't admit guilt, so the prosecution was not very happy with him. In retaliation to this, the prosecution decided to mention the porn films just before the judge threw the book at him. I watched him with breath baited as he stood up to take what was coming in that big glass box thing when the judge ordered for all to rise in that courtroom. There he was, stood there in his funeral suit like a little boy lost trying to look all innocent. At that moment, the prosecution said to the judge: "Your honour, please let us not forget the type of films Julian Davies was selling;

235

films like Shaving Ryan's privates, Bangkok Chick boys and Up the Arizona Dirt track." And every single solitary person in the room (even the cleaner) turned to face Julian and stared at him. With that, Julian scanned the room and then looked straight at me glaring, as the tears rolled down my face as I tried desperately not to laugh my head off in front of the judge. The gavel went down, and the judge fined him £14,527, which he had to pay in one lump sum, and he also ended up doing a few weeks porridge (prison time) for good measure; he wasn't a happy bunny, to say the least.

The following week it's gone off with a rugby team yet again. Keith, 'a true gentleman' who I'd worked with for years on the doors but never actually seen throw a punch – that was just how personable he was – everyone loved him, so he didn't have to get his fists out. Anyway, what has happened is some man has 'for some reason' taking a disliking to Keith and caught him with a cheeky shot, and that's it, Keith's off like a bull in a china shop. When we watched the CCTV back, we witnessed "Mr Nice Guy, Keith," smashing them all to pieces. Obviously, I wound him up all night saying, 'fucking hell Keith, he must have upset you? That's the most work I've ever seen you do!' From that day forward, we started calling him "bomber." Joking apart, it just goes to show how rough it was in that place to get "Mr. Nice Guy's" back up.

The following week had been really quiet; the snow had settled so we must have only had about twenty people in the nightclub. Anyway, I went upstairs to check it out, and one of the doormen is talking to this girl who's a bit of a rocker at the top of the stairs; the doorman tells me she's after a job as a stripper and the next thing you know she got her boobs out, *'shy girl'* I was thinking to myself as I walk off shaking my head chuckling.

Ten minutes or so later someone tells me that the doorman has disappeared into the toilets with this tart. So, we bang on the door and wait at the end of the corridor; the doorman walks out like he's some sort of king doing himself up while walking towards us smiling from ear-to-ear. He then goes to take a sip of his lager when one of the other doormen shouted, 'what the fuck is that running down ya' can of lager?' The man turn's the can wipes it off and carries on drinking it while we are all gagging and laughing – without the need for me to get to verbally graphic, I'm sure you can use your own imagination.

Another time the owner had asked me if I'd go into the nightclub an hour early before for a hen do, apparently, they had ordered a stripper, and we know how rowdy that can get. So, there are all these drunken women waiting for some sort of gratification, at which point the stripper calls in and cancels the gig. Now, I can't remember if the girl was a lesbian or not, but next the thing you know all of her friends have her sat in a chair as the music start's to play. The manageress at the time was a nice woman, but totally crazy, and suddenly she starts to strip with everyone cheering her on. Let me tell you, this is no half-hearted show, this is the full fucking work's, it was so graphic that in the end, the owner of the pub had to step up and put a stop to it. There's me shouting, 'that's enough!' while trying to wrap a coat around her "scantily-clad" torso; fortunately, she got dressed and went about her business as if nothing had happened.

Later that night, as we were drawing to a close, the Beast I and are bored leaning on this balcony. This tall young boy comes up to Beast, and he's blowing him kisses, winding him up. Beast ignores him, so he makes his way over to me, saying things like, 'ooh, you're a big boy, I bet ya' good in bed!' And a load of other stuff. With that, Beast step's in and said to him, 'listen now mate, I'm warning you, don't wind him up!' All the while I'm stood thinking to myself, we're closing in five minutes, what is this man's problem. I then stand up from leaning, and he gets in my face, at which point I thought it was a setup, but I'd finally had enough and slapped him to the floor, dragging him down the stairs where the other doormen took him off me. Things take a turn for the worse because just then he started asking to see the boss 'cos he wants me sacked. On looking at the CCTV you could clearly see he had provoked us, and my job stayed.

Around this time there was a documentary company from London filming my life on the door's and also my involvement in a wrestling promotion, and they also ask for permission from the Vulcan to film, which it was granted. I told them on the day, 'I hope you aren't disappointed, 'cos it's not every night we get trouble in here.' Nevertheless, they were happy enough to have a pint and simply tag along with their cameras in tow and on red alert. Also, that night there had been a fighting event in our town, so a few of the locals were under the illusion that they were some sort of fighters. Anyway, I'm on the door, and it's gone off upstairs, and without giving the camera people a thought, I ran up there to do my job.

When I got up there it was complete mayhem, and all these people who had been to the show are fighting, so I grab hold of this stocky man who had just knocked another big man out, he's screaming and hollering saying, 'I'll walk out Shirl!' With that, I grabbed these other two men with Warren and try and drag them down the stairs. We manage to get them out then suddenly one of the prick's tries biting me, so I've smashed him a few times in his face, splitting him wide open; he's hanging onto me, ripping my radio and shirt off me in the process, but we finally get him through the outside gates. Warren's then smashes this other one, and it's complete chaos; the whole of the outside street looks like a scene from the Wild West. Fortunately, the police turn up and arrest a few of these lunatic wannabe's. I go off and grab a t-shirt from behind the bar and go back to working at the club door as usual. In the mayhem, I'd forgotten about the Film crew, who had, unbeknown to me managed to get a lot of it on film; it was pure gold to them for the documentary. Most of the clip's made the final edit, however, no channel picked it up to run it for TV. Apparently, BBC Wales wanted to run it, but they wanted to shorten the whole thing by twenty minutes, the film maker's refused, so it still lies in some draw somewhere today. One of the filmmakers moved to Australia, and I recently found out that the other Chris passed away. I was gutted on hearing this news, and I hope one day they do manage to release it as he was quite proud of the finished product.

Then one night another door team came to the Vulcan and asked the owner if they could put a bid in to take over the running of it. They wanted me and Beast to stay on and also work for them elsewhere if they got the contract. The owner refused, and said she was happy enough with how it was, however, not long after she began getting problem's with some of our door staff week in, week out and had to get rid of them; I couldn't blame her 'cos some of them were getting drunk on the job, and I was fed up of covering for them.

Then one weekend she wasn't happy with another of our doorman and a few days later she ring's me up to tell me, now she didn't know I was getting married that day so you can imagine I had a lot on my mind. Anyway, there I was in my suit and tie, and she's moaning about this and moaning about that, and in the end, I just tell her to go forth and multiply, and I slammed the phone down on her. My boss then rang me later, and say's we have lost the contract and the new firm was in there two days later. I really had a fuck full of the place anyway so coming back from my honeymoon in Rome I was out of a job, but I knew as soon as I advertised, I'd be back in the game.

CHAPTER SEVENTEEN

(Wannabe a Gangster)

Over the years, working on the doors some of the boy's had lent me a video of the Guvnor, Lenny Mclean, and I started studying him, and all these other characters from the London underworld. Then, my mate Julian started an internet page dedicated to the unlicensed boxing scene, and I started a Lenny Mclean page to run parallel. The underworld scene had really taken off, and the books of the same were coming out almost weekly from a glut of colourful characters. Soon after, Julian decided to write a book called 'Streetfighters', and I travelled all around the UK, meeting all these different people while he interviewed them.

Over time my interest grew, and I started collecting stories for my Lenny website and thought maybe I could write a book one day: another tick for my bucket list. I was also in touch with people who ran the Roy Shaw webpage and the "yellow pages" of crime, Dave Courtney, and at the time there was nothing like this out there on the internet. Unlike today when every fucker has a webpage.

At the time Dave Courtney was big news; he had recently had his first book out and was appearing everywhere, and I was interested 'cos I'd seen a photo of him and Lenny McLean in his book. I managed to get hold of his number and so now I was walking around thinking I was some sort of gangster. I finally built up enough courage to ring Dave and ask him if he had any more pictures of Lenny for the website. Next thing I know he's offering us up to his house (Camelot Castle) the following week. So, I, Julian and my brother Steve made our way up to London to find Courtney's house; he met us and took us straight out for breakfast; it felt like he'd known us year's. Now there's a lot of mixed comments on Courtney, but I can only speak as I find, suffice to say, every time I met him; he was always great to me.

We spent a few hour's in Dave's house, I was going through thousands of pictures looking for Lenny ones in his kitchen. Dave's misses at the time was cooking food, and some man walks in, it turns out it was the television license man, and Dave has shouted for him to come on in, Courtney's laughing his head off and his misses his attacking him screaming abuse, I'm just sitting there, and Julian comes in and says, c'mon Ant, we are off!' I didn't give a fuck because I wanted pictures and Julian repeated it, so we left in case thing's got messy. This was the first of many experiences into the London underworld scene, I was striving on it and couldn't wait to see what happened next. The following month there was a big show in Gloucester at the Crime through time museum, with a show in the evening that Dave was yet again the star of.

When it came to the auction Dave pulls out this knuckle duster which had apparently been used in the past; me being young and dumb got into a bidding war, and I ended up winning it for £150, and I thought eh, now I'm a proper gangster, 'cos I've got Dave Courtney's Knuckleduster. I didn't mind about the money because it was for charity but travelling back in the car, I noticed the thing was so big it would fall off your hand - and as anybody would tell you, I have big fucking hand's. If Courtney had used that in the past, he must have had a pair of MMA gloves under it to keep it on, anyway, I thought, who gives a shit, at least I could tell everyone I had his duster, I laugh about it now as it was over 15 years ago, and it never got used anyway, it just sits in a draw in my house.

Hundred and fifty quid's worth of fucking "paperweight!"

I contacted another man on the internet who apparently met Lenny: his name was Billy Cribb, otherwise known as "The Tarmac Warrior." Over a few conversations, it was clear to see that me, him and Julian got on exceptionally well. Now Billy had been involved and appeared in a documentary called, Bare Fist which also featured Lenny, and he was also involved in a new Channel 4 Documentary about fighting. They'd not long wrapped the project up, and a premiere party was held in some club in London. Billy couldn't make it, so he asked Julian and me if we wanted to go instead. And due to the fact that Roy Shaw was one of the stars of the documentary, and we both wanted to meet him, so we travelled up.

So, we got to this venue and would you believe it, Billy had only forgotten to put our names on the fucking list. With that in all our 'suited and booted' finery, the two of us are now walking away gutted, not happy, until Julian said, 'Right, let's give it half hour… we are early anyway…'
And swiftly comes up with a plan that he's some big-time journalist reporter, and I'm his bodyguard.

As we arrived back, we could see that a different doorman was minding the place, so we went up quick, and on our approach, we spotted Roy Shaw and a few other's walking in; the doorman was all over Roy, distracted so we walked past and make our way quickly up the stairs. At this point, I

243

was shitting myself thinking we were going to get thrown out and with that, Julian headed straight over to the free bar with me in his wake.

The room was full of these celebrity's and Julian got straight onto Nosher Powell and started chatting like they were the best of mates. Julian shout's to me, 'Ant, can you get Nosher and his wife a drink while you're up there?' The cheek of him, I was ready to burst out laughing and goes for the drink like the excellent servant he thinks I am.' Now, like I said it's a free bar so every time I'm up there, I'm having one and then taking another back with me, doubling up and slowly getting pissed. I turned to Julian and said, 'I've got to take this leather jacket off!' He grabbed me by the arm and said, 'don't you dare, you look huge in it, and you're my bodyguard.' But from the weight of the coat sweat was pouring down my back from the heat.

Throughout the night we had started chatting to all these people like Joey Pyle Senior (the man who started the Unlicensed boxing game) who reckoned I looked a bit like Lenny, and we also got round to talking to Roy. I'd mentioned that I run a Lenny page and managed to get a few numbers off them for an interview in the future.

Towards the end of the night I was hammered (drunk,) and god knows what I'd said to Roy Shaw, but I'm guessing it was to do with Lenny 'cos Julian's says, 'c'mon Ant, we are off!' And after seeing the pictures the next day it dawned on me that I'd argued with Roy about Len, but me being drunk meant that I didn't give a fuck.

A few months later Julian ended up taking over the Roy Shaw Page, and we popped round to his house. A funny story: I remember Julian was in this swivel chair looking at the pc screen, and Roy's telling him stuff what to do in a fight. Roy's then starts getting a bit worked up as he's shadowboxing explaining to Julian, so Julian swivel's round fast in the chair to witness Roy, who I don't think was wearing any pants under his tracksuit, so this thing (that a Grand National Winner would be proud of) is swinging about and nearly takes Julian's eye out. With that Julian then says, 'fucking hell Roy, you should have hit Lenny with that thing; you would have knocked him spark out!' Roy saw the funny side of it and was laughing his head off. I got to meet Roy quite a few times on my travels to London, and he was always a proper gentleman. And although I was running a page about Roy's archenemy, Lenny Mclean, Roy hardly brought it up and spoke quite highly of Lenny when his name was mentioned.

Another time we went to his house, and he had two Rottweiler's the same as mine back home. So, I went over, and I'm stroking one of them, while Roy was wrestling the other one like a bear.

I went onto meet a lot of the UK Hardmen, and most of them ended up having a book written about themselves. Many people like, Decca Simpkin, Tyneside's, Richard Horsley and Teesside's fist fighting "Taxman," Brian Cockerill. Oh, and not to forget the late Bartley Gorman King of the Gypsies. Bartley had a lot of time for Julian and me, and once Julian had interviewed him, he took us out for food. Julian mentioned I was boxing at the time and he jumped up and said: 'c'mon Ant, let's have a spar?' I've gone all shy, while Julian's laughing his head off. With that, he got me up and was showing me how to go into a stance and move around; I didn't have the heart to tell him I knew what I was doing, so just smiled along with him. Nevertheless, it was a nice moment, and not many can say they've shaped up and moved about a bit with a legendary "King of the Gypsies." After the success of Bartley's story in Julian's book, Bartley went on to have his own life-story written before he died, much like Lenny, Bartley never lived to realise the success of his book.

Another big name which you'd think wouldn't need looking after was the late gangster Charlie Richardson. Not to mention, another well-known figure from up North, George Craig. Now, at the time I'd become friends with a man named Jimmy Andrew's, and I had also helped him write some of his book when he was down in Wales staying with us for a few weeks. Jimmy had put a charity night on up north somewhere, and we were invited as his guests. Jimmy had booked us into a lovely place for the night and after all of us having a meal we had a limousine booked to take us to the venue. There I was sitting in this limo pouring Charlie R and his lovely wife, Veronica champagne with my mates Bernard and Brendan. Arriving at the venue, we quickly realised that it was a dive of a place; it looked like a rough shithole. They had this big doorman there who knew Jimmy, but he was on the front door most of the night. Even though we were drinking, Jimmy asked me to keep an eye on Charlie at all times because there might be some disrespectful idiots out trying to make a name for themselves.

The snooker player, Willy Thorne was the highlight of the evening, and then it was announced that Charlie was in the building, and quite a few people came down to have pictures and a chat with him. However, as soon as that had finished, Charlie, his wife and George said we have had enough, and we are going back to the hotel. So, we saw them to their limo, safe in the knowledge that they were safe before heading back.

I met Charlie R various times after that, at show's in London etc; he even gave me his phone number and did a good interview about Lenny Mclean for my first book: 'The Guv'nor, Through the eyes of other's.'

I also got to know Charlies two sons and one of them, Lee, even did a bit for my first book too. Jimmy had some film maker's doing a trailer for a film called One-armed Bandits up North, and me and my boss Bernard was invited up to play 2 of Jimmy's henchmen. Now, here's the exciting part, Charlies two sons were to play his real-life rival's the Kray Twins in the movie, and all the papers were extremely interested in it. The trailer was sorted but no more came of it, because apparently, no one would invest in a full film which was such a shame as I was going to have a part in it. Jimmy had also taken Charlie on in a business deal selling tube-shot drinks. They were big news at the time, so Bernard and I took a few pallets off them and had them delivered down to wales. We were supposed to have sold the drinks cheaper so we would have to order more, but we sold the lot in 2 weeks flat, made a quick buck, and then decided it was too much trouble travelling them around.

Jimmy helped me get some useful contacts for a new Lenny Book I was writing and done a good write up himself. Jimmy would spend a lot of time back and forth to Wales, and we got on really well, but he was suffering a few illnesses including Bi-Polar, which made things a little fraught.

One-night Jimmy had put me in touch with this man named Billy Martindale, a right head banger who had a book out but wasn't happy with it. So, I'm chatting with Billy and having a good laugh then he asked me if I'd write his new book. I spoke to Jimmy about it and made a joke about something and Jimmy mentioned it to Billy. Next thing I know Billy's making threats to me, but I just didn't have a clue what he was on about. When he finally came up for air, I thought, right son, now it's my turn. So, I'm walking around my garden screaming and hollering down the phone and Billy goes all quiet and immediately apologised. We amicably sorted out the indifferences, but he then had the hump with, Jimmy. Strangely enough, within the next month, Billy was murdered with a pickaxe handle and died of head injuries. It was mad to think I'd only been speaking with him a few weeks earlier.

Not long after Jimmy asked if I would help finish his book. He said it was almost halfway done and so we began working on it for a few months. I finally got it wrapped up, and we got to the stage where my mate Julian was going to edit it, and Jimmy and Julian were talking over the phone. Next thing I know Jimmy's accusing me of taking things out of his book, but if the truth be known he was so off his face when I interviewed him; he hadn't even told me any of the stuff. I bit back at him, but even though he apologised, I no longer wanted anything to do with it, which was a shame because it was a good book and I had worked hard on it. Also, we had a publisher waiting as well. A few years later, he started speaking to me again and started advertising on social media that the book was going to be coming out soon. However, as quick as he appeared, he promptly disappeared off the face of the earth. To this day, I still don't know if the book was ever released.

I started speaking to a man online who had bought an unlicensed boxing video from me. Over the course of the next few months, and after building a friendship, he decided to inform me that he was accused of being a mafia hitman and had been pulled in by the police. Now, to be honest, I found this quite funny, I mean c'mon, a mafia hitman talking to a man from sunny Wales, 'well you just couldn't write this stuff.' Anyway, we continued to chat, and it was extremely interesting because he told me some dark stuff about the London Underworld that could never be printed in a book, 'well not if you like ya' kneecaps.'

Then one day he messaged me and told me that he'd found a copy of the ITV documentary on this Italian mafia family which he had appeared in, and the very next day I received a copy in the post from him, which I slipped it into the video recorder and sat goggle-eyed waiting for his appearance. Just a few minutes into the video, low and behold there he was, true to his word, as large as life on my TV screen. Now, for me, this was on another level, and for the next year, we talked constantly, and he even asked me to write his book sometime in the future. One day I happened to mention to him that I was up in his neck of the wood's interviewing for my new Lenny Mclean book, and immediately he asked if we could meet up. So, I travelled up with my mate Bernard and met him at a service station, the reason for this "rendezvous" was that he didn't want us near his house 'cos he was always under surveillance. With the meet underway, we sat down and ordered food and then spent the next 4 hours listening to his exciting stories; it was an incredibly surreal moment. After our meet, we said our goodbyes and went our separate ways but continued to chat for some time to come. Unfortunately, after a few years, we lost touch - I never did get that book out.

Around this time, I was writing to the notorious prison inmate, Charles Bronson. I'd send him papers and stuff, and he even managed to do a write up for my Lenny book. I was in regular contact and was also invited to his wedding in London; obviously, he wasn't there, but the reception was held in one of Dave Cortney's pub's, and the place resembled a 'who's, who' of the London underworld. Who would have ever thought that 15 years later I'd still be involved in this scene? And here I am today with my new writing partner, Lee Wortley doing an interview with Bronson's new wife Paula for our Gangland Podcast show. Not to mention the fact that the two of us even received invite's to the wedding reception, but due to work and Lee's other commitments, unfortunately we couldn't make it.

While on the subject of Bronson here's a funny little story. My mate Julian was also speaking to Bronson, and a conversation came around that Bronson wanted flowers delivered to his mother's house on mother's day. So, Bronson's agent was talking to Julian and mentioned it and Julian (presuming the address she was living wasn't far from us) arranged with her to deliver them. I pick him up, and he pulls the address out then I said, 'are you fucking real, this is Aberystwyth? It's North Wales, you nutter!' Julian goes, 'oops! I just saw the Aber part and thought it was Abergavenny, 'which was 25mins away'. We arrived a few hours later, and there was no one there, so we waited in the car and soon after she came back home from her trip. It was worth the journey just to see the surprise on her face;

with an added bonus of her on the phone to Bronson while he was shouting out thanking us.

I was also asked to appear in two new book's that were in the process of being written. One was called bouncer's, by Julian Davies and Tel Curry and also Tel had teamed up with Bronson to write a new book called Heroes and Villains, and I was to feature in that. I had quite a few story's and Pictures in Bouncer's and my picture and story even made it into Bronson's book, where I was identified as, Big Tony Thomas. Also, at the time 'FRONT MAGAZINE' wanted to do a spread on the Bouncing book, so Julian arranged for them to come to Merthyr on a night out. Me and a few other's booked a night off and gave the reporters a bit of an eye- opener. Furthermore, my photographs thankfully made it into the finished article.

I continued to work on my Lenny site, which got more prominent by the day. Until one day it got hacked, I lost everything, and it was back to square one. By now, I was flat out back and forth to London on my own doing interviews. I got in touch with a man called Stilks who had had his own book out and knew Lenny. Stilks had been interviewed for my mate Julian's book a few years before, and I'd always kept in touch with another doorman named Max who was Stilk's mate. Then after speaking to Stilks he offered me to stay in one of his flats for a few days, and he would line up interviews for me, and I could also work the doors for him and earn a few quid into the bargain.

Now, I'd heard of all these gangster stories of shooting's and attempted hit's, so I'll be honest I was a little nervous, but it was time to leave the Valley's behind and head up the M4 to London. Silk's was a genuine man and helped me no end for the next few days; running me around for interview after interview. I was put in this venue with this other man names Lenny and the night had been a bit quiet, so Stilk's picked me up, and we went to this new venue full of pool tables that Stilks had boy's minding. So, we sat down with these two big doormen and ordered food. Then, halfway through the meal, it went off over by one of the pool tables; the two men I was sat with ran in, so I went to go with them, and Stilk's shouted at me, 'stay there and don't move!' Now, I don't know if he thought I wasn't up for the job or something because I was his guest, but by fucked am I some man who just watches what goes on, so I ran over to give them a hand. There was a lot of commotion, and people were getting dragged downstairs, and I didn't have to do anything, but at least I knew that I had their backs. We then go back and eat our food, and Stilk's said, 'I told you to stay there Ant?' I laughed it off and said not a chance mate.

The following day Stilk's took me round to Dave Courtney's house; he had a quick cuppa with Dave, and then he arranged to pick me back up a few hours later after I'd finished the interview. Courtney did a brilliant interview, and his misses made me some food before I left. I was back in the pub that evening, and it was a lot busier but no trouble whatsoever. At the end of the night, we went on the piss up this big long stretch of pubs with a nightclub at the end. Every pub we went to the doormen were all over Stilks, and the free entry and drinks was a bonus. I drank a good drop but made sure I kept my bearings – I didn't need another Roy Shaw scenario. I met Stilk's a few times after that until I heard that he'd moved to Cyprus and we lost touch. 'By this stage in my life, my little black book was turning into a "who's-who" of the London scene, and all of them had a lot of time for me when I asked them for interview's.'

Another funny one was when I met Joey Pyle, who turned up with this man who was his bodyguard. We went for a bit of food and drink, and then I slipped my Dictaphone on asking him questions. We were going through London, and Joey ring's some number to pay the toll, and he's reading his credit card detail's out over the phone, and with that, the man with him said to me, 'you're not taping, are you? Can you please knock it off,' I apologised and made a joke saying, 'would I be that stupid to give his credit card details away?'

This other time Frankie Fraser was advertising bus tour's around London while telling stories about his life. I managed to get his phone number off him, and we started chatting every night. A few days later, I booked for four of us to go on the tour, and the money was paid. Now apparently it was a 10-seater bus, and then my other 2 mates' wanted to go, I managed to get them in on the tour, but Frank said I would have to pay another £40 on the day because he had to upgrade the bus. Now, I knew this was bullshit and probably one of his scams, but I went ahead with it, to avoid letting anyone down. We arrived on the day and got booked into our hotel, jump on the tube and make our way to where the tours depart from. Now, I could see this was the same bus he always used, and there wasn't no upgrade. We went on the trip and ended up in the 'Blind Beggar' having a drink, and a chat, and then the tour finished, and we were supposed to go back to a pub. Now, call me tight, but no way was I going to be tucked up for £40, so the others and I shook his hand and headed back to the tube. We then all went out in the night, and Frankie kept ringing me and leaving messages about the money. My boss who I'd gone up with was now buying us all £100 bottles of champagne in this nightclub, and I was hammered. I finally answered, and Frank says, 'I want my money' now I'm not one for threat's and says, 'well come and get it, I'm in the West End somewhere,' and I hung up on him laughing.

The following day I had messages again off him until he finally gave up. My mates would say 'you can't tuck Frankie Fraser up Ant,' but only one person was being tucked up, and that was us.

Now, one name that would always come up in my town and put fear into most people was Malcolm Price. Pricey was a legendary street fighter and well-known around Britain. I'd seen him about in pubs but always stayed well clear of him. One day when Julian was writing his book Street fighters, I went along with him to his house and to my amazement he was one of the nicest men you could ever meet, much so, that we all become friends.

After appearing in Julian's book, Julian went on to put Malcolm in touch with another author, and from this link-up, Malcolm's life story was written and later, published. I've got to tell you about how we first met though.

Picture this…

We knocked on his door, his wife answered and invited us in, we shook hands and Malcom said, 'sit down lads.' so I've gone and planted myself next to him in this plastic chair. Next thing you know the legs have snapped and I'm down like a dyeing fly on my back; well I didn't know what the fuck to do or say, and Julian was crying, laughing while the toughest streetfighter around was trying to pull me back up. I think it broke the ice, which was the start of many visits, and cups of tea in the future. In the background on this journey, I came across many hurdles; firstly, I was told that I couldn't write a book on Lenny Mclean. Peter Gerrard who had done the Guvnor, had teamed up with this film producer, and both were threatening me with court action. Peter also told me that Lenny's wife, Val didn't want a book out and I'd later find out he hadn't even told her. I'd been working on this book for over a year by now, and no way was I stopping. I was then accused of making money off Lenny's name, so I said to Gerrard to prove I wasn't, that anything my book makes, he must match it, and we give the money to charity, I heard no more on the subject on that one. After various chat's to Len's wife she was now on board, so she was sent a manuscript, then all of a sudden Len's son ring's me up ranting and raving that he doesn't want a book out, I could see where he was coming from and offered to take a few things out and put different stuff in but he wasn't happy. Thing's finally calmed down, and I then went to London to meet his son, we shook hands, and nothing was mentioned about the telephone call.

A few months later the book came out in hardback and I'd finally done it and proved to people I was no pushover. Id later on in life go onto to do another book about Lenny called the Guvnor Revealed with Lee Wortley which went on to become a number one best-seller on Amazon for many months.

I was also offered once to go in some land rover and just look the part with these four other men, It was a nice pick up but I knew it was all about drug's and it just wasn't for me, I thought if I get a taste for that fuck knows where it could end up, so I turned the man down nicely.

As I got older, I no longer felt the need to be a gangster; I'd met everyone from the land rover runner's to the Mafia Hitmen and learned a lot and made many friends. I was still interested in that scene and stay involved in writing book's, starting a Gangland Podcast Program on YouTube with Lee Wortley, but that was it for me.

CHAPTER 18

(The Bodyguard)

Whilst bouncing I'd always fancied having a go at body guarding but the courses cost a few grand and there wasn't much call for it locally. I saw a few stars appear at nightclubs before I started bouncing and I noticed the way the bouncer's looked after them and thought I'd love a go at that, but in my eyes, it was just a dream at the time. Then one day Bernard, my boss rang me up and said: 'A job has come in Shirl, do you fancy doing a bit of body guarding for me?' So, I said, 'Yeah, book me in for it Bernard.'

'So, I'm thinking, I wonder who the star is, and where is it ect… until Bernard enlightened me.'

Turns out it's on a farm in Abergavenny and the owner of the farm has split with her psycho boyfriend and they can't get him off the land until it's gone through court. Apparently, he was living in a caravan a few yards from the house and was being a bit of a nuisance. So, I was booked in for the second day after Lee Callaghan had done the first day. Anyway, at 5.30 in the morning I was driven over there to take over from Lee at 6. I'm now out in the middle of nowhere, no mobile phone's work with some nutter from one flew over the cuckoo's nest with a mood on. I've got my diary noting everything the man gets up to, jotting notes down in the bedroom in darkness watching this nutter come out of his caravan. All of a sudden because he knows I'm watching him he turned a massive set of spotlights onto the house. He then start's doing exercises in his boxer shorts, running up and down the field at the back. He briefly, disappeared from sight; we know he was close to the house and it was starting to feel like a scene from a horror movie. The woman's starts saying to me: 'He's trying to break in! He wants to kill me!' So, I'm doing my best to calm her down. And if I'm honest my arse is going a bit as well.

Not long after that I heard a gun blast, which must have been a 12-bore shotgun, and now the arse is really twitching, 'cos I can't see this lunatic from any of the windows. I could not wait for daylight to appear. The woman had to leave in the car at nine, so I saw her to her car, and that's her gone for the day. It's just me, the nutter, and his sawn-off – cheers Bernard!

So, around dinner time I could hear a noise; he'd only reversed a jeep into the backdoor so that no one can get out of it. Then about ten minutes later I hear another noise and I run into this room and his head is poking in through this window; he's opened it with a screwdriver - so abruptly I said, 'what the fuck are you doing?' and he replied, 'I want my shoes?' So, I throw's the shoes at him and demanded, 'right, don't come near here again!' And off he trotted, quietly. I finished the shift and was glad to get home, obviously I put the wind up the new guard before I went – boys will be boys eh? Fortunately for me, I never had to go back there because two days later he was arrested when he'd tried to drive the woman off the road, and because of this she finally got her injunction letter from the courts, and he was ordered away from the property.

Not long after The Kooler's had signed a contract that would see celebrity's appearing at the club every Friday night upstairs. Bernard, myself and Beast were to meet them and guard them throughout and then escort them back to their vehicles. A few singer's such as, Kym Mazelle,

Chico Slimani (who my writer pal Lee interviewed for one of our Lenny McLean books) and many more appeared. I now felt like I was a proper bodyguard.

One night we had Lee Ryan from the boy band Blue who is currently appearing in EastEnders. We met him in a car park and brought him in through the downstairs.' I can't remember now if another band member was with him, but there was two of them that night. Now Bernard had told me if there was any fighting in crowd to ignore it and leave the other doormen sort it, and to just get any celebrity straight down the back stairs into safety. Now up until now we had never had any trouble and it would always be packed. So I'm in front of Lee walking him on and Beast his behind him. We get onto the stage and about 8 doormen are positioned all around him. They play a song and I could see it wasn't everyone cup of tea has some are booing. Sean Jay the DJ then start's asking Lee question's on his mic and about a minute in I could see this full can come out of the darkness heading straight for Lee's head, the doorman little Ray had seen it and jumped in front of Lee taking the full smash of the can; the drink's gone all over us and me and Beast have covered Lee like a turtle shell. A few doormen have run to where he came from, Ray part's the crowd for me while Beast to get him out. We got him out in second's and back downstairs, he looked shook up and then the owner Vicki came and couldn't stop apologising, him and his mate didn't say much and left ten minutes later after me and Beast took them to their car, nice little pay day for him even though he was cut short.

Talking about EastEnders, we had quite a few of them down one month including, Bill Murray who played Johnny Allen; after telling him that I was writing books about Lenny Mclean we had a good chat about the London underworld. Johnny went down really well with the crowd with all of his underworld and Kray Stories. Not long after we had Louisa Lytton, who played Johnny's 'on-screen' daughter Ruby Allen, who today is back in the show. She was a top girl and after her appearance she stayed on with a few others who had travelled up with her, so me and Beast stayed with them and kept a close eye.

One Friday night we had Dean Gaffney who play's Robbie in EastEnders; Dean finished his Q&A and we then took him back downstairs. Now, after these stars had appeared upstairs the public could queue up downstairs to have a picture with them and maybe a quick chat and an autograph. Robbie was downstairs waiting and just two people turn up for a pic, which was a little embarrassing. The owner thanked him and paid him then Robbie enquired, 'Is it ok if I hang about and have a drink?' The owner looked a bit worried and asks me and Beast to stay with him right up until he has had enough and wants to leave. Robbie ended up staying over two hours' with hundreds of people asking for a picture with him. To be honest, I think earlier on, no one knew he was downstairs, and so didn't bother going down. The night was quite surreal, and by the time he was leaving we were all on first name terms. And when we put him in his car, he just couldn't stop thanking me and Beast for looking after him.

The celebrities continued to appear including: Abby Titmus, Fran Cosgrove, Dale Smith from the Bill; Michael Greco from EastEnders; Ben freeman from Emmerdale and Ziggy from Big Brother. Will Mellor from 2 pints of lager and a Packet of crisps also made an appearance and Wendi

Peters from Coronation Street came too. And through all of these engagements we had no trouble whatsoever.

One Friday night two porn star's Cathy Barry and Michelle Thorne were doing an appearance. Michele hadn't long been on X Factor and came to sing her new single. What people didn't know was Michelle was three months' pregnant, and her boyfriend and personal minder was with her. Me and the other doorman Warren were big fans of the girls; I mean we had heard these names around, that's about all, 'yeah-yeah,' I hear you saying. But joking apart, it was a good chance for us to grab a picture in their dressing room before the show. After the introductions we took them up onto the stage alongside Sean's DJ Booth, Cathy Barry went on stage first, and she did her bit of a show while Sean asked her questions. It was all going well until they announce Michelle Thorne on to the stage, and as she was walking on stage some drunk from the crowd booted her up the arse, fucking about. With that her boyfriend stepped in and pushed the boy, but he retaliated and hit the "Minder" boyfriend.

Now, I was on the opposite side standing by Cathy, so the doormen have rushed the boy and dragged him out. I immediately got hold of Cathy and take her and Michelle back downstairs, and that was yet another show cut short; although the owner apologised and still paid her for the appearance. The boyfriend was downstairs, and he wasn't a happy chap, so to make sure there's no more trouble we take them out through the side door back to their vehicles in the car park. The "Booter-boy" ended up with a life ban for being an idiot.

Soon after, the act's finished in the club. I'd hazard a guess that it was to do with the two incidents as, they were all booked through the same agent. Mind you, later on, we did have some strange acts in which weren't so famous on a Sunday night, from fire breather's to half naked stilt walkers, not to mention, midget's doing trick's. I started following my mate Jolly's band and I also knew the singer Marcus from the boxing gym. The Band Foreign Legion had been going for over 25 years and had a good following; I'd follow them all over the country standing at the side of stage just in case there was any trouble. Very rarely did I have to have a word with someone or get them off the stage, and I even travelled as far has Germany with them which was a right eye opener. One night after a gig in Germany I'd gone back to my room and was just nodding off when the door came flying open and Marcus was stood there with a balaclava on and a gun in his hand screaming 'give us your money?' It was quite scary for a few seconds, but obviously I found the funny side of it.

My next big security job was down in the Morfa Stadium in Swansea where the singer Pink was head lining. I got asked by my mate if I wanted to work security, it was a good pay day and I was hoping I'd at least see her perform; however, as there were hundreds of security men there that day, I didn't hold my breath. I was working for one firm and there was about 20 of us on the firm. We all get briefed and this man started picking people for different positions in the venue. First came "the pit" which was situated at the front of the stage, 'fuck, I'll have some of that!' I thought to myself as my hand hastily went up. Anyway, he picked about ten men including my two mates, Jolly and his brother Martin, and I'm left "stuck on the bench." It gets down to me and another man left in hope, then we're told that they want us backstage in the VIP section at the side of stage. So, there I am, with an amazing view, being paid to watch a superstar. Then I get told by the man from the "snatch squad" who I'm working for that even if there was a fight a few feet away I'm not to leave my post. The amount of people who tried getting backstage to the VIP area was unbelievable, 'I'm a singer...' 'I'm on TV...' You name it, we heard it... But unless they had a neckband on, I was having none of it. About 30 minutes left into Pink's performance the other security man said to me, 'fancy a change?' So, there I was on stage behind the curtain a few feet from Pink as she's performing; now and again she would run behind the curtain to do a costume change, while I'd be laughing and joking with her crew.

Looking back this was one of the highlights of my security career; a few feet away from this famous American singer, scanning my eyes everywhere, with fifty thousand fans' looking back at her. It was another surreal moment in my life, and to top it off at the end of the gig she passed me, smiled, and said 'thanks!' with a big American, Rock star high-five – I was an extremely happy man.

Then one day a funny job came in with my boss Bernard, and me and Neil (Beast) were chosen for it. Now, not only was we looking after a certain person, we were also looking after their equipment as well, and we had to guard with our life. It was at a 'Masonic lodge' centenary do, and people were coming from all over Wales for it, and some extremely powerful people to boot.

I wasn't available in the day and was there just for the night, but Neil had to go with Bernard and Pick this Belt up worth a lot of money, as well as other stuff. We were told that our priority was to watch the stuff and make sure it was back away and on its way to its destination, safe after they had finished. We also weren't allowed to go into the halls when they done whatever it was, they were doing, and I was quite surprised when people we knew walked in dressed up. They finished, and me and Neil collected the stuff up, gave it to Bernard so that he could take it all back. It was quite an interesting night and me and Neil would wind a few up throughout night. I said to Bernard the next day laughing, 'Bern, are you sure you're not in the Mason's?' because a few times in the past, I'd gotten off with stuff that I'd been in bother for when it looked like it was about to go pear-shaped – Bernard never admitted or denied it.

The following year I was contacted by my mate Lyn who was one of the organisers of the Merthyr Rising festival. What had started out as a few bands and speakers was now getting bigger by the year, and they were upping their game. The stages and bands were getting bigger, with more guests coming to every event and it was growing fast. In the first year no doorman were employed, but by this time they required at least six doormen – so you can see how it was escalating. The event was to start at 12pm, and the organisers had booked the controversial British politician, George Galloway to do a talk at about 3pm at the 'Soar chapel' which was just up the street from the actual event.

Now one thing I've never been into is politics…' I have no interest in it whatsoever, all I knew of him was that he was the man who had appeared on Big Brother with the beard playing a silly cat. So, the day before the event I received a phone call from Lyn and he says, Right, I need you and another man to bodyguard George Galloway! We're expecting trouble from the National Front and I want the pair of you with him at all times.' By this time the police had been made aware of the threat of the National Front coming, and the whole event was the talk of the town.

So, I arrived on the day and had a little team talk with the boys who were working for me. At the time we had taken on this new "up and coming" doorman named, Kevin who was about 6ft 7inches tall, the sheer size of him would have scared many a man I'm sure. We also had our obligatory "loose cannon" Warren turn up saying, 'when they come, shall we just smash into them and get it over and done with Shirl?' This was Warren's answer to everything and being a Cardiff City supporter he wasn't shy of the odd few rumbles on the terraces. I was then told that the NF were already there and were sitting in Witherspoon's, so me and the team made a beeline for them, we walked straight over to the window staring at them to make our presence known, letting them know that we didn't give a fuck for them. Turns out there was only about twenty-five of them altogether, but my first thought was that we were outnumbered but after putting the boy's in their position's and walking round talking to people I knew that some of the other tough blokes who I knew would jump in and help, and this was confirmed when they started saying, 'who the fuck do they think they are, any trouble, and us lot are behind you boy's all the way.' So, within half an hour I'd assembled a little army, who were all up for a battle.

Then came 2 o clock...

I took a boy named Jason with me (Tomo) who was ex-army and a brilliant boxer, and we made our way up to the Soar chapel. When we got there the two of us had a good look round and all seemed ok, then we were radioed up to the other doorman who kept an eye on the NF's movements. Suddenly, it came over the radio that there was about 10 of them making their way up to the venue. Now, the venue was off the high street and had big open gates that lead up to the venue, so me and Tomo ran down to these gates and as I'm slamming them shut and bolting the gate, they walk up to us and say, 'Alright lad's, where do we get a ticket for the talk?' Anyway, I turn to them laughing and said, 'Do you honestly think your lot are going to get in here?' I'm laughing at them like a psycho when one of them said, 'I know you, your Shirly, I wouldn't fuck with him lads...' I honestly didn't have a clue who he was but I for the obvious reasons I played on it. Moments later, they started laughing and walked off knowing they couldn't get in and a few minutes later 2 PCO's were sent to stay with us, and they stayed on the gate while we went and met Galloway. Galloway turned up with his wife and a little baby, we met him at the back entrance then together we travelled up in the lift. The next hour was intense watching everyone's movements, and after he'd finished his talk, he stayed on speaking to everyone, drinking endless cups of tea. There must have been an insider from the "NF" in there, 'cos the split second he was about to leave the whole 25 or more of them left the pub and made a protest line in the car park opposite. However, come this time there were more numbers in police standing directly in front of them. Anyway, we got him to his car safe, and he thanked me and Jason, Jason then apologised, but George replied, 'Listen boys, I'm used to this by now, thank you again boys for looking after us.' And with that off he went with the NF shouting obscenities as he drove by them. As soon as he'd gone the whole lot of them fucked off, not one of them had started trouble. My mate Warren who was bouncing with us goes, 'how the fuck could you bodyguard him, he's a horrible man?' To which I replied, 'Look Bolt, (which is his nickname) we're here to do a job, I don't know fuck all about politics;' our priority was him, his wife and the baby, anyway, he can't be that horrible 'cos he's just given me and Jason £50 for a drink.' Warren looked at me with shock in his face and I strolled off laughing. George hadn't really given us the cash, but hey, the doorman didn't know that.

The following year Roland Gift from the Fine young cannibals was playing at the festival; I was working with a mate of mine Tom, who was running the security at the event, and he and I were on opposite sides of the stage with Roland doing his show in front of us. When leaving, I had to run across and join Tom while we escorted Roland back to where he was staying through the extremely busy crowd of piss heads.

I was also asked to bodyguard the Welsh TV actor Richard Harrington who was also born in the Gurnos and was doing a talk in a local venue. This should be interesting I was thinking to myself, and the place was rammed out on a Saturday afternoon. So, I escorted him in, realising immediately that the talk is only in Welsh, so I'm stood there for the next two hour's pretending to laugh along, with everyone else; without having a fucking clue what he was going on about. Strangely enough, I'd taken Welsh in school but to be truthful, I'd have had more chance learning fucking

Chinese. After the show Richard said to me, 'did you enjoy the show?' I had to own up and tell him that I couldn't speak a word of Welsh. I even told him that I'd laughed along with the crowd, so not to look like an idiot, Richard found it to be quite funny.

A few job's came in regarding boxer's and a few shows were set up in my town to bring boxer's to the ring. It was a good chance to catch up with a few people like Enzo Maccarinelli backstage as I'd gone through the amateur's with them. The unbeaten Joe Calzaghe was also doing a show in the town and we had a good team there protecting him. My main priority was to meet him in the car park and bring him in with his belt's, not taking an eye off him all night until he left. Another sound guy was the great Ricky Hatton, I'd met Ricky year's earlier in his gym up north where he was training for a title fight. Lyn from the Rising festival was doing a gentleman's evening and wanted me and my mate to bodyguard him. So, we turn up and wait in this car park, Ricky turned up with his own bodyguard, so we introduce ourselves and this man just looked at us like, 'what the fuck are these pair going to do?' We then took him up to his changing room and the man start's talking to my mate Warren about football; this broke the ice. He could see Warren was some sort of psycho, but I couldn't be arsed talking to him. Then we had to go into this room where people were drinking, and Ricky was to join them. Now, there was some right character's from our town in there, but fortunately we knew them all. One or two of them started getting a bit rowdy 'cos they'd been drinking all day, but they calmed down a bit after we had a word in their ears.

The rest of the show went brilliant - without a single bit of trouble.

CHAPTER 19

(The Wanderer)

A new club was to open in the town named Play, by a man called Naz. It was going to be the first of its kind with an outside roof balcony. It was officially due to open Black Friday and we were set to mind the door. However, the owner decided to open up a night early, as a test-run thinking it would be a quiet one, but by fuck was he wrong. We had a phone call from our then boss Bernard, asking could we go down and throw a pile of boy's out who were kicking off. As we arrived, we could see that it was rammed full, and I knew quite a few of the faces that were in there. Immediately one of them kicked off with big Payne and the place erupted; we were dragging them down the stairs and they were now outside making threats that they would come back.

The following day a few of them past by with their heads down, and nothing comes of it. We put a few out during the night and for a black Friday it was quiet, until one of the last men started on Payne yet again. Payne was twice the size of this skinny fucker and he was thrown out. Then one night this gang of local boy's kicked off and immediately turned on the doormen. Bald Lyn's got the main one tied up and the others are kicking off, one then rugby tackles me, and I went down about a few stairs when Big Payne's grabbed me and smashes the boy. It was a close call, but we managed to drag them all down the stairs and get them out.

After they have gone Beast noticed his phone and car keys were missing, and looking back on the CCTV, it was quite clear to see who had them. So, come end of night we all jumped in my car and waited outside this other nightclub in the town. We spotted a few walking off, so I mounted the kerb in front of them and jumped out. I knew one of the boys 'cos he worked with my misses and he immediately pulled Beasts phone out of his pocket and tells us he was bringing it back. We tell him that we know who has the car keys and we want them back by tomorrow and nothing will come of it, come the following day the keys were returned.

It bugged me all week how this boy had tried to rugby tackle me down them stair's and how he had managed to pinch the car keys. So, a few days later I popped into the Crown Pub to see the boy's in work and spots the idiot in there, I immediately saw red and smashed him straight in the face, he went flying back and his mates (not knowing what had gone on) started shouting at me, so I've pushed one of them and then two doormen run in and try and calm me down; I tell them I'm off and with that they go and check on the man.

A few months later I saw him in a club, and he apologised saying he was off his face on cocaine. Not being one to hold grudges, especially when I had had my revenge in the Crown pub anyway, I shook his hand.

Now, this is a funny little story...

Like I've said before, it's not all doom and gloom when you're working on the door, and to pass most evenings away we would play practical jokes on each other. Anyway, one Friday after just passing my driving test I was driving through town in my new car when I saw my boss in front of me. So anyway, I beep's on the horn. Next thing you know this speed cop has pulled me over and is giving it the big one, he wasn't well liked in the town and did you no favours, so gave me a producer (a ticket to take my documents into the station) and I was on my way. So, come the following night I'm working upstairs in Play, and one of the doormen comes to see me and says that a speed cop has just pulled up outside and put a notice on my car; I'm boiling inside calling him rotten, thinking that he's got it in for me, and promptly goes outside to confront him and their all laughing out there winding me up.

Come the next night Beast has driven into work, parked his jeep by the nightclub opposite and hung the key's up. Someone then came up with a trick for Beast, which went like this. What we did was we put him upstairs in his doorman position, then one of the boy's grabbed his keys, drove his jeep two miles to his home with me following We parked it up and I brought the doorman back to the club. We then discretely hung his keys back up on the hanger – and this was all done in the space of ten minutes. At the end of the night we go to walk off as Beast is looking into space swearing to himself; I'm holding the laughter back and say's to him, 'you ok beast?' To which he replied, 'my fucking jeep's gone Shirl!' By now all the doormen are around him and in on it, everyone's giving explanations and I said, 'I bet it's that traffic cop! He's had it towed away…' Some even accused him of losing the plot saying that maybe his misses dropped him to work and he'd forgotten all about it. He then asks me for a lift home, I obliged, and all he went on about on the drive home was that he definitely brought his motor with him. Seconds later I dropped him down his street and says, 'there's your jeep there you nutter!' Beast gets out my car, all puzzled looking at it staring into space as I drove off with tears in my eyes. He called us everything under the sun when we told him the next night in work.

Play had started to go quiet and most Sunday night's we would just be stood on the door the whole night. My boss Bernard had taken a new venue on over in Blackwood and there had been trouble there all weekend, it just wasn't worth the hassle, however, me and my mate John Scriven's were sent over on the last night to collect my boss's money. So, we're up on this hillside in this place on some council estate, with tons of youngster's everywhere. We had been there for about two hours with not a single problem. Then out of nowhere this man started arguing with his girlfriend. John asked them to leave when these other idiots join in giving it the big one. They're now outside, and some of them are issuing threats, saying,

'You're dead boy's, he's a boxer.'

Well, this boy is going off his face and John goes outside to fight him, there must be ten men in circle, and they have a scrap; I'm getting warned not to jump in and then it abruptly finishes and me and John go back in. Now, John's blowing, but as far as I knew, it was all over. when all of a sudden, they all start playing fuck by the front door; we manage to kick them out of the place and close one of the door's, then someone phones for the police 'cos we were totally outnumbered, although still holding our own. Anyway, here's where it went tit's up.

Picture the scene:

One of the door's is locked solid, and I'm trying to punch out at them around it and in front of the door's; I'm smashing a few in the face and John's smashing them too, when all of a sudden, I've thrown a straight right, my shoulder's hit the door which puts my arm straight out of its socket – dislocated. The pain was fucking immense, so I had to back off and immediately start screaming at John to lock the door. So, then the two of us lean on the door putting all of our weight on it. Then, thankfully the next thing we heard was the sound of a police van, with that the kicking to the door stopped and they scattered like rats from a sinking ship. An ambulance turned up and I was put in the back, in agony with my arm, and after a lot of poking and pulling, they manage to put my shoulder back into place. My boss Bernard had heard what had happened and drove over with Paul, and you can imagine the shit I had off them, I said to Bernard, 'You can stick your Blackwood up your fucking arse!' And he replied while laughing, 'never mind all that Shirl… did you get my wages?'

A few days later we ended up losing the 'Play' contract, 'cos a few of the bouncer's had caught a man sniffing cocaine in the toilet and when they were putting him out the owner asked them to leave it, and that he wanted him to stay and just have a warning, turns out they were best mates. The boy's argued their case, then rang our boss who said get my wages, we're fucking finished with that Shithole! The owner refused to pay the wages so me and a few others who were working elsewhere had a phone call to go over there as soon as possible and get it. On hearing this the owner paid up, in full straight away and saved us a trip. It had been a good few month's there, and I got on well with the owner Naz and his son's, but it was time to move on.

This one Night in another venue I hadn't been working and this boy that I knew who had just been released from jail was out celebrating with his mates. Come the end of the night the boy kicked off and the doorman hit him and there was murder's. Now, a few nights later, it was a Wednesday and I was working with this man named, Andy in the Splash Bar on Glebeland Street and the doorman who had hit the boy was working his night job has a mobile security guard and was driving round and had popped in to see us for a cuppa. After a few minutes the boy who he had hit was passing and shout's to the doorman, 'you're dead!' With that the doorman goes to front him but he ran off. The doorman came back, and I said to him, 'I'm telling you now, he won't leave this alone.' Fifteen minutes or so go and we are there chatting away and the next thing you know from the alley next door this boy appears with a flare gun like you see at football games; the light is blinding, and It still hadn't fully kicked in, but in the brightness of the flares flames, I spotted a knife. The two doormen are now in the pub doorway and he's stabbing out at them; I'm screaming at him while all the time backing off away from him, and even though I knew him he was off his head and I just wasn't taking a chance. Suddenly, he ran off and the police arrived within seconds. The following day my mate not wanting anymore comeback's had had second thoughts about it and didn't push it no more. Soon after I received a message from a mate of mine who knew the boy and the boy had said it had nothing to do with me and the problem was with my mate.

I told my mate *it was lucky the doorman dropped it, or he'd be back in prison by now.*

Then came May, and a new event in the town was about to be born: 'Merthyr Rising' named so after the infamous Merthyr riot's which had seen many people killed in the town and an innocent man hanged in Dic-Penderyn in 1831. The event was the brainwave of two good mates of mine, namely, Anthony Bunko and Lyn Williams and it was held in the square where the actual battle was once held. The event was a success with no trouble whatsoever. One funny little thing I do remember though, was when I was in charge of watching the stage and the equipment on it overnight, me and another doorman, Ray were taking it in turn's, Ray was knackered 'cos he'd just finished his night job and finished at 6am. So, I took over and I'm sitting in my Jeep, to be truthful I'd only had 2 hours sleep myself, so I was still tired too. About an hour later there was a bang on my window and this man's stood there ranting and raving that he's just come in and there's stuff missing, and he said apparently someone was fast asleep on the equipment; obviously the first thing that ran through my mind was that someone had snuck in while Ray was on shift and I hadn't seen anyone. With that I ran over only to find no one there, so I goes back to the man who still wasn't happy and tells him what "I hadn't seen" but he's still ranting and having a go. I could feel myself going off on him but kept myself professional until the organiser Lyn arrived. Lyn told me not to worry about it, then all of a sudden, the man comes back and says, 'sorry, I owe you an apology.' Turns out one of the stage crew had been winding him up, well his face was a picture and we all just laughed it off. Ray came in for the night shift, and I played the trick on him too, telling him that we had almost got the sack 'cos someone had snuck in while he was on shift.

During this time, I started spreading myself about a bit, doing a few extra gig's in different town's and I even ventured to the Brecon area working at a nice little club called Harley's. I did a few week's there and there was hardly any trouble at all, that was at least until one Sunday night when it had been the local Brecon Jazz festival. The regular boys' had apparently been having some trouble from some other doorman who used to work there. It had been a pretty good night and it was kicking out time, the police were all parked opposite and we all left together. However, as we get round the corner one of the main boys' who had had a problem with our doorman said something to him and, Payne shoulder barged him knocking him to the floor. With that some other man goes to run in, so I grabbed him and we're wrestling up against the wall when suddenly I was pushed into a wall with a policeman screaming at me pointing a can of 'CS-gas' in my face, and due to the fact that there was police everywhere, I held my hand's up to show that I didn't want any trouble. Fortunately, the police had been made aware of the arguments with these other doormen and said to our boss that they would have a quiet word them. They then politely saw us to our vehicle and escorted us out of the town. I don't know if anything else came of it, because I was only sent over there now and again to fill in for other people's shifts.

Shortly after I was working in Crick Howell on a big job which again Bernard had taken on. Bernard was in with the owners of the 'Glanusk Estate' and they were organising their yearly polo match where there was always a lot of high profiled people in attendance. My pal Beast and I had even been fitted for a suit and we were put in charge of the VIP section of the show. There were all these celebrity's there drinking bottles of champagne, that looked like alcopop's and the sites we saw were laughable. The only thing was you had all these army people there and a lot of biker's who were watching the live bands; so, from seven onwards, the radios would be going off with trouble constantly. It got to the stage where the police got sick of being called out, and simply decided to stay at the event.

During the evening, the VIP section was closed, so I was back and forth in a jeep going to the trouble that was called out on the radio from all over the whole park. We had got to one fight and these two idiots' had drug's on them, so we put them in the back of the jeep and was driving them out of ground's, when one of them started to kick off in the back. So, to sort it out we stopped the jeep, then suddenly him and his mate dived out of back doors; we went after them, but they ran off through some wood's close by. Next thing you know it's going off again in one of the tents, so obviously we had to head back. When we arrived at the tent, this big horrible lump was kicking off, so a few of us walk him out as he called us all wanker's, so one of the boys who was on our firm, rugby tackled him to floor and began laying into him; the rest of us calmed the situation down then held him there until the police arrived, all the while he's going off his head, spitting at us, so I dropped a knee into his torso, which took the breath out of him for a bit. The night finished and I was glad to be home.

I was then asked by a different company if I wanted to do the 'Green Man Festival' over in Crick Howell. It was going to be four, 12-hour shifts in the day, which was a long haul 'cos I was also working at night in my hometown. Anyway, I agreed and was positioned by myself in the bar; I didn't mind though, because I had a brilliant view of the bands on stage from where I was stood. Now, the man who was in charge of everyone was some ex-army man and was full of himself. Anyway, he turns up first day and introduces himself; I'm sitting outside at the bar on a chair and smoking a fag 'cos it was boiling hot and this point there was no punters about. So, this Army bloke turns up and tells me that I can't sit down or smoke because it look's unprofessional. But I'm thinking to myself, there's no one here and it's a festival for fuck's sake, nevertheless, I bit my tongue and did what he asked of me. He also said that if there was any trouble in the bar or outside, I wasn't to leave my position at side of bar watching the till's and must radio him immediately and his team would be there. If I'm honest, I felt like I was back in school, he must have thought I'd never done anything in my life, but the money was too good, so I just nodded and listened.

The following day the place had filled right up, the bar was getting busier and rowdier by the hour and out of the blue this man has butted another man by the bar, so I radio's it through and old superman told me he's on his way. This one man was now on top of the other, with people screaming and hollering, so I ran in and choked the man out while dragging him from the tent. By the time the Calvary arrive I've got him round the side of the tent, and they place the man in this jeep and take him away. Ten minutes later the jeep returns and out jump's Army boy,

279

who says to me, 'I thought I told you to radio us and not do anything?' And with that and after having a fuck full of him I said, 'listen here now, that man was caving another man's face in who he'd knocked out with a head-butt, and you want me to do nothing and just stand there waiting for you to turn up, well you've got the wrong fucking person if you think that's ever going to happen!' This reaction of mine had obviously showed him that I was no mug and all of a sudden, his attitude changed, and to be honest, he was sound for the rest of the weekend.

A funny thing happened the following day not far from me when the bands were on, when this man, a streaker appeared, 'fuck that' I thought, I'm not chasing him and like the man said I've been told not to move, so I quickly radioed for superman and his team. A few minutes later they turned up in the jeep and could they catch him, could they fuck; the man was stark bollock naked and moved like lightning, there were all of these security driving around after him, it was like something out of the Benny hill show. That gig turned out to be quite a hard few days, and to be truthful, I was glad to see the back of it all.

Sometime after, a bit of work came up in a different town at a pub called the 'Market Tavern.' We had taken the door over there; it wasn't a bad little pub and we hardly had any trouble. Then one night I was working with Lee Callaghan after a quiet night and no trouble there. Anyway, it was chucking out time and we were doing the normal rounds, asking everyone to leave. Five minutes later having asked them again and there's one or two ignoring every word we were saying; so, we gave it another five minutes and then I asked this man by the bar to leave when he replies quite abruptly, 'I'll go when I'm ready!' So, with that I replied, even more abruptly, 'no, you'll go now mate.' And the he says, 'why don't you fuck off!' So, I've seen red and grabbed him from behind taking him off his stool and as I'm dragging him to the door, I notice his leg's getting longer and longer then suddenly it's finally off and on the floor. I'm now thinking oh goodness me, he's only got a wooden fucking leg. With that, the landlord came running across calling me a bully and Lee step's in and slap's him to the ground; I've put the man on the floor outside and he's rolling about calling me every name under the sun, and Lee then says, 'oh fuck 'em Shirl, are you ready?' And we walk off to Lee's car laughing our fucking heads off!' Shortly after, I sent a text to our boss saying: Sorry boss, but we think we've lost you the Tavern.' The following morning my boss Bernard ring's me up laughing his head off, saying, 'what the fuck have you pair been up to?' And I'm laughing, trying to tell him what had happened. Thankfully, we kept hold of the contract, but the owner said to him, 'don't send those two over again, 'cos they're fucking nut's!'

This one day we were doing a rock festival at Merthyr Football Club, the gig was on the field and over two thousand people were in attendance. We had ten people working with us, and true to form, Warren Lewis turned up late. Around this time, I was doing a comedy show with Warren on a YouTube channel called 'Valley Adventures' - with Bolt and Bass, and our videos were that popular we hit over a million view's. Anyway, back to the story. Half hour later Warren turned up beeping his horn on his moped as he was coming up the drive, he hasn't a care in the world – but that's Bolt for ya.' My mind was now working overtime but got back on the clock and put him in his position near the stage 'cos he likes to listen to the bands. I then say's to the other doorman Kristian, 'Kristian, bring the work van and come with me?' We then went to the car park and reversed the van up and lifted Bolts moped into the back of it. And next we moved the Van from the area and put it out of the way.

Come finish, about ten hours later, we all and make our way to the car park, and by this time I've got every doorman in on the prank. Anyway, Warren walks up to where he's parked his 'ped' (moped) and he's stood there looking all confused while we walk off to our cars. Next thing you know he's ranting and swearing that someone's pinched his bike, me and Kristian are crying laughing and the one doorman says, 'when I passed the gate earlier, I'm sure I saw a big pick-up truck carting your bike away Warren!' Well, we kept him going for about twenty fucking minutes asking him stuff like, 'are you sure you parked it here, 'cos you were late and rushing Bolt?' With that, he rang his misses telling her his bike's been pinched. He then goes to ring the police and we open the van and reveal his bike to him; he called us rotten, but it was one of the funniest times I'd ever had while working, we even filmed the whole thing – mind you Bolt is also a top prankster, so I watched my own back for a while.

I also got asked to work Merthyr FC club one Boxing day because they were playing Hereford and were expecting trouble. Being Boxing Day, it was double the money and was always good hours. So, there's about six of us working and we are all split up. I was on the main door with all of the VIP's and footballers and had an easy shift. But apparently, unbeknown to me all through the game, certain Hereford fans were causing trouble and being nuisances in the ground. The police were also in the ground with a

bunch outside in wait. Anyway, I don't know whose
Brainwave it was, but common sense would have been to
hold the Hereford fan's back ten minutes, and let the
Merthyr fans leave beforehand; but did that happen? Did it
fuck! They decided to open both gates at the same time.
So, all of the fans are now spewing out of the ground and
about to meet on the roadside outside the gates of the club.
Our job was simply to protect the bar's and the venue
itself, which we did, by which point they were all empty –
so, job done. Next thing you know it's gone off and there's
loads of people fighting, then one of the doormen said to
me 'Shirl, shall we go in?' Now I'm thinking to myself,
this is outside the ground and out of our jurisdiction, but at
end of day we can't just watch 'cos there were kids out
there as well, so with that we ran down the bank and
jumped in to assist. There were only three policemen there
trying to stop the fight's, so me along with a few doormen
and stewards plus a few men from club stand in line
holding the Merthyr fan's back from going at them and
vice versa. Anyway, it's gone off again and I've barged
one or two to the ground. I then pull's my phone out and
started recording them while shouting, 'carry on boys, 'cos
you're all on film!' I hoped that this would make them
think twice about fighting anymore, and this along with the
other police cameras calmed it down and loads of them
started to walk off with us escorting them down the street,
like a scene from some battle. They did all meet down the
bottom of street by another pub where there was loads of
police, but then they were escorted back on to their
awaiting coach, and quickly shown the way out of town.
Let me tell you, we had defiantly earned our money that
day and then one of our doorman Gavin Borstal say's to
me laughing, 'do I

get a bonus for that Shirl?' and I handed him a packet of crisps, laughing.

I was working this one festival and it was a lovely sunny day when me and Keith's daughter Rosie was walking around checking on everyone. We noticed a few girl's up against a fence and a bit of a commotion started, so we headed on over there. It turned out that one of the girls had passed out, so me and Rosie tried to put her in a recovery position. Now, you always have some girls who think they are nurses when they are drunk and this woman was one of them, and she's screaming telling me what to do, yet all the while I'm just ignoring her. She continues to abuse me until in the end I said to her, 'look do me a favour love and go away!' To which she replied, 'why what the fuck are you going to do about it?' So, I replied, 'look I won't do fuck all, but see her over there, well she will rip your fucking head off!' At which point I waved over at Rosie. The girl soon shut up and let us carry on seeing to the girl. A few hours later I goes to the toilet, the cubicle's locked and I can hear talking inside. So, I waited outside ready to throw the men out, 'cos it was obvious to me that they were up to no good, sniffing cocaine. Ten minutes go by and they're still in there, so I tapped on the door and shouted, 'c'mon lad's, you got to go!' Suddenly, one then shout's back for me to fuck off. Now. I've seen red and shoulder barged the door open, this one boy's naked bent over and the other black boys just finished and his wiping his penis. I'll be honest I wasn't fucking expecting that, and I walked outside the toilet embarrassed. With that, one of the boys came out, so I grabbed his arm, pointed him toward the exit and said, 'right son, off you go!' I'd radioed to the doorman to take him out while I waited for the other one who by now was doing his fucking hair; I told him he had to go, but it just wouldn't sink in what he had done wrong. They were then both outside wanting to come back as they couldn't work out why it was wrong to have sex in the public toilet. The rest of the day as the word got around, I had shit off everyone; people were coming up to me laughing and blowing me kisses. I finished there and had to go onto another venue. As I got to the next venue one of the doormen said to me, 'how did your day go Shirl?' And I said, it went well mate, but as I was walking away, he shouted, 'by the way, some black boy's been here looking for you, he's left his number behind the bar Shirl...' Obviously, it quickly sank in and I told him to fuck off and went off laughing. True to doormen form, word had certainly gotten around fast about the day's incident.

I was still moving around different venues and ended up on a rugby international working with my mate Nick in Merthyr Labour Club. Then with just fifteen minutes to go after a seven-hour shift, this bunch of pricks decided to kick off. So, there we were dragging them to the door and there was murders going on; another doorman Mathew jumped in to help us too, and ended up outside, so as we were dragging him back inside these pricks started jumping on the cars and trying to come back in, however, we kept smashing them before they got in, and they did a runner when they heard the police siren's.

The following day I ended up working in Merthyr rugby club, it was an under eighteen night and as any doorman will tell you it's hard-fucking work. I was working with my mate Dynamite Dan, and we were putting loads out for doing drugs and fighting. With just a couple of hours left to go out of a five-hour shift It then kicked off, and we had to clear the whole building because the owner no longer wanted it open. Mind you, we didn't mind, because they had already paid us upfront for the entire shift.

Valley Adventure's continued to grow in popularity, we even had t-shirts printed and later was offered to feature on the TV show, 'Gogglebox.' Another night then we were offered by a Gun's 'n' Roses tribute band singer Gav to pop down and watch them perform local. He was a fan of 'Valley Adventures' and had one of the biggest names in the Porn industry, his name was, Ben Dover (who is also a friend of John the Neck) and he was playing drums with the band. Now, Bolt and I were fans of Ben Dover's work, so we arrived with another mate of ours called, Spam for the night. We filmed an episode through the night and was also called on stage to sing with the band. After the gig they all came around town with us and onto a nightclub where we had to keep an eye on Ben Dover. It was a surreal moment walking up through town seeing Bolt trying to worm his way into the porn industry.

I then received an interesting phone call which would change my life for the next two years; this would also take me away from the doors for a while, it was going to be hard work and a big challenge, but I jumped at the opportunity.

CHAPTER TWENTY

(Now, I'm The Boss)

It wasn't long before I received a phone call from my mate asking for a meeting. Turns out he'd got into a spot of bother, and the security company he was running was about to go under, so he offered me the chance to take it over. If I'm honest, I wasn't interested at first, but after pondering on it for a while, I thought look, you've run the doors for years and collected money for different people too, and this would be a totally different challenge, not to mention a good test of my character as well. So, I took the bull by the horns and immediately had more than 50 security men and 20 doormen working for me, however, running all of the above wasn't really looking good for me while I was still working the doors, so with that I packed the door work in; that's it, I'd finally finished, well that's what I thought at the time.

So, there I was 'suited-and-booted,' sat in my own office with various rooms for secretaries and other staff. I'd finally made it and was earning good money without having to use my fists for a change.

One Saturday night, I popped round a few venues to pay my doormen as they arrived for work. Now, as I was talking to the doormen it kicked off inside another place called the Venue, my mate Wayne Bevan was on the door, and it was just a few buildings up from where we were. With that, I ran up the street and into the pub to find a massive brawl going on in the beer garden out the back; the doormen were grabbing people as I jumped in and was breaking up the fights. Suddenly, near the door, I noticed this big boy had the owner of the pub in a chokehold, so I ran straight at the boy and put him in a chokehold and dragged him through the pub. As we got to the door, he was still putting up a fight, but his legs went dead on me, therefore, I let him fall to the floor outside. I ran back in the pub to help the other's drag the rest of them out, but by this point, a big crowd had gathered, so I was aggressively screaming at everyone - but no one wanted to know. Fortunately, a few of the instigators mates picked him up and took him away. So, back to the job in hand, I paid the boy's and told them, *I was off home, 'cos the kids will be waiting for their food.*

After a few months had passed by, I got rid of the old accountant in work and took my brother on instead (keep it in the family) however, with my brother on board it immediately dawned on us how much of a state the company was actually in (had I taken over a dead duck) was all I was thinking. Basically, the previous owner's had been spending more money than the company was pulling in and the company was in a lot of debt. I immediately had various meeting's with my brother in tow to try and sort out the problems. We were then trying to pay the old debts off in the hope that we didn't get shut down, I was writing cheques for thousands of pounds, and it seemed like a never-ending battle. I had to cut back on staff a bit, and various other thing's in order for the company to start making money again. And obviously, the money coming in was simply going back into the business to pay off the company debts. The thing's I saw while running the company was something of an eye-opener. I was a hands-on boss, and made it my business to get to know every guard on the firm, and I'd like to think they thought I was a good boss. Because prior to my take over some of the guards had been getting away with murder and I shook the place right up. What I found out was that a few of the guards had been leaving various sites and doing the check-in-calls from their own homes, so obviously a few of them had to go, and P45s were issued.

Then on one of our primary contract sites, one of our guard's was caught with two others on a big scam pinching diesel, so obviously, the police were involved. The guard pleaded guilty, and they split a price of over 50 thousand pounds between the three men, and our company was made to pay back one-third of it on the guard's behalf – what a load of bollocks. The only problem was, now the major contract refused to pay us anymore wages for the guard's that were employed unless we paid in full our guard's split of the 50 thousand, they basically had us by the bollock's and we hadn't done anything, And this, along with the other debt problem's set us on a downward spiral, and in order to keep the contract and have the guard's wages released, I had to write a cheque in full for the man's stupidity. It got to the stage where come wages time some Friday's, I started using my own life saving's to pay our guard's, simply because the cheques were late coming in. Now, don't get me wrong eventually, I'd be getting my money back, but this would go on for months, and every month I seemed to be giving more and more of my own savings – which is no way to run a business.

Later, another one of our sites was attacked, what I mean by attacked is someone had filmed the site overnight for 7 days in a row showing guard's not doing their patrol's, and one of the guards was even leaving the site when there was supposed to be two men at all times. This was the site where 'Trago Mills' department store now stands, and we were going to be in the running to have the security contract there when it opened in the not too distant future. To be honest, a deal such as this would have set me and my company up for life, but due to the guards disrespect for our company and its contacts, the owners of 'Trago Mills' decided to cut my workforce down to just one guard, so there we were losing money hand-over-fist yet again. And before we knew it, they went all out and sacked off our contract totally, *cheers boys.*

It seemed to me that someone must have had it in for the company, but I could never get to the bottom of who the low life fuckers could have been. Talking about low life fucker's, two of my guards who I thought I got on well with were apparently planning to do an insurance job on the company; basically, they had planned to have an accident on site which would involve one of the firm's jeeps. Then they were planning to sue the company and me for everything we had. The news of this was brought to my attention, and I had no other option than to react to it straight away. I went straight over to one of the sites and told the guard to pack his bag and fuck off; he looked at me laughing thinking I was joking, then noticing how serious I was he did as he was told. Apparently, this man had bullied people for years and was being dealt some of his own medicine in reverse…

Soon after, I went and told the other man the same, and he said, 'you can't suspend me!' Anyway, to cut a long and tedious story short neither of the men came back into work and the next thing I know they were asking for meetings for unlawful dismissal. One man then pulled out and took what was coming, he then went to work for someone else, while the other no good slimy bastard continued with his meetings.

It had now come to the stage where the company was on my mind day and night, and the only way to survive was to let an "umbrella-company" come in and help out with the wages, but some of our contract's refused to have an umbrella company, and because of this the end was obviously nigh.

Around this time, one day my teenage daughter came downstairs with her mother and immediately broke down crying. Turns out for the past year she had been bullied in school and had even started self-harming. I'll be honest. I took one look at the scars she had been covering up, and I cried, and nearly smashed a door down with my hand in temper. She'd been too scared to tell me 'cos she thought I'd go up there like a psycho and kick-off (which I would have.) We got in touch with the school, and it was arranged that she needed to speak to certain people. To be honest, I had never felt so useless in all my life; what with me being bullied as a young boy and now my precious daughter (which was even worse) was going through the same thing, I was terrified at the thought of what might be around the corner. Anyway, she promised us the self-harming had stopped, and we just kept an eye on her. Then one evening she came home and said that the girl was bullying her again, and it turned out she wouldn't fight back cause she was frightened of getting in trouble with the teachers, not to mention the fear of what I might have to say. She then informed us that the girl was going to beat her up in the morning, so I say's to the misses, 'right, I've had it with this, I'm taking over now!' And I said to my daughter, 'in the morning, as soon as she comes up to you, you're going to hit her first, pull her hair, and do anything you want!'

With my daughter now smiling I told her, *not to worry about the teacher's, I'd deal with them!* And for the next hour, I gave her a crash course on what the girl was going to do and how to fight her back; within the hour she was ready. The following day I had a message saying, 'dad, I've done it…' I was so fucking proud but then I'm getting pulled in 'cos some kid's filmed it and put it all over Facebook. The girl continued to give her a mouthful but never attacked her again, and if she did my daughter would simply answer back, 'I've beaten you once already…' People will say that I was encouraging violence in young ones, and if that's the answer then yes, I fucking am; especially if it stops kid's getting bullied.

Anyway, onto pastures new, and like I mentioned earlier I had always wanted to be a wrestler; I'd started watching it from a young age and was hooked, I travelled everywhere, even to America to meet these people. So, when a chance came up where a local man Karl (Caiman) was starting training, I jumped at it. I picked it up easily and before long, I was performing on the shows. I quickly went on to have hundreds of matches and won many Welsh Heavyweight titles in the process; I even ventured into England winning Belt's there too with my brother.

One particular evening Caiman had been hospitalised and asked if I could take the training session. For the training, we used to hire a hall, and we all chipped in money towards it, and any money's that were left over went straight towards the shows. Halfway through the session, one of the boys who used to film for us felt a bit faint, so he went outside to get some air, as we gave him water. I told him to leave it for

292

the rest of the night, but he wasn't having any of it and wanted to start where he'd left off. Anyway, I put him and a partner up against another two boys, and one of the boys just happened to be my brother. So, they went away and sorted their match out between them. They began their match, and only a few minutes into it one of the wrestler's had the "fainting boy" in a chokehold and with that, the boy collapsed. Unfortunately, due to the match being staged for a few second's I thought the boy was acting, but suddenly realised he had actually collapsed completely. So, I immediately ran in and stopped the match, we then put the boy in the recovery position. Someone phoned an ambulance, and they tell us to keep talking to him, and fortunately, first aider's from the Centre were seeing to him, while I was on my hand's and knee's holding his hand talking to him. Within a short while, the paramedic's turned up and take him away.

I went up the local hospital, and an hour later, I got told he had to go to Cardiff for an operation because he had a bleed on the brain. His parents are there, and fortunately, because I had filmed the training session, I was able to show the doctor's what had happened. His father wasn't at all happy and blamed some other boy who had hit him in Cardiff two weeks earlier. Apparently, he had been taken to the hospital and then promptly released. He was then taken to a different hospital in Cardiff, and I stayed all night and left at eight in the morning in a daze from the whole event.

For a spell, I was down that hospital for hours on end for the next few days with his parent's because they weren't sure if he would pull through the brain surgery. It was a horrible few days, and once again, my depression kicked in. Fortunately, on a visit one day his parents were smiling from ear-to-ear, because apparently, he was up, talking. I kept up the visits with some of the other wrestler's for the next few week's taking books and DVD's down until he was finally released.

One Friday night we had a show in Cardiff, and he wanted to go but didn't have a lift down, so my brother Steven and I picked him up and had a good laugh with him; it was so fantastic watching him getting back to his old self. Then about two months later comes the bombshell, Caiman had received a letter asking for his insurance details for his training sessions. Now, like I said we just hired the hall, and everyone just trained there together, so basically there wasn't any insurance and there was nothing they could do. But what do they do next? You've got it, they came after me 'cos I had been in charge of the session, and they tried to do me for negligence; they also went after my brother and the other wrestler for assault. After all, I'd done, going back and forth to the hospitals for weeks on end out of concern, this broke my fucking heart, *then came the kicker!* There was talk of them suing me. I just couldn't believe it, and no solicitor would take the case on for my brother and me, so we just had to defend ourselves. Their solicitor's claimed that he wasn't a wrestler and that he was a new trainee and had never trained or been in a ring before. However, what he had failed to tell them, was a few weeks earlier he had been training (which I had on videotape), and he had also been involved in one of the match's on one of the show's, this of which, I also had on videotape. The boy's parents had also taken the video of the incident to the police, and they had said there was no assault because we were all friends just training. Fortunately, we didn't hear another thing about it, however, regarding the wrestling, the whole affair left a big black cloud over my brother and me. And even though they had all turned on us, I still kept in touch with people and always asked how he was doing – because after all the boy was a friend.

Shortly after I received a phone call off Caiman asking if I wanted to take over his promotion Celtic Wrestling. I thought about it for a few weeks then I went for it. I was now the boss of my own wrestling promotion as well has Security Company. I started putting on a load of shows, and everyone was leaving happy. I was also staging big shows in Cardiff which were selling out - all was going well. Then one night I had a show in Cardiff and was supposed to be back working in the nightclub by 11. I told the boss I'd be a bit late because I was in the main event and was on last. I was fighting this man from Cardiff called Chris Recall who I'd become good friends with, and due to the fact that all the fight's before us went off fantastic, he and I had to go all out in our match to follow them. So, we stepped outside the ring, and we're smashing each other with anything we can get our hands-on. The students in the crowd were going nut's, then suddenly he picked up a steel chair and smashed me clean across the head; I've seen star's and hit the floor, and he's strangling me with someone's scarf. I'm thinking to myself I've got a fifteen- minute match to go here and then I've noticed my head is all warm and blood is pouring into my eyes. Apparently, the chair had sliced my head open and gifted me a six-inch gash. We got through the match although I was fucked all the way through it. I drove back to my town, and the owner of the club said, 'you can't work like that Shirl, get yourself up the hospital.' I said, 'it's only a graze!' But an hour later I ended up with 16 staples across my head and then bandaged up. I still went back to the club after it for the last ten minutes but stayed backstage with my head looking like a mummy.

A few months later I booked a show in Cardiff which sold out again, I booked all the wrestler's and four men came down from England. They were running late and being the promoter, I went and checked all was ok before their match. Now one of the men I had booked hadn't turned up, and another man had come who was friends with them. The match went ahead, but a move had gone wrong in the ring, and one man was in a bad way; apparently, he couldn't move. The referee then noticed it and stopped the match and started doing first aid, paramedics were also called, and the man was moved. I was having a hard decision whether or not to continue with the show 'cos there was one more match left. Anyway, after speaking to a few people, I allowed the show to continue. After the show, I was straight on the phone to the hospital and said that I'd ring in the morning for more news.

The following morning, I spoke to the man's family member, and I offered them any lifts and anything I could do to help. I then found out the man had been paralyzed and couldn't move and it broke my fucking heart again. I then asked could I visit the following day and the wrestler said he'd like to see me, so all arranged. Then an hour before I'm about to leave, I receive a message that there's no visitor's, I continued to massage the boy's family, and no one would answer me anymore. I tried asking other wrestler's, but I couldn't find out how he was doing, I got told then his family want nothing to do with the wrestling world and who was to blame them.

A few months later I received another letter yet again that I'm being sued for negligence, this was like déjà vu has like the other boy I had offered help and spoke to the family. Anyway, to cut it short I explained everything, had all my insurances for the show and nothing more came of it. I had finally had enough of the wrestling and packed it all in as a promoter. I came down with deep depression and as anyone who knows me will tell you I had feelings for those people that had been hurt and it was hurtful when they turned on me, especially when in my eyes, I had done nothing at all wrong. I did another few show's for charity, one for Cancer Aid, one for a second cousin of mine who had passed away in a car crash. The shows went exceptionally well, and we raised some money for her kid's, it then came to the show at a local club in my town. The event sold out with over 200 tickets taken.

I rushed straight from work to the venue where I had hired a ring. I was sweating, running around putting chairs in position. Then I noticed that the ropes were very loose, so I jumped in to try them out, and after running back and forth, I nearly fell out of the ring. I told the man whose ring it was, and he said he would tighten them up for us. The show start's an hour later, and I'm still organizing thing's, and my match is due on in an hour, to cut it short I didn't put my knee support's on and hardly warmed up, and my music hit the speakers; as I ran in around the crowd, with drink all over the floor, I slipped; I went down laughing to myself thinking I'd made a right fool of myself; nevertheless, I still got up and continued shaking hands.

I was in a tag team match with my partner Danny up against these 2 English men. Now the end of the match was nearing, and I've gone up on the ropes ready for my big dive onto my opponent, I'm sitting on the top rope with my feet on second ropes, and people were cheering 'top rope.' Now, I was 21 stone at the time, and if I landed on them wrong, it would have been game over, but adrenaline overcome me, and I went off the top. Now, I'd made this move loads of times with no problem at all, so I went to the top, one little bounce then leapt through the air landing with my elbow on the man on the floor. The only thing was as I jumped one of the ropes buckled and I felt a shooting pain in my leg like I had been stabbed, I half landed on the man and was in agony, bad cramp I'm thinking to myself as I go to get up and I've got no movement in my leg at all and drop to the floor in agony, I roll's out of the ring and everyone's probably thinking it's wrestling, he's only acting and it's part of the show. I'm in fucking agony, and these kids are cheering for me to get up. My partner got the win in the ring, and we were now the new tag team champion's. With that my brother, Steven ran out from behind, picked me up while my wrestling partner and I raised the belts for the crowd as they were cheering. I then hobbled my way to the back with my brother supporting me. When I got to the back, I knew there was something wrong; I then went white and felt like I was going to faint. My other brother Barry then took me to the hospital while Steven took over running the show with my misses. I was in the hospital all night and sent home with my leg bandaged 'cos they couldn't tell what was wrong until the full swelling came out.

A few days later, my knee's twice its size and my leg's purple. I could still walk and put pressure on the leg but was on crutches. Then a doctor asked to see me, and put one of those scanners that they use for woman's stomachs to see if they're pregnant and he says 'I've got some bad news, you've snapped your quadriceps muscle and you need an operation as soon as possible, and by the same time the next day, I'd had it done.

After a few days in hospital in absolute agony, I was back home with plaster up to my groin covering 37 staples which looked like a shark bite scar, so I was now off work and couldn't even get up the stairs. Had a few weeks in the house but there were a few problems at work, so I had Kristian come and pick me up, he also had to put me in back of van 'cos I couldn't bend the plaster to get in the car.

So at this time I was somewhat disabled; all plastered up! To my best ability I had tried everything I could to keep the company going, and my brother had been flat out contacting everyone, but unfortunately, we just weren't having any luck, Christmas was two weeks away and I could have just shut up shop but the guards wouldn't have had no wages with a few day's to go to Christmas so I had to put all the money I had in to pay everyone and then go and break the bad news we were finished. I tried my best to go and meet every man and tell him myself but by the time I got out of one site word was spreading. Kristian, my operation's manager, came with me and I shook every person's hand and apologised, and they all thanked me, I think they all knew deep down it was coming. My brother had got in touch with a liquidation company, and a meeting was set up, and a final close down date on the company was given to the guards.

The next week was a nightmare just waiting for cheques to come back in just so I could get my money back, once that was done, I could sleep at night tidy.

It was horrible seeing these people coming into the office taking computers, chair's, phones, anything they could get their hands-on, including jeeps and vans. Alison, the secretary and Kristian, stayed right till the end with me helping out until I handed the keys in. *It was totally gutting, but on the other hand it felt as though a big weight had been lifted off my shoulders.*

CHAPTER TWENTY-ONE

(Back to Square One)

'There's a saying that goes 'nothing lasts forever' and just how true could that be; I'd gone from being the boss of my own security company and a wrestling promotor to having nothing...'

The next few months, I was more or less stuck in the house with my leg. I finally got the plaster off and was in a leg brace. I started rehab in the local hospital only to be told that the leg brace had not been working because it had been adapted for the wrong movement. Also, the pin's they had put in my knee was now sticking out, and I was told that I may have to have another operation to shave them down. Fuck that! I thought to myself, especially after the last surgery which was like a scene from a Saw movie. I was honestly at the stage that I didn't even know if I'd walk again properly and due to this fact, the depression set in and raised its ugly head.

After a few more months I started in a local gym, just walking at first on a treadmill, I knew my running days were over, and I was even scared to pick up the pace a little, 'cos even with straps on I thought my knee was going to snap. It was also apparent that the wrestling was over so I got back into the metal detecting instead and would walk miles on end, every day. After a while the money I had saved was going down which made me think that I had got no other option but to go back to what I knew best, more life on the door's, but this time I didn't have full movement in my legs and being the type of work, I did that obviously worried me.

I received a message from a man named Alan (Shaky), now me and Alan hadn't quite seen eye to eye in the past but had spoken since, and he'd asked me for years to go and work for him when he had other pub's, but unfortunately, I was always in work when he asked – sods law, I guess. However, things were different now, and I needed the work, not to mention that he was now offering me three night's in the 'Belle Vue' where I had started all those years ago.

The first night back was a Thursday, I was working on my own and even though I had it strapped up all I could think about was my leg holding out. Anyway, it's gone right off with these boys' from the pub's pool team and some other local's; I managed to throw a few of them out onto the street, but now there was murder's, and the police had to be called in. Déjà vu had kicked in, 'cos it felt as though I had never fucking left the place.

After a year off, I was back in the game, and the leg had held out on me. The following night I was back working with mad Kristian who used to work with me at the security company. I had got to know Kristian well, now, he wasn't the biggest, but he had your back whoever they were. One of the first time's I met Kristian was when I was working the door in this other pub and he would always chat to me; I could see he was never quite right, but he made me laugh all the same. So, he's there drinking, and some idiots are screaming and fucking about outside, he turns to me laughing and says, 'is it ok to throw this bottle at them, Shirl?' And me thinking he's messing about says, 'Yeah son, crack on.' Next thing you know he's launched this bottle at them, and it smashed into the wall; these boys' shit themselves and fuck off. With that, I said to him, 'are you fucking real, I can't believe you actually threw it at them?' To which he replied, 'well you said crack on Shirl!' I just looked at him and went off laughing.

One night after having my birthday celebrations there, the owner Shaky turned up in his mini and said, 'Shirl, I've got your birthday present here for you.' So, there's me thinking he's got me some chocolates or something when out he pulled four pool ball's in a sock, then just drives off laughing his head off - the man was completely nut's but funny as fuck.

Back at the Belle, it had been a busy night, and this boy I used to know from another pub was kicking off. He was a lot bigger than when I knew him, and he's giving it the big one, so I grabbed him and put him outside, and he's doing all the usual, ranting and shouting stuff before he walks off. The boy then returned, and he's got an enormous martini bottle in his hand, he's looking at the people who are stood by the door, and he's threatening to throw it, all of a sudden Kristian picked a stool up and gave it to me to use as some kind of shield. The boy then ran off kicking my car window on his way. I did see him a few times after this, and he was still giving it the big one, but eventually, much like the rest, he apologised.

Due to the owner being known as some sort of psycho, there wasn't much trouble going on in there. This one night a boy was arguing with his misses, so I asked him to leave, with that he gave me this look like I was a piece of shit, so I asked him again, and he ignores me. So, without notice, I choked him out and threw him outside. Suddenly, just a few minutes later, he launched a brick through the window and did a runner. The owner went out to find him, they brought him back and made him apologise and pay for the window.

Then one Rugby International day it was rammed to the rafter's, and there's fighting going on out the beer garden. So, I've run out there and drag someone through the pub. When I came back in one of the owners, Tanya, has hidden one of the other doormen inside a storeroom 'cos apparently, these boy's wanted to kill him; this one boy has snapped a pool cue in half and is screaming by the pool table, threatening everyone. I quickly went flying at him, screaming, and he gave me the cue, apologised, and left. The following day he came back and paid for the cue and again, apologised to everyone for what had happened.

'Then came Christmas!'

The owner made a joke one night saying that I was going to be Santa Claus for the children's Christmas party that was coming up. Anyway, I agreed, and as it just happened a mate of mine Adam who had been working elsewhere in Merthyr has Santa had a proper costume, so I turned up in full Santa dress, I met over 200 kid's, and they all left extremely happy.

After having a go at RM's rock club in the past, I knew the Belle Vue had an upstairs that was empty and threw the idea up to the owners to start a Rock club up there; they jumped at the idea and trusted me with the organization. So, I began buying posters and other rock memorabilia to stick up on the walls, and it didn't look too bad. I then sorted a DJ (my nephew Jake) and I bounced it and left a relative of my misses Dai Davies on the main door, and the first night we had over 150 people in there. I even tried having a few live bands, but in the end, the number of punters diminished by the week. A lot of people moaned, saying that it smelled in there and needed a new paint job, but I couldn't be arsed investing money into that: it died a death, and I called it a day. A few months later as we were heading towards summer the owners of the pub had handed their notice in, so a final date was set for closing just 2 weeks later. Then one Thursday night I'd been working on my own when this man had come in late with one of the local's. I was just asking everyone to drink up when this man step's out in front of me. "With attitude." I knew straight away that he was going to kick off. With that, he walked up to me and said, 'what's your problem?' And before I had the chance to answer he smashed me straight in the face and I must admit, I saw stars. Anyway, still in a daze, not knowing what the fuck had just happened, I grabbed hold of him, all the while he was still hitting me. I managed to get some good shots into him and threw him through the door; he's then kicking the door's and police are called, then suddenly he disappeared.

The following day I receive a phone call from a local man wanting to know what had happened; the man knew me well and couldn't work out why his mate had started trouble. Also, there were rumours that this man was coming back up the following week, but I know deep down the man must have known he had started it, and so nothing actually came of it. The following day, and with a cracking back eye, I was working up the martyrs club doing security for a charity boxing show, after all the fight's I'd had this

305

was the first time I'd ever had a black eye, so everyone was laughing and giving me shit.

The following week the Belle Vue was shut down and again, it was time to move on. Some work came in for the weekend at a new place called the Walkthrough bar. Around this time, Anna gave birth to our third daughter Natalia, and it was back to square one with the sleepless night and nappy debacle. Once again, I contemplated packing the door's in to help out with our new baby, but we had bills to pay.

A few days later, a job came up in the old, 'Three Horseshoes' pub, which had now changed its name to the 'Celtic Bar' and my name had been offered up to the man that took over. I had heard of the owner, Kevin (Kego) but never spoken to him, so, as is the way, an interview was set up, and the rest, as they say…

CHAPTER TWENTY-TWO

(The Celtic Warrior)

I'd worked a few times in the Three Horseshoes in the past, and it had died a death. Then a businessman named Kevin (Kego) had taken it on, they'd painted the outside Green and white, smashed a few posters on the walls and renamed it, The Celtic bar. After getting the job, I was asked to find some doormen to work there with me. The first weekend went well with live band's upstairs and the place was packed; it had really taken off. Now, we would get the occasional argument now and again, but this was unlike other venue's I'd worked in where I'd end up fighting or getting arrested most of the time.

I was then offered to go with the owners of the belle who I worked with as they were opening a new pub up in Merthyr, but like I told them I was on four night's here and couldn't just walk out and drop down to two. One of the jobs in the early days was walking this 7ft tall man in a leprechaun costume over to our local town to do some promotion. All these people were having their pictures with him like some sort of celebrity, but there would always be one fucking dickhead. This one-night a doorman who worked with us named Walshy had gone into the costume to pass an hour, and we are in the square in town when I spotted about seven rugby boys coming towards us! I've clocked one of them who looked like he was going to go for the leprechaun head. Now, Walshy was a quiet boy but had a hell of a temper if goaded, but remember, he can't see with this massive head on his shoulders, so a few walked up for a pic and Mr. dickhead goes to grab his head off. He's pulling, but I've got a grip on it, and the head came clean off, so now Walshy has full vision and is offering to fight the boy. The man's mates apologised and dragged the prick away; I couldn't stop laughing at Walshy in his costume and told Kego he's either no good for the job or possibly a bit too good.

Another night this man's kicked off because he's caught his misses carrying on with some black man. He's going nuts, so we've dragged him outside, and with that, he ran at me, and I hit him with a jab, and he goes flying backwards. He must have had second thoughts because he soon went off on his way. While writing this, I've been at the Celtic bar for over five years, and I'm proud to say that other than that jab, I haven't had to use my fists once, and haven't been pulled by the police either.

Anyway, back to that night, an hour later it's gone off with this group of men from down the valley's, but we managed to drag them out and get them all outside. There's me trying to be "Mr. nice guy" calming it all down when shit's your thanks', and this fucker's rugby tackled me to the floor, only I had a curb behind me, and I've made easy pickings for him, much to the point that I was even laughing as I went down at the shame of it. Momentarily my head flipped, and I manage to reverse the situation - so now I'm on top of him instead. I tried to smash him, and the three fucking doormen started pulling me off him, they were screaming at me saying I'm going to get locked up if I don't give it a rest. The police arrived a minute later and move them all on. Now, it's not very often I turn on my own doormen, but I just had to tell them in scenarios like that at least let me get a few shots in first so that I'm at least a little bit happy.

Doormen come and go, and every time we got a good team together, this man or that man would promptly leave. A good team were two boy's named Steve and Simon and the trouble started to stop, but they then left, another man that shocked me was a man named Alan Robert's or has people knew him from his comedy show the local morning weatherman, he was a professional doorman like myself and no comedy from him when working. One man who was there from day one with me, and was a long-time veteran was John Agi. Now, Agi had been doing the doors for over thirty years, and I'd even been thrown out of clubs by him when I was a young man of eighteen. He was a straight-talking Cardiff man who everyone respected in the town, but for the first few week's he would hardly even look at me. Then one night the two of us were sitting at the end of the bar after work, at a time when he had got to know the real me and he said, 'see you, Shirl, I was dreading it when I got told you were coming here, 'cos I used to hate you!' And just as I was about to reply, he said, 'let me finish… I didn't know you, but people would say stuff, and I'd listen to them, and from what I've seen so far them people were all wrong. You're a gentleman, agood doorman and by no means a bully.' I'm now smiling to myself saying, 'ah thanks for that John,' I could see where he was coming from because I worked next door in the Kooler's nightclub for years and was fighting every night; so when I think about it, half of those stories were obviously getting back to him and being turned around to make me look like a bully.

After a good few month's it was all getting to Kego. The four nights were now down to two, it was nothing to do with the gaffer, it was just that no one went out on those other nights anymore. This as well as his other businesses, he came close to packing it all in, and he asked me for a meeting and wanted me to take the pub over. A stupid move by one's self, as I'd probably be a wealthy man by now if I'd have taken it on, but it just didn't make sense what he was offering, so I turned it down and told him to keep at it and that it would all take off eventually. Fortunately, he took my word for it, and it worked. Kego was a sound man and one of the boys who would do anything for you at the drop of a hat, we soon became extremely good friends.

Not long after, the upstairs' was turned into a rock venue for a few months, and other different ideas were tried out until it was decided that it would be turned into a fully-fledged nightclub. So basically, you walked in, paid at reception, and either went downstairs with the older lot with "more mature" music and upstairs for the rowdy young lot. This wasn't a fantastic mix, but for some reason, it worked, and the place was busy most evenings.

I also got asked to work a charity night for a boy who had just passed away in a car crash. I was working with Keith and the bar manager Craig from the Celtic bar who was doing his drag act. So, Keith and I were in hiding not to get any shit off him. Then this older woman comes up to us after an hour and says, 'there's fighting in the girl's toilet's boys!' Now, we'd only been there an hour, and it's rammed, so we thought she was joking. Then with added urgency, she repeated it, so we ran inside the toilets and found these girls fighting on the floor, so obviously we parted them, and I took the main one out. The police were there, and we now had to make statements. The rest of the night went well, but a little while later we are due in court, fortunately, one of the girls pleaded guilty, so we went straight for breakfast.

One night down the Celtic bar I was working downstairs with Jason; (Tomo) we had been up and down those fucking stairs all night helping with the trouble. After having thrown a few people out, next thing you know, some of them had snuck back in through the fire exit. This one boy stood in the way and refused to move, so, after I had pushed some girls' out of the way who'd been fighting I went back to the stubborn boy and once again politely asked him to move, this idiot was having none of it, I can see his fist clenching so I then grabbed him and threw him at the door through to the outside; he's trying to fight back, so I slammed him with force, to the floor. This prick has gone too far, and I've seen red, just then I spotted a big black wheelie bin full of empty glass bottles; he's still trying to get back up to fight me, so I just lifted the bin up and smashed him with it then attempted to put it over his head. Jason starts grabbing at me trying to pull me back 'cos he knows that I'd gone off on one. The man soon fucked off but came back the following week and apologised.

Another night while I'm standing on the front door, a big gang of boy's who are inside in the club started kicking off. And as I ran in this big boy was ripping his shirt off with two bodies on the floor at his feet, who he had knocked out and he's screaming for anyone to fight him. So, with that, I came up behind and put him in a simple chokehold, then I just dragged him to the front door. This boy is putting up a

311

bit of a fight, so I simply tightened the grip, suddenly his legs have gone to sleep, and he fell to the floor outside – he didn't have a clue where he was. About five minutes later he comes round and say's to me, 'get that man out here who done that to me?' So, I said laughing, 'I can't bring him out mate, 'cos it was me who did it!' He immediately started going nuts, but the police turned up and move him on.

A month later and I'm on the door on my own again it's flat out inside, and as I turn around the boy from before is there with a few of his mates; I told him that he was banned, and he starts apologising, and his mates vouch for him saying he'll be ok. Now, rather than cause a scene 'cos I was outnumbered I did the stupid thing and let him in. Inevitably, just two hours later, the radio's goes off, and I'm being called upstairs. Immediately, I ran up and spot one of our doorman, Warren, by the bar with another two doormen hanging over him; turns out Warren had been fighting with him. I glance at Warren and notice his thumb has been bitten and is hanging off, and not one doorman had gone for the boy who's done it, which just happened to be the same fucking boy that had been banned earlier.

With that, I went flying over; he was in a rage with all blood over his mouth. His mates then told me that they will walk him out of the club and knowing what I'd done to him last time he walked all the way out with no trouble. Now that's sorted, I immediately ran Warren up to the local hospital, his misses turned up and said laughing, 'don't be a baby, it's only a scratch!' The police weren't involved, it was bandaged, and Warren even turned up for work the following night and all night as we passed him, we'd give him the thumbs up.

Talk about more lives than a cat!

We had finished work one night, and as usual, I was dropping a few of the staff off around Merthyr. So, we were just going up this high street, in a place called Cefn Coed, all having a laugh and a joke when I spotted this car coming down my side of the road and it appeared to be flipping onto its roof. With split-second reaction I had no choice but to mount the kerb while almost hitting a wall; everyone was screaming in our car like their lives were over, and it only turns out the driver was drunk, speeding, and hit some bollard which caused his vehicle to flip. It was like in slow motion coming towards us, stopping just a few feet away upside down. We are all in shock, and Craig jumps out shouting, 'they could be dead!' But then immediately decides that we have to help. To be honest, I was frozen for a few seconds, but quickly realised that he was right and that we had to help, and while Craig and I are rescuing the girl from the passenger seat, the boy driving suddenly did a runner, and an police and ambulance was called because the girl was in complete shock. Anyway, we got home about two hours later when they opened the road back up.

The following week, after just getting into work I told the boss I'm going to get petrol now to save me time later when I run people home. So, I went to the garage, and it's closed, so I thought I'd take a short cut up through this housing estate to another garage. So I'm going up this hill and just come over the brow when I can hear this car motoring towards me at high speeds, It's coming straight for me, so I had no other choice than to mount the kerb yet again but this time I've smashed a wall down, and I've been hit all around the car, I'm fucking and blinding in the car but happy to be alive. The neighbour's come out and can see I'm shaken up and make me a cup of tea. I then went to the garage and then back to work not happy about an hour later. I posted online about it, and a few people contacted me; I was approached by the boy's family and asked if I would leave it there and that they would deal with it.

Another time, I'd bought a wrestling ring and this big blue transit and was doing shows around Wales. One night, Warren and I were coming back from a show when the nut's on the wheels snapped and we went off the road into this bank. We both just looked at each other thinking yet again we are still alive. Police were called, and it cost me hundreds of pounds to get it towed away and fixed.

One last one on my luck of cars or being in them, one Saturday morning I was going metal detecting with my two mates Mike and Steve, Mike had been driving, and it was really early when this massive arctic lorry pulls out of a junction without looking, and we are heading straight for it, now I'm guessing it would have been instant death or we would have been in a bad way, but Mike's slammed his brakes on and we have mounted the curb and on this embankment, we are all in shock, and then Steve says, 'chase the fucker, Mike,', Mike's then gone round this roundabout and got his foot down chasing him, we are doing 60mph by the side of him and Steve's screaming out of the window to pull over, I'm not sure if the man had seen us go off the road, but he's not pulling in, I'm laughing my head off at Steve has I'd known him has another psycho all my life, we then gave up has not far away was our turning off, we got out of the car lit a fag up

314

and talked about what had just happened and how we were all still alive.

It felt as though someone was watching over me with the number of lucky escapes I'd had.

One night though I'd finished working in the club and had gone down to local petrol garage to fill up, and when I was driving back past this local college, there's was a few of these boy's in the road and they are not moving; with the drink in them they obviously thought they were the terminator. So, I beeped my horn, and a few of them move and this one cocky fucker his just standing there shouting abuse, and he's not moving, the psycho switch goes on, and I just hit the accelerator and put him up over the bonnet and slam brakes on and he goes flying off to the side of the jeep, I'm laughing like a psycho and drive off has a few of his friends are screaming abuse, I panicked for a few days as I thought there might have been CCTV but heard no more.

My smoking habit had got really bad, and with the weight, I was putting on from not training I had ballooned to over 24 stone. I then went on a diet after doctor's advice and tried packing the fag's in. I managed to go three months' on one of the Joking vape machines Id had off my mate Warren and was doing well when I had one of the worst months of my life, Firstly my aunt Margaret passed away, then a week later my uncle Jeff who was like a father to me died suddenly of a heart attack and I'd only spoken to him a few hours earlier, then my other uncle Sid dies a week later as well as one of my good mates from the wrestling Ryan. I just couldn't take it all in, and I left one funeral halfway through to go to my uncle's on the same day, by the end of it all I was back smoking as normal. It's still hard to

315

believe I didn't have my first fag at my dad's funeral until I was 35 after a mate had asked if I want one 'cos I was stressed.

I've always been involved in raising money for charity, doing walks, fancy dressed, and I even climbed the odd Mountain. I also put on a few wrestling shows with my brother for the Alzheimer's Society and for Cancer Aid Merthyr. Around this time my wrestling trainer Karl Griffiths (Caiman) contacted me after I'd left a comment on his previous challenge congratulating him, and over a chat, he came up with a brainstorm for him to fight me for charity on top of a mountain one Sunday morning coming soon. This was for the "Movember" charity that supports testicular cancer. One of our good friends Ryan, who had joined Caiman for it had sadly passed away, so Caiman wanted to dedicate it to him in the process.

Now, me being an ex-boxer, the next thing I know, I'm being challenged by Caiman to a fight in which he to last a full three-minute round with me. Fortunately, he had already raised £300, and a week later we had smashed his target and shot it up to a staggering £1000. Fight day arrived so Caiman and I went up the mountain in the morning, and we got our friend Mad Charlie to referee us. Now, I'm not going to lie to you, it was a fucking bitter day, especially at the top of a mountain, and I even had to piss on my hand's to get some feeling back into them. The fight started, and the cameras were rolling a live stream to Facebook, with hundreds of people watching and donating.

Now, I'd trained with Caiman for years and knew he was no mug, and the first minute he threw some massive punches; unfortunately for him I soaked them all up and caught him with a body shot that dropped him to one knee. Horses are now surrounding us wondering who the fuck are these pair of nutter's. Caiman fought with all he had, and managed to come back, catching me with some heavy head launcher's, however, I dropped him a couple more times in the process, but with just thirty seconds to go he must have had a second wind, and he caught me with an uppercut and a few hooks. The fight finished, and my mouth was bleeding a bit. Nevertheless, he had managed to last the round out to the three minutes, we both hugged and declared the winner – it was fantastic for the charity and Ryan, and all for a worthy cause. I'd like to think Ryan was with us that day laughing his head off as we went into battle.

Another time I was talked into walking up Pen-y-fan mountain in the Brecon Beacon's for this kid's cancer charity, which we were collecting for in our pub. My only problem was it was only a year after my knee accident, and I knew it was going to be one hell of a challenge. Anyway, I've strapped up my knee and one of my mates Warren (Bolt) said he would stick with me; we even made a comedy video of the day for our channel Valley Adventures. The rest of the pub got up there in an hour and were passing us coming back down. My knee wasn't too bad, but due to the lack of training my back kept pumping up with immense pain. Warren and I finally got to the top, although it had taken us three hours, and by the time I reached the top, the rest of the pub was in Merthyr back at the pub. Nevertheless, I had done it, and we raised thousands of pounds between us.

Back in the Celtic and it's another regular night, rammed and trouble now and then when someone calls me over, and this man's got this woman by the throat and slapping her, I grabbed him in a neck hold and dragged him out, as I get to the door the woman, he was hitting is now hitting me, shit's your thanks' I'm thinking to myself. They then go up the road arguing with each other. Next thing you know the next day the woman's put a post on Facebook how Shirly the doorman of the Celtic had beaten her up, she even showed pictures, and I hadn't even touched her. So, I did a post and had hundreds of comments how good I was and how I'd never hit a woman and before you know it everyone was messaging her calling her a liar and she took the post down.

Around this time, I started a few groups on the town's history called, 'Merthyr Tydfil – The Past' which now has over thirteen thousand members; Merthyr Tydfil Metal Detecting club and many more.

I then got involved in doing the detecting in my local park after meeting the park ranger Ian. The park was once owned by the famous Crawshay family in the 19th century. In the next year I spent over 260 day's there and started finding Roman stuff everywhere. An archaeologist named Graham was brought in and we hit it off and became friends. Between me, Ian and Graham we managed to pull off a community dig in the park. I then appeared on a Wales Online article saying Bouncer may have found a Roman town and the media world went nuts for it, and even the daily mirror rung me up for an interview. A community dig was held with hundreds of people from our town all helping out, I even made the ITV wales at six news, and stuff was found on the dig, but as I write this my quest continues because I still ain't found the buildings yet. However, I won't give up until I succeed.

One morning I was out detecting with my mate Steve Davies and came across an undiscovered Roman road. We then spent some time cleaning the ash tip on top of it and showed it to a few archaeologists who confirmed it was Roman. Now you'd think this would be a major discovery, but no one seemed to care and up until today it hasn't been mentioned or documented. Fortunately, I was finally given our Detecting club's display's cabinet in the local museum which I had been asking for years, and I was also writing history news for a local newspaper called the Tydfil Times.

I also came up with an idea about making little video's for a YouTube channel about all different places in my hometown and some of the 75 videos were even played in school's to show the kid's. I was then given a recognition award online for all I did for my local town by my mate Lee who runs a page with over 15 thousand members', it was only an online thing, but it was nice to get some recognition.

I was also asked to give a few talks in my hometown and further afield, not bad for someone who left school with no qualification's, and now even my history teacher Val is on my pages. Also, I had started a new comedy series on YouTube with my mate Julian; we had toyed with the idea for years because in the past everyone had commented on how funny we were but due to Juggy finding out he had an inoperable brain tumour he decided to film the episodes anyway, so that his grandkids could look back on them in the future. The Juggy and Shirl show took off, and our videos would get thousands of views every time we put a new one on. On a serious note, Julian had to stop driving so I would taxi him around a lot, and has I write this we never let the brain tumour get to him and we continue life, as usual, playing fuck with each other.

I also started work on a new book about a man called John The Neck, now John was Lenny Mclean's good friend and work colleague and once getting on board with book author Lee Wortley we spent over a year putting together nearly 100k word's for a possible bestseller.

After many chats on the phone, I travelled up to Lee's to finally meet the Neck, he was a true gentleman, mind you, you could see in his eyes he was the real deal unlike a lot of the other so-called people I'd met on my travels'.

Back to the Celtic, we had a few incident's but now has the upstairs' was being used as a nightclub, and like I told the owner the trouble would now double, and people would go out every week but we stayed on top of thing's and In all my year's there I'm proud to say I haven't thrown one punch, Ok I've had to put a chokehold on a few people but only when they have asked for it and needed to be put out straightaway.

Now in the year's I'd been in the Celtic bar a few accidents with cars had occurred outside. One night this boy I knew mounted the curb and parked his car with not a care in the world, on the path sideways. I said to him, 'you can't park that there you nutter', he then threw me the key's and asks me to park it and I throws them back; he then decided to move it himself, reversing into a lamppost while a police van past just yards away. He then crunched through the gears and was off, just as fast as he'd arrived.

Another night this man kicks off outside with some boy's, and he's gone and got is car pissed, then came back and ploughed it straight into a crowd of people; how he didn't kill somebody is anyone's guess. However, our resident DJ got hit as well as a few others who had to go to the hospital

Then last year in the summer, this boy came into the club who I'd chatted to and got on quite well with, in the past. Now, in the past, he had attached something that everyone thought was a bomb to a lamppost where I lived, and there were crowds of people, as well as police making sure that it was safe. He also came to the Belle Vue and asked if he could go in; I was working with a relative of my misses called David, and we said, 'yeah, of course, you can come in.' And with that, he pulled out this big machete and said, 'is it ok if I bring this in with me too?' Dai said, quite abruptly, 'what the fuck is that?' And he goes on to tell us that he was having some trouble with some boys' and had the machete on him just in case. We stepped back a bit as he had it in his hand and refused him entry. With that, he put it above the door on a ledge and said, 'so, can I go in now?' Well, I looked at Dai laughing, he's just as shocked as I am, and we refused him once again. He then went off saying, 'ok, no hard feelings boy's!' And minutes later a police van came shooting down the road to us and asked us where he had gone because apparently, they had been watching him on the CCTV and noticed that he'd pulled it out on some boys' minutes earlier, at the bottom of the town.

Anyway, back to the Celtic bar night, it was coming up to the end of the night, and he was sitting on the floor upset, so the doormen took him outside. Then, he went off up the street, got in his BMW and sped back and forth until coming to an abrupt stop. Seconds later, the Police turned up and tried to take his key's out of the ignition, he then reversed off dragging a policeman about ten feet across the floor until another police vehicle got in his way; it was nut's, he was subsequently arrested and sent to jail for eighteen months – it was covered in the newspapers along with his mugshot.

This one night this boy I knew kicked off and run at me, instead of punching I just shoved him to the floor twice, he ran at me again throwing punches, and I have grabbed him so hard Iv torn my shoulder and bicep out, Dynamite Dan's jumped in and grabbed him and we have thrown him out, I locked the door, and my shoulder is hanging, it must have been when Id dislocated it before, the police pass and he goes away. It was another visit to the hospital who said I'd done nothing although the next day I was purple all over my side and chest. Someone then told me you've torn your pectoral muscle. The next night I was in agony but went in and said to Dan that he will have to carry me through the night if there was any trouble, we got through trouble-free thank god. I see the boy the following week in town, and he couldn't even remember being in the pub and apologised. To this day the injury hasn't gone away and the slightest of movement sometimes sees me in agony.

On one bank holiday we were open for three nights and Id managed to choke someone every night, and it got to the stage it looked like I was doing it on purpose when there was nothing further than the truth, I was put down stair's on my own and when it got nasty it was easier to put a hold on them and get them out.

The owner then decided to put another doorman named Dan in with me thinking the trouble would stop, and within a few hour's this man has head-butted this man knocking him back, so I've grabbed the head butter in a choke, and Dan's only got a chokehold on the other man he was fighting and thrown him outside the door. Dan had a bald head and goatee like me, and people started saying he was my son and we would wind everyone up because I'd call him son, and he'd call me dad.

Then one night's it's gone off and Dan's run through grabbing this man and dragging him out. Iv then run in, and these two other big men are on the floor, and we can't part them, even the door girl Emma's on them, I said to Dan, 'fuck them, leave them tire' and then next thing you know these three men turn on Dan and Ray has no one was on door, and people kept coming back inside. I then just scrum down and run at the three of them getting them all out in one hit, their faces were a picture. I then told Ray to stay on the door, and by then the bigger ones were fucked, and the other doormen were parting them, we got them all out, and they were fighting until police locked them up.

Had a few little problems here and there, one man split his head open outside, we rung him an ambulance, but they had a habit of coming late so Id, take him up the hospital and he spewed all in my jeep. The same happened for another man who had his lip bitten off and another man whose leg had been broken.

One strange little one that puzzled me for days though, was when a woman had been thrown out of the club one night and she had snuck back in at the end of the night. So, she's gone up to this chair where a carrier bag is, and the doorman grab's the bag, she goes nut's and a split second before the doorman Ray shout's, 'she's got needles' I felt a needle-like pain in my leg, so me and another doorman, Andrew, grabbed her by one arm each, and we put her out. All of a sudden I can feel my leg going dead and said to the doorman Ray, 'did you say she had needles, I'm sure she's had me with one' he then tells me to get upstairs straight away, I'm now panicking and drop's my trousers' has Rays got his torch on, he said your all clear and I said to him laughing I owed him one for looking. I still for the life of me could not work out what I had felt.

Finally, after 18 years in Swansea road we decided to move to a new house, we needed a bigger room because the girls were getting older. We had made some good memories there but also a lot of bad ones, from being broken into countless times to my car being done over although the last few years it had gone quiet has everyone knew me by then. Although it still didn't stop has a month before I was due to move, I'd made a schoolboy error and came home from town rushing and left my jeep key's in the back door of the boot. I didn't even realise until I went to go to work a few hours later and couldn't find keys then I noticed they had taken everything from inside jeep. I was now in the awkward situation as the jeep's still open, and they could come back and take it, my house keys were also on there, and my misses and kids were at home. On looking, I noticed one of the robbers from up the street who was with another robber who had come out of jail the day before, as they saw me they turned around and went back into a flat which made me suspicious. Anyway, I got a lift to work and took the chance they wouldn't come back. The misses also left her keys in the door so they couldn't get in. The following day my cousin Daniel came up and changed my house door locks. I then went to go out with the misses and kid's, and I can see one of the robber's walking down the street, I jumped out of the car and run at him hitting him to the floor, I just went with my gut instinct he knew where the keys were, by now he's crying on the floor and I tell him he's got to six to get the key's back to me or he's a dead man. I then received a phone call from my misses around five that night that the man's son had knocked on the door and given key's back. I then saw the son, and he reckoned his dad had told him, and he went asking about, and someone gave the keys back. I didn't ask any questions because it was going to save me hundred's the next day sorting the jeep lock out. We packed up and made our way to where I had lived all my life, on the Gurnos Estate.

All the way through my journey of life a few things never took off, me and Warren (Bolt) had lost out on a part in a BBC Program because I had the kid's one day and couldn't make it. Then we got offered Gogglebox, and that went tit's up. Id pulled out of a channel 5 documentary about paranormal doormen, and they were mocking us. Also, the trailer for the One-armed Bandit's movie was good, and a part was promised for the feature film, but it never got the backing. Also, Warren and I ended up with a part playing our characters Bolt and Bass in another film called Svengali being made by Merthyr born actor Jonathan Owen, but we never made the final cut which was also gutting has we had told everyone we were in it.

Then a new film was being made called My name is Lenny about Lenny Mclean who Id run his page and written two books about and they were looking for extras. My mate Julian and I then travelled to London for 2 days to film the final fight scenes. It was a good experience, and this time unlike other times, we made the final film. Ok it wasn't a talking part, but you could see us in it, and another tick off my bucket list. Julian and I then had a small part playing 2 bouncers throwing a man out in a new music video by Merthyr singer Chris King.

Then came summer 2018 when I came up with the idea of starting a page on Facebook making people aware of the paedophile's that were all around us in our local town. It went nuts, and people were messaging me daily, and I was pulled in by the police a few times, but it was all sorted. Before I knew it, the page had over eight thousand member's and had taken over my life yet again, I was going to bed sometime five in the morning, and my black eyes were getting blacker, but it was all worth it as we were helping people out and they felt like the whole page was now behind them. It just felt like there weren't enough hours in one day with all the project's I was running and not for one financial income, all in my own time.

I'd now been in the Celtic Bar for over five years and every time I'd pass John Agi by the door taking someone out he's would say at the top of his voice 'Warrior' and laugh at me as I walked back in and then he said to me one night going home in the car, 'you are the Celtic Warrior' has we laughed all the way to McDonald's.

Throughout the years I've worked with various bouncers, some good, some bad, some who would hide and some who just didn't give a fuck and steamed straight in every time. I put myself in the "don't-give-a-fuck" department. No matter how big or how many there are, I'm straight on them without allowing them time to think. It's worked well for me so far, and the day I start leaving other people to do the work will be the day I'm ready to hang up my leather gloves.

Bouncing is the only job that never gets easier the longer you do it, don't get me wrong, you pick things up the more you experience it, you know when that fights going to kick off minutes before it happens, a bit like déjà vu. You keep running it through your mind what you're going to do repeatedly, and usually, the game plan works, you walk into a bar, and within seconds you know who the dealers, pissheads and troublemakers are. You sense things quicker than the average person, and some of the things you see would scare the life out of most people.

The months were flying by, and we then had hardly any trouble all over Christmas and New Year in the Celtic bar, and we were now heading into 2019.

CHAPTER TWENTY-THREE

(Epilogue)

So, as we conclude, I have to say with one thing and another it's been a terribly fractured year, with 'peaks and troughs' like you would not believe. First and foremost, my eldest daughter got lost in her own mind for some time; the poor girl was suffering in silence, and she'd thrown herself deep into her own murky and cynical thinking mind and all too disastrous effect. Unfortunately, in her desperation, she turned to illegal drugs with the vague hope it would dissipate, only to make it worse.

Then one night I was just about to go to work when I received a phone call saying she was acting a little strange at some house; she'd only left us two hours earlier. Anyway, we went to the house to pick her up and then we took her home, however, she wasn't at all right, she was cracking up. After a few hours, she told us that she had taken a few Acid tablets and other stuff, and as there was no change in her mood, we took her to the hospital. The next few week's I can only describe as one long nightmare, I broke down numerous times through the course of it, but I knew I had to stay strong. We basically had to put her under house arrest for over a week.

My wife and I didn't know what to do – it was mental blitzkrieg for a while, with trips to and from the hospital for help. Basically, for the first few days, her brain just couldn't shut off, and she went through every memory from her seventeen-small year's; her emotions were up and down like a yo-yo, and she had no idea what she was doing or saying.

As is always the case, our family was there to mop up after the mayhem; which was, and always is a godsend. My wife Anna had been going through all this with me in the house and breaking down too, and I was fearful that this could have quite easily tipped her over the edge. But no! True to form, she dealt with the onslaught in much the same way she has had to deal with my dark and treacherous life over the years. Smack bang in the middle of all of the madness our family pet 'Ali' passed away; this obviously broke our hearts, but the pressure of what was occurring with my daughter took precedence.

Now, as we write this, thankfully, our beautiful girl came through the worst of it and is growing stronger and stronger by the day. Furthermore, the dark depths she had sunk herself into, today seem a distant and less harmful memory. With my family 'that I hold dearest' now back in the safe bosom of tranquility once again. Mind you, I take it all a day at a time as there's always something lurking around the corner waiting to spoil things; hopefully, the black cloud that engulfed us is well and truly behind us now.

So, as I approach my 50th birthday (a time of life that many people refer to as "halfway there") I think I am way past the halfway stage; I take seven tablets a day to keep me alive, and my fingers are fused from fighting. My arm is shot from being dislocated twice, and my knees are shattered with arthritis from all the sport I have entertained on my journey. Nevertheless, I had a go at it all and enjoyed it, making many people happy in the process.

And today, as I approach my 25th year on the door's and have finally earned my stripes to bring you a no holds

329

barred look at a thankless job that has seen me close to death on many occasions. I have been bottled, stabbed, knifed, shot at, sued, locked up, had fireworks shot at me and I've even been run over by a car and more, but somehow, I've lived to tell the tale.

As for the door work, how much longer can I go on? Some say it is a young man's game and I am certainly not getting any younger. However, at the moment, I have a family to support and will continue to do the doors until I know it's my time to finish. A man said to me recently, 'ain't you retired Shirl? You're too old for all this shit now.' I looked at him, held my fist up and said, 'See that, well as long as I can still knock them out, I'll be ok.' His face was a picture as I laughed and walked away.

So, what's next on the journey…?

Well, as we end 2019, I've just wrapped up two appearances in new TV programs, the first called Paranormal Mind's and the second a Paedophile documentary coming to BBC Wales next year. I've also been asked to do a few talks about Metal Detecting find's in my hometown later this year and hopefully will be involved in a few community archaeological digs too with an archaeologist named Graham I've got to know well. I continue to write constantly and have a few book projects on the go which will probably be released in good time.

I continue to help with any charities I can and recently in the Celtic bar we have raised over a thousand pounds to help some little kid surpassing my 40 thousand pounds in the past few years.

Add all this with running a Predator Awareness page and also trying to do comedy video's there just isn't enough hours in the day. I've now also taken the Predator thing to the next level and become a hunter, yeah you heard that right, and have so far caught over 21 of these sick, vile creatures, but that's another story.

'From being bullied at a young age, leaving school with no qualifications, transforming myself into a town idiot, and turn it all around to be to one of the most respected men in the town.'

No part of this has ever been easy, some of the things on my journey have brought me to the lowest points of depression; a pathway to nowhere, but I've always managed to steer my way past it and keep it from the gazing eyes. There's a saying that goes 'it's all sent to test us' and believe me, I have been tested over and over, but nothing will beat me, I've grown confident in age to where I am today.

'I had a load of dreams, a bucket list of stuff, and I managed to tick off every single one of them on my journey.'

I'm not here to preach to anyone, all I'm saying is if you put your mind to it, you can do it; I went from Zero to what some might say is a "Hero" during my life's journey, and in some form or another I'd like to think I left my mark on the town. However, It ain't over just yet.

During my tumultuous journey, I thrived in many things. From different sports to writing books. And as luck would 'ave it, I'm not just respected for the door work, no, that's just one small but vital part of it. Besides, I like to think that I've helped many people out in life and all of its struggles. From the charity work to running pages with thousands of members for my little town with a population of sixty-four thousand, which I don't think is bad for a bullied little chubby kid with curly locks and a girl's nickname,

Shirly.

Printed in Great Britain
by Amazon

40323862R00195